AMERICAN CRUSADE

AMERICAN CRUSADE

CHRISTIANITY, WARFARE,
AND NATIONAL IDENTITY,
1860–1920

BENJAMIN J. WETZEL

CORNELL UNIVERSITY PRESS
Ithaca and London

First published 2022 by Cornell University Press

Library of Congress Cataloging-in-Publication Data

Names: Wetzel, Benjamin James, author.
Title: American crusade : Christianity, warfare, and
    national identity, 1860–1920 / Benjamin Wetzel.
Description: Ithaca [New York] : Cornell University Press,
    2022. | Includes bibliographical references and index.
Identifiers: LCCN 2021060340 (print) | LCCN 2021060341
    (ebook) | ISBN 9781501763946 (hardcover) |
    ISBN 9781501763953 (epub) | ISBN 9781501763960 (pdf)
Subjects: LCSH: War—Religious aspects—Christianity—
    History. | Spanish-American War, 1898—Religious
    aspects—Christianity. | World War, 1914–1918—
    Religious aspects—Christianity. | World War,
    1914–1918—United States. | National characteristics—
    Religious aspects—Christianity—History. | National
    characteristics, American—History. | Christianity and
    politics—United States—History. | United States—
    History—Civil War, 1861–1865—Religious aspects—
    Christianity.
Classification: LCC BT736.2 .W44 2022 (print) |
    LCC BT736.2 (ebook) | DDC 261.8/73—dc23 /
    eng/20220111
LC record available at https://lccn.loc.gov/2021060340
LC ebook record available at https://lccn.loc.gov
    /2021060341

To Joan B. Wetzel (1958–2003) and James H. Wetzel

Contents

ACKNOWLEDGMENTS

Many thanks are due to the multitude of friends and colleagues who helped me write this book. I first want to thank D. G. Hart, who put me in touch with Cornell University Press. At Cornell, Michael McGandy believed in the project from the start and patiently helped me navigate the editorial process. Sarah Elizabeth Mary Grossman became my editor at the book's final stages and ably guided it to completion. The book is much better thanks to the valuable suggestions of Cornell's two anonymous peer reviewers.

In its earliest stages, the project began at Baylor University. In that regard, I wish to thank Barry Hankins, Thomas S. Kidd, and Barry Harvey. Baylor's Guittard Fellowship allowed me to pursue my graduate work without financial worries. The project matured at the University of Notre Dame. Mark Noll, a Christian scholar and gentleman if ever there was one, mentored me there, as did Rebecca Tinio McKenna and James Turner. Harry S. Stout at Yale also deserves special thanks. The members of Notre Dame's weekly Colloquium on Religion and History offered helpful suggestions on several occasions and shaped my intellectual growth. Philipp Gollner supervised my translation of German passages.

Notre Dame also provided unusually generous financial support during my seven years there. I thank the Department of History, the Graduate School, and the Institute for Scholarship in the Liberal Arts for providing research and travel grants. Postdoctoral fellowships provided by the College of Arts & Letters and the Cushwa Center for the Study of American Catholicism provided space to revise the manuscript. I would especially like to thank John T. McGreevy for the former and Kathleen Sprows Cummings for the latter.

At my current institution, Taylor University, I would like to thank Michael Hammond, Thomas Jones, and Kevin Johnson for their support of my research and writing. Daniel Bowell, Lana Wilson, Jan King, and the staff of the Zondervan Library consistently helped with research and interlibrary loan requests. I am grateful to Barbara Bird, Kris Johnson, and the Bedi Center for Teaching and Learning Excellence for providing subvention funds to help with the book's publication and for providing a grant to hire a student to help prepare the index. Mallory Hicks did an excellent job in that regard.

The following archives generously granted permission to quote from their collections: The Congregational Library & Archives; the Brooklyn Historical Society; the George J. Mitchell Department of Special Collections & Archives, Bowdoin College Library, Brunswick, Maine; and the University of Notre Dame Archives. I thank Cambridge University Press and the *Journal of the Gilded Age and Progressive Era* for permission to quote from an article that became an earlier version of chapter 4; Oxford University Press and the *Journal of Church and State* for permission to quote from an article that was an early version of chapter 3; and the Congregational Library & Archives and *Bulletin of the Congregational Library* for permission to quote a few paragraphs from an article that became chapter 1.

I thank the leadership and members of Redeemer Church in Niles, Michigan, for their friendship and spiritual support during my years at Notre Dame. Now I am pleased to call Upland Community Church home, and I thank Pastor Mark Biehl and the congregation for their friendship.

Personal thanks are due to my family—first and foremost to my wife, Megan. I would also like to thank my Stanton in-laws in Michigan and my extended Wetzel family in Pennsylvania and Virginia. This book is dedicated to my parents, James and Joan Wetzel, who supported me in every good endeavor.

AMERICAN CRUSADE

Introduction
Christianity, Warfare, and National Identity, 1860–1920

"Dr. Newell Dwight Hillis, pastor of Plymouth Church, Brooklyn, preached a sermon last night on Lord Lansdowne's peace proposals," reported the *New York Times* on December 3, 1917. Lansdowne had written a letter detailing a proposal for peace to end the Great War and stop the mass slaughter occurring in Europe, but such ideas only offended Hillis: "I abhor the letter because it lays too much stress on human life," Hillis was reported to have said. "What is human life? All the great things of the world have been done through martyrdom." Hillis was not alone among New York clergy in his militaristic posture and aggressive stance toward the Germans. The same *New York Times* article reported on the declarations of various clerics across the city concerning the war. Dr. Hugo Black of the progressive Union Theological Seminary also rejected any premature peace plans, stating that Germany's "sinister philosophy which brought this war about" must first be crushed. In Union Square, Robert A. Kells of the Bible Readers' Institute drew comparisons between the Kaiser and the Devil in the course of his homily. And uptown, at St. Patrick's Cathedral, the Catholic priest John E. Wickham got in on the act when he added a nationalistic word as well: "The Christian remembers that patriotism is not only a civic duty, but also a Christian duty, and the man disloyal to country is disloyal to God."[1]

The comments of New York's clergy on Advent Sunday 1917 were simultaneously remarkable and ordinary. They were remarkable since they featured ministers of God roaring for German blood and exalting the American nation-state. But they were ordinary too, for in linking Christianity with nationalism, associating America's enemies with the devil, and equating dead soldiers with religious martyrs, they were following a pattern that had a long history in the United States—but one that has yet to be fully appreciated or understood.

This book seeks to recover this sort of mentality. Far from anomalous, ministerial blessings on America's wars often reflected the consensus among the mainline Protestant leadership in the Northeast, the nation's religious center in terms of influence among elites. Repeatedly during the Civil War, the Spanish-American War, and World War I, the white Protestant religious leadership endorsed the nation's conflicts. They did so in ways that evoked holy wars or medieval crusades, imbuing their political commentary with religious import. When Hillis's colleague, the Reverend Lyman Abbott, baldly declared World War I a "twentieth century crusade" in 1918, he said only a bit more loudly what his clerical friends and colleagues commonly declared from their pulpits. Although there were dissenters and outliers who nuanced or rejected such language—and their stories will be told here too—by and large white Protestant churches tended to be churches militant.[2]

Yet as much as Hillis, Abbott, and their kind spoke to, and for, their colleagues (and by extension a sizeable portion of the national Christian community), they did not speak for all American Christians. The opinions of religious groups far removed from elite Protestant leaders' ideological convictions and lofty social position offer a striking contrast in their interpretations of America's military conflicts. Whereas Northern white Protestant leaders tended to lend religious sanction to armed conflict, groups on the margins like Black Methodists, conservative Catholics, and Midwestern Lutherans—what I call "counterpoint" groups—often refused to do so. Their specific theological positions and social location impelled their alternative approaches to war and peace.

Juxtaposing vehement support for America's wars with the views of Christian groups less a part of the cultural mainstream reveals much about the history of the era from 1860 to 1920. The attitudes of Catholics, Lutherans, and Black Methodists did differ substantially from those of mainline white Protestants. Each group dwelt on the margins of American life and advocated a theology at odds with proprietary Protestantism. These factors could prompt strikingly different political commentary, as when spokesmen for each group rejected the idea that America was a Christian nation.

The writings of these groups, then, reveal a different version of the American nation—a version completely missed by confident white Protestants. Counterpoint groups regarded racism, imperialism, and an unholy civil religion as sins in ways that the mainline establishment never could. Their marginal social location and differing ideological and theological commitments allowed them to make especially incisive comments on both the promises and perils of living as minorities in the United States.

The ordeal of American warfare prompted these groups to engage in sharp internal debate and also to challenge opinions (like those of the New York clergy) about the righteousness of the nation and its military conflicts. For these outlying communities, military conflicts did nothing less than remake their relationship with the American nation. Although the mainline Protestants undeniably played the main melody during the wars (in terms of national influence), those with ears to hear can also listen to the strains of an important counterpoint. When we hear all of the tunes playing at once, we appreciate a richer composition than when we listen to only part of the score.

This book argues that a combination of ideological interpretation and social location decisively molded American Christians' views of America's wars from 1860 to 1920. A key aspect of ideology was theology. Theology influenced answers to questions such as: Was the United States a Christian nation whose military victories were ordained by God? To what extent were democratic liberty and Christianity inherently intertwined? Was it ever permissible for Christians to hate their enemies? Was fighting despotism around the world a religious endeavor? How America's Christian communities drew on and developed their theological understandings of the nation in responding to these questions mattered tremendously for their interpretation of the nation's wars.

Social position also played an important role in Christians' reactions to these problems. I use the generic terms "social position" and "social location" interchangeably to designate nonideological factors—such as race, class, gender, and geographical location—that also impacted attitudes toward the nation and its wars. Individual chapters flesh out which elements of social location mattered most for each group. For a privileged white Anglo-Saxon Protestant minister who circulated in upscale Manhattan or Boston, as well as for Black Methodists or Midwestern Lutherans who inhabited much humbler venues, social position inevitably affected outlooks on the nation and the righteousness of its conflicts. At the same time, the wars themselves helped remake social location, as the counterpoint groups especially learned well. Taken together, ideology and social position shaped American Christians' attitudes toward the Civil War, Spanish-American War, and World War I.

No study can adequately account for the views of all American Christians in this era. This book is an intellectual and political history of Christians' debates about the righteousness of American wars. As such, it privileges the voices of ministers, editors, and denominational representatives. These people enjoyed a particular prominence in their communities and set the terms of debate among the ordinary members of their churches and denominations. To balance this approach, this book also considers dozens of letters to the editor, published in a variety of periodicals. Written by unheralded, ordinary people (even if selectively printed), these letters provide a sense of the extent to which the masses reflected the views of editors and pastors.

This book focuses on the conflict of ideas central to American self-understanding that warfare provoked—an intellectual conflict mirroring the physical violence of the battlefield. In the Civil War, Spanish-American War, and Great War, Americans decided who they were and who they would become. Religious understandings of the nation, both in support of and opposed to armed conflict, played a major role in such ideological contestation. By grappling with the views of America's religious leaders, supplemented by those of ordinary people, the book provides a fresh way of understanding the three major American wars of the late nineteenth and early twentieth centuries.

New Insights

This book makes at least three distinguishing contributions to our understanding of the period from 1860 to 1920. First, it redirects our attention to big questions about the American relationship between religion and nationalism. For the first two-thirds of the twentieth century, American religious history, like American history generally, focused on great white Protestant men, the institutions they built, and their place in the American nation.[3] The rise of social and cultural history in the following decades revealed the inadequacies of the older approach as younger historians stressed race, class, and gender. In addition to offering a more inclusive understanding of the past, the newer histories demonstrated beyond serious doubt how social location indelibly influenced historical experience. They also showed how wars themselves helped (re)make social identities. Such accounts, however, did not always attend to more comprehensive questions about American religion and national identity. The admirable focus on neglected groups meant that attention to powerful white Protestant men and their relations to the halls of national power sometimes fell by the wayside. In particular, we still do not adequately understand the relationship between popular Christian justifications for war and middle-class white Christians' conceptions of the United States. To rectify this important omission, we need to re-examine the traditional figures and sources, albeit in a more sophisticated fashion. As Harry S. Stout has argued, "For religious history to correct social history's overcompensation it will have to re-engage the original preoccupations of historians with politics. It will also have to re-engage the old preoccupations of 'church historians' with theology and ideas . . . as an aspect of the history of nationalism and millennialism."[4]

Because they can incorporate the insights of the past forty years, today's historians are unusually well positioned to take up the older questions. This book speaks to the issues of religion, war, and nationalism by paying attention both to ideas and social location. Such an approach allows us to bring together disparate stories in American religious history that for too long have been told separately. Moreover, it takes up Stout's challenge "to engage 'great [white] men,' albeit in a prophetic vein that understands the meaning of America at its deepest, most problematic level."[5] Focusing on leaders like Abbott or Hillis while putting them in conversation with representatives of the counterpoint groups allows us to develop a greater understanding, but not triumphalism, about the record of American Christianity vis-à-vis America's wars.

Second, in examining religion, war, and national identity, this book focuses on the benefits we gain when we analyze the question over a large swath of time, 1860 to 1920. We need to study this longer period because, while the general subject of American war and religion has burgeoned in the past few years, most studies have focused on individual conflicts rather than offering comparative analysis.[6] In addition, by starting in 1860 and ending in 1920, this book allows us to grasp fresh insights about American history because it rejects standard periodizations. This book shows that the three wars under consideration must be understood as a unit, suggesting that divisions between "the Civil War Era," "the Gilded Age," and "the Progressive Era" are too often exaggerated.

The wars must be understood together because they represented a distinctive, perhaps unique, period in American history—a period where white mainline religious leaders tended to sanctify American wars with few reservations. While criticism, caution, and dissent characterized ministers' responses to (for example) the Mexican-American War, World War II, and the Vietnam War, commentary on the Civil War, Spanish-American War, and World War I was much more supportive. This book will explain how ideological and social factors caused this phenomenon, while the conclusion will flesh out at greater length how this period differed sharply from the decades preceding and following it.

Third, our understanding of the intellectual culture of the late nineteenth and early twentieth century is incomplete. Sometimes, historians have concluded that during this period the United States showed signs of entering the modern world and making a significant break with its antebellum past. Intellectuals in the late nineteenth and early twentieth century, the argument goes, adopted a secular, post-Christian outlook.[7]

This narrative is problematic for two reasons. First, this book demonstrates the persistence of ideas more commonly associated with even earlier periods.

Fine work on colonial and antebellum history has shown how Christianity and American nationalism became thoroughly intertwined in these eras.[8] Less well-known is the extent to which such attitudes continued to bear on public life in the twentieth century. Growing up in the antebellum period, a figure such as the Social Gospeler Josiah Strong imbibed then-current ideas about religion and nationalism that he continued to advocate through World War I. While the world changed rapidly around him in all kinds of ways, it failed to affect his Christian patriotism.

Moreover, the secularization narrative is not persuasive when applied to the middle and lower classes. While some intellectuals in the Northeast undoubtedly rejected their ancestral Protestantism, they exercised relatively little influence on the nation's culture as a whole. Ordinary Americans at the turn of the century, for instance, continued to flock to the popular revivals of Dwight L. Moody and Billy Sunday. Middle-class editors and ministers, moreover, spoke to far more Americans than professional philosophers or other intellectuals. Although Christianity lost cultural power in the nation's elite institutions, it continued to flourish outside the ivory towers. Jon Butler has shown just how pervasive religion remained in New York City in particular through the mid-twentieth century.[9] Accounts that do not acknowledge the way that many ordinary middle-class Americans continued to use religion to buttress their political and cultural views miss the persistence of a kind of Christian culture through at least the first half of the twentieth century.

Chapter Outline

The book is divided into three parts. The first chapter in each part analyzes mainline Protestants' positions on a particular conflict, and the second chapter puts them in dialogue with the views of one of the counterpoint groups. These groups were chosen because of the salience each war had for the particular group (for example, African American Methodists on the Civil War).

Chapter 1 analyzes Northern Protestant commentary on the Civil War, featuring sustained engagement with the arguments propounded by prominent clergymen Lyman Abbott, Henry Ward Beecher, and Horace Bushnell. In their view, God ordained the conflict, blessed the Union cause, and would pronounce divine condemnation on the Confederacy. For Abbott, who lived until 1922 and commented extensively on public policies during his long life, such an interpretation of America's wars would remain, mutatis mutandis, more or less the same over the course of the next half-century. Abbott will serve as a key voice in this book since he reflected so well the consensus of the Protestant mainline and since he left a lengthy record of his views on all three conflicts.

Chapter 2, which examines how the Civil War debate played out in the African Methodist Episcopal Church, emphasizes that invoking God's blessing on the war depended on a specific ideological orientation and social location. Many Black Methodists, for obvious reasons, welcomed the war, appealing to God and the Bible to justify their views. Others, however, demonstrated that easy conflation of God and country was neither unanimous nor inevitable. These dissenters laughed at the idea of America as a Christian nation, distrusted President Lincoln, and sometimes discouraged Black enlistment in the Union Army. Historically significant in and of itself, this debate, which was carried through the denominational newspaper *Christian Recorder*, also helps reveal the ideological and social assumptions of Abbott, Beecher, and Bushnell.

Chapter 3 analyzes white Protestant support for the Spanish-American War. In this conflict, prominent religious leaders championed the United States as a tool in the hand of God to deliver helpless Cubans from despotic Spanish misrule. Their commitment to "democratic Christian republicanism"—the idea that free institutions and Christianity were intimately connected—also led to clerical enthusiasm for the war. That Americans had a Social Gospel duty to spread democracy around the world rounded out their three-pronged support for the struggle. Chapter 4 elucidates the contested nature of support for the Spanish-American War among American Catholic communities. Where some prominent spokesmen echoed Protestants' convictions about the righteousness of the American cause, others bitterly opposed the conflict throughout its duration. This antiwar crowd often based its stance on a conviction about the unrighteousness of the American nation.

Chapter 5 focuses on white Protestants' enthusiasm for American involvement in World War I and the apotheosis of their extreme rhetoric in its support. Even more than in other conflicts, patriotic ministers painted the United States as a Christ-like nation, Germany as a devilish foe, and the struggle as a holy war for democracy. Chapter 6 features a group much less supportive of the conflict: Missouri Synod Lutherans, German in origin. As national debates about the war raged, this denomination's leaders advocated neutrality or the German cause. After the United States joined the Allies, they only grudgingly supported the conflict. Their distinctive theological orientation and social position provide an insightful contrast to the more vocal white Anglo-Saxon Protestant point of view.

Finally, the conclusion surveys the relationship between mainline Protestantism and warfare over the course of the rest of the twentieth century. Ultimately, the Christian-inflected support for America's wars that the Gilded Age and Progressive Era generations offered stands out as unique in American history. Neither before 1860 nor after 1920 did any generation of mainstream American Protestants offer the kind of unqualified endorsement of American conflicts that those generations did. This period must be better understood in light of its historical distinctiveness.

Shrewd readers will notice that this book does not deal extensively with the American state's conflicts with Native Americans. A few remarks on this topic are therefore in order. First, we must see clearly that violent clashes between American soldiers and Native Americans began in the early years of the nation's existence and continued well into the twentieth century. Harry Stout, for example, has identified twenty-nine such conflicts. It is emphatically not the case that the periods between the Civil War, Spanish-American War, and World War I were punctuated by domestic peace. By contrast, armed conflicts both at home and abroad (some major, some almost unknown) have marked the experience of every generation of Americans.[10]

America's white Christian leadership also had a good deal to do with Native Americans in this period. An extensive literature has shown that both Protestant and Catholic missionaries had a long history of evangelizing, manipulating, coercing, and naively struggling to help American Indian groups (often with government backing). While some natives accepted or affiliated with Christianity, more often than not they rejected missionaries' overtures or appropriated the Christian faith in ways the missionaries found troubling. Sometimes missionary encounters ended in physical violence, and they almost always ended in cultural violence. Tragically, America's religious communities bear part of the responsibility for what Jennifer Graber calls the "physical and cultural dispossession" done to American Indians, an act of colonialism on par with the more well-known form that developed after the Spanish-American War. Perhaps Henry Warner Bowden put it most succinctly when he observed in 1981 that "nearly five hundred years of American history show that interaction between Indians and Christian spokesmen produced tragic results."[11]

However, there are also some differences between the conflicts with Indians and the nation's foreign wars. Congress, for example, did not declare war against the Lakota, Apache, or other groups. Similarly, Congress never issued a draft during the Indian conflicts, as was done in the Civil War and World War I. Finally, the ongoing conflicts with Indians were terribly frequent but also somewhat episodic. Thus, they did not occupy the nation's attention in the same way that the conflicts analyzed in this book did. This book does not devote an entire chapter to Indian wars, but it does frequently bring in the conflicts with Native Americans as points of comparison to the more well-known, major wars waged by the American government. In particular, the birth of

America's foreign empire in 1898 (and religious support for it) can be much better understood when examined against the backdrop of the domestic colonialism the nation had been practicing in prior decades.

Religion and warfare call forth some of people's deepest impulses and loyalties. Both involve transcendent experiences of life, death, and sacrifice; both have impacted the lives of most Americans in one way or another; and both have indelibly shaped the character of the nation. We cannot understand American history unless we reckon with the ways religion and war have reinforced and challenged each other. Examining mainstream Christian nationalism, contrasted with the alternatives offered by other Christian communities, is a good place to start.

CHAPTER 1

"The God of Justice Is the God of Battles"

Northern White Protestants and the Civil War

The Divided House

In the fall of 1860, the young republic stood on the brink of crisis. For the previous thirty years, the Northern and Southern states had grown farther apart as disputes concerning economics, law, and above all slavery revealed sharply differing visions for American society. From the Southern perspective, an agrarian economy relying heavily on Black slavery constituted a legitimate social order; Northerners who disagreed were meddling idealists blind to the abuses of their industrial society. Abolitionists led by fanatics like William Lloyd Garrison and John Brown, in the Southerners' view, constituted an even worse threat. When radicals like Garrison proposed to ignore the Fugitive Slave Act, enacted as part of the Compromise of 1850, Southerners saw vigilante justice and lawless deprivation of their property.

Many Northerners saw things differently. Beginning with South Carolina's provocation of the Nullification Crisis of 1832, it appeared that Southerners had shown a dangerous penchant for ignoring laws that did not suit *them*. Moreover, the South's increasingly strident defense of slavery as a positive good often seemed maniacal when viewed from Boston or New York. Bloodshed in Kansas and Nebraska, the Dred Scott Decision, the caning of Charles Sumner on the floor of the Senate in 1856, and a dozen other instances of Southern malevolence convinced Republicans that the South would stop at nothing to entrench its slave system permanently. "I will tell you how you can secure peace with [the South]," a young Lyman Abbott declared in December 1860. "Deliver to slavery the National territories, and open to it the portals of the free States . . . swear allegiance . . . to a universal and national slavery, and you will have secured peace—the peace of death."[1] For Abbott and like-minded Republicans, the South was locked in the grip of a Slave Power conspiring to deprive the nation of its liberties.[2]

Ultimately, the center would not hold. Despite Abraham Lincoln's conciliatory inaugural address in March 1861, his election in the previous fall had already precipitated the secession crisis resulting in the Civil War. Over the next four years, about 750,000 soldiers lost their lives in an agonizing conflict that would determine the future of the nation's divided house.[3]

The carnage of the war and the stakes for which it was fought demanded religious justification. Moreover, the fervent religiosity of many antebellum Americans required spiritual explanations for the conflict, which proliferated from 1861 to 1865.[4] The Almighty was alternately thought to be on the side of the Confederacy and the side of the Union; the champion of the South's godly republic and the defender of the United States; the chastiser of His chosen people and the protector of soldiers. But everywhere, at all times, God was present.[5]

Although Protestant ministers provided the most widely read commentary on the conflict, historians are divided concerning the extent to which they uncritically championed their section's cause. For a long time, scholars held that the vast majority of Northern Protestant clergy unabashedly supported the war, with few qualms about enlisting God in the Union cause.[6] A nearly endless supply of quotations from Northern Protestants imploring God to smite the rebels supports this view. Research from Timothy L. Wesley alters the picture somewhat. Wesley argues that the Northern clergy did not constitute "a monolithic group of cheerleaders for the nation"; instead, they showed considerable diversity and dissent.[7] Some ministers explicitly refused the temptation to blend earthly and heavenly matters.[8] Wesley is correct in that the Northern ministry did not speak with one voice. However, among the most elite and influential of Northern preachers, such as Henry Ward Beecher and Horace Bushnell, few doubts surfaced concerning the righteousness of the conflict or God's preference for the North; for them, ideological convictions combined with social location to influence their wartime commentary.

This chapter analyzes the wartime views of three such Northern ministers: Lyman Abbott of Terre Haute, Indiana; Henry Ward Beecher of Brooklyn, New York; and Horace Bushnell of Hartford, Connecticut. These figures are especially well-positioned to illuminate the thought of Northern white Protestants for several reasons. First, the three held pastorates, respectively, in the

Midwest, Mid-Atlantic, and New England states, thus providing geographical balance. Second, Beecher and Bushnell can be thought of as the two most prominent Northern clergy, bar none.[9] (Abbott was not well-known at the time but would gain increasing national prominence in the coming decades.) It would be impossible to sample the writings of every Northern clergyman; instead, the chapter probes into the thought of three ministers who offered representative positions on the conflict. Even so, to add further context and granularity, the writings of these men are supplemented with the statements of other Northern white Protestants.

Ultimately, ideological commitments and social location best explain how and why these spokesmen employed religiously charged language to support the Union. In particular, their ideological statements fell into two categories: American Providentialism (the view that God uniquely blessed the United States) and Christian Republicanism (the view that Protestant theology and political liberty were inherently intertwined). This chapter analyzes how these ideological constructs came to justify holy war against Confederates. When the ministers blurred the boundaries between sacred, eternal principles and earthly affairs, the latter took on a religious cast that lent an otherworldly imprimatur to the Northern cause. It was one thing simply to differ on political philosophy; it was another to oppose God Himself. The kinds of statements emanating from the Northern ministry during the conflict, in other words, demand explanation. Social location—in this case, these ministers' status as Northern white men—rounds out our understanding of their vehement support for the conflict. A religiopolitical worldview, then, combined with racial and class privilege, best accounts for the positions taken by these men.

American Providentialism: Lyman Abbott

Although it is not entirely clear whether nineteenth-century American Protestants typically viewed the nation as the perfect expression of God's will, the Reverend Lyman Abbott (1835–1922) certainly did.[10] In his view, God had blessed the United States and chosen it to accomplish His purposes in history. Abbott was born in Roxbury, Massachusetts in 1835. Raised in Farmington, Maine, Abbott graduated from New York University in 1853 and went to work for his older brothers' law firm in the city. Events in the late 1850s changed his professional course, however. Influenced by the Businessman's Revival of 1857–58, charmed by the friendship of Henry Ward Beecher, and convinced of a call to the pulpit, Abbott abandoned the law to become a minister. He was ordained in the Congregationalist Church in 1860 and immediately left with his family to pastor a church in Terre Haute, Indiana.[11]

Abbott's convictions about God and country were formed at a young age. As early as the fall of 1855, the nineteen-year-old Abbott foresaw a coming cataclysm for the nation. On November 6 of that year, he wrote to his fiancée Abby Hamlin that his family had "all taken a strong interest in politics" and had "even done a very little electioneering." Although this political involvement was "unusual" for the Abbotts, the stakes could hardly be higher: "America will either remain in God's service, an exponent of individual freedom, or it will go over to Satan's, and relapse into oligarchy and thence into monarchy." He feared that "we are near where the two roads branch off."[12] Abbott believed that maintaining freedom was not simply a worthy goal; instead, it was a question of the United States remaining in God's service or betraying His sacred trust.

This espousal of American Providentialism helps to account for the strong rhetoric Abbott employed during the war. I use "American Providentialism" to indicate a belief that, for the most part, God was pleased with the United States and its institutions and was using the nation to accomplish His purposes.[13] According to the historian Peter J. Parish, most Northern clergy expressed a "widely held and deeply rooted belief in the God-given mission of the United States—the confident assumption that the United States had been specially favored by God, in its resources, its liberties, and its opportunities, and that, in return, America would be required to play a unique role in the divine plan for the future of the world."[14] Abbott expressed this perspective by arguing that Northern victories were providential, by suggesting that civil war would help usher in the millennial age, and by demonizing the South.

In Abbott's mind, God had ordained Northern victory. He said this clearly in an 1865 address to the American Home Missionary Society. In this speech (later published in *The Home Missionary*), Abbott declared that "through the smoke and carnage of the two Bull Runs, of Gettysburg and Antietam, of Fredericksburg and Chancellorsville, and the seven days in the Chickahominy, God led the army."[15] This assertion reiterated themes from an earlier article, "Southern Evangelization" (1864). In it Abbott maintained that God had ordained the war. In a plea for Northern churches to assist in the effort of Reconstruction, Abbott contended that "the trumpet of God has been sounding through the land these three years . . . and the heretofore impregnable Jericho is impregnable no longer, and the voice of God speaks clear and loud above the din of battle to the American churches, 'Go ye in and possess the land.'"[16] This use of Old Testament imagery served to reinforce the notions that the

Northern cause was divinely ordained and that the South (Jericho) was nothing less than the habitation of God's enemies.

From the earliest days of his pastorate, Abbott used the pulpit at least occasionally to discourse on political themes. Although he was only in his mid-twenties, the prestige of his clerical office would have helped to secure a respectful hearing. Abbott's local newspaper in Terre Haute, the *Weekly Wabash Express*, for example, sometimes printed his sermons in full for the greater edification of the community. On one occasion, the paper's editors explicitly advised readers to "go to church," reprinting an editorial arguing for the wonderful intellectual and spiritual benefits of heeding one's minister.[17] The cultural context suggests that when Abbott offered his views on national affairs, people listened.

In fact, Abbott's social status as an Anglo-Saxon Protestant male minister did more than guarantee him a voice in middle-class society; it also helped frame his outlook on slavery and the character of the American nation. In 1862, for example, Abbott recounted in paternalistic tones the ways in which old-stock Americans had welcomed Europe's "peasants, her common people—those whom she called her dregs." Although he went on to praise such immigrants, Abbott drew social distinctions between European newcomers and native Americans like himself and his audience. Likewise, Abbott's ethnocentrism influenced his remedy for racial problems. He came to advocate emancipation in part because freeing the slaves would mean that African Americans would stop coming north. "Let us remove that from which they flee, and they will seek the Northern States no longer," he advised in 1862.[18]

Despite the impact of his ethnic outlook, the Terre Haute minister framed the conflict primarily in moral terms. In a December 1860 sermon titled, "The Crisis—Its Cause and Cure," Abbott noted that the slavery question was really a matter of "whether we that are strong shall use our strength to beat down or raise up the weak." This principle remained important for Abbott; he would invoke it again in his justification for World War I. Then, as here, he based his views on Jesus's statement in Matthew 20:25–27, portraying it as the foundation of righteous political arrangements: "Ye know that the princes of the Gentiles exercise dominion over them, and they that are great exercise authority upon them. But it shall not be so among you: but whosoever will be great among you, let him be your minister; and whosoever will be chief among you, let him be your servant." For Abbott, this text taught that governments, inevitably controlled by a strong few, existed to serve the weak and the many. Only the North even came close to fulfilling this high standard; a slaveholding society by nature was part of an oppressive governmental structure and therefore opposed to God's purposes.[19]

Two years later, in a September 17, 1862 evening sermon, Abbott made such principles even more explicit. The founding of the United States meant that the Matthew 20 passage had been put into practice for the first time in history, the Terre Haute minister declared: "America was built upon this text as its chief corner stone." Although circumstances in the North were not perfect, Yankees might look "with Christian pride" at American history over the past seventy-five years. Abbott's theological view of the nation, so central to his justifications of American wars, came through clearly here: "To-day in the free states of America the prophetic words of Christ are realized. Our great men, our chiefs, our governors and legislators, and the President of the Nation himself, are set, not to be ministered unto, but to minister unto and serve the common people. And with all our defects and short comings it is nevertheless true, that the sun never looked down upon a people, whose Government has been founded, and on the whole maintained, on so Christian a basis as that of the free states of America." Given the evil Confederate alternative, Abbott believed that the Almighty must invariably uphold the Union: "It is impossible that God means to overthrow a Christian Republic, that He may found on its ruins a slave oligarchy." Anticipating President Lincoln's preliminary emancipation proclamation by five days, Abbott used this occasion to ask his congregation to "consider" the necessity of freeing the slaves.[20] Such a measure, adopted primarily for pragmatic reasons, would secure the military objective of defeating the Confederacy.[21] Most important from this sermon, however, was Abbott's belief that the United States was a model Christian nation. With this conviction, it became easy to make the Civil War a crusade.

At times Abbott even implied that the Civil War might result in the beginning of the millennial age.[22] Indeed, as early as 1860, Abbott identified the preservation of the Union with the coming millennium. Although the United States was being tested, he maintained, "I have no fear of a final disruption of the Union." Troubles might come, but "these I believe will be but as this furnace whence we shall come forth as gold tried in the fire, the dross of our national corruptions and sins cleansed away." Rather clairvoyantly, Abbott declared that he saw in the future "the Union of these States stronger in the hands of fraternal affection than ever before" as well as the disappearance of slavery. Less accurately, he also foresaw "the light of christianity growing brighter and brighter unto perfect day" because he could already see "the first dawning signs of the Millennial day." Ultimately, God's special plan for America would not be thwarted: "Trusting in those foundation principles, on which as on granite our Union is built and in the power and love of God who has so signally blessed us as a nation in times past, I look into the future with hopeful— with joyful—anticipations, believing the time to be not far distant when the words of the Psalmist, already partially fulfilled, shall be true of the whole American continent, 'Then shall the earth bring forth her increase, and God, even our own God shall bless us.'" Current national problems only represented "the labor pains of the world which are to give birth to liberty, and love, and the Kingdom of God."[23]

If the Union was accomplishing the will of God from 1861 to 1865, logically the Confederacy was in rebellion against the divine order. Accordingly, Abbott demonized the South, especially its clergy. In 1864 Abbott held that the Southern clergy were experiencing divine judgment for their failure to preach a "full and free gospel." Abbott began his attack on the ministry by accusing Southern pastors of preaching an "emasculated gospel" from an "expurgated Bible." After relating that several prominent Tennessee clergymen had refused to swear an oath of loyalty to the United States after the fall of Nashville, Abbott jubilantly noted that they found themselves "exiled" and their churches closed. He concluded by rejoicing that "everywhere throughout the South the priests of Pharaoh have perished with their masters beneath the Red Sea."[24] Abbott's allusion to Exodus 14 recalled God's destruction of the slaveholding Egyptians, further undergirding the theme of divine judgment. Applying military metaphors a year later in his Home Missionary Society address, Abbott continued to argue that God was behind the effort to expel the Southern clergy. He warned that the new battle would be a struggle of "thoughts, ideas, of truth against falsehood, of civilization against barbarism." Even though "Lee has capitulated," he declared, "the devil has not." Accordingly, "there will be Lees, and Johnstons, and Jacksons in the Southern pulpits. And we must send there Grants, and Shermans, and Sheridans to wield our sword of God's truth."[25]

In his condemnation of Southern society—and especially its clergy—Abbott used the most loaded religious terminology available. Naming the Confederate chaplain Moses Drury Hoge and the New Orleans Presbyterian pastor Benjamin Morgan Palmer specifically, Abbott warned, "We can not trust the cause of Christ to the Judas who betrayed it."[26] Abbott then upped the rhetorical ante by characterizing the antebellum South as the province of Satan. In calling for Northern volunteers to occupy the South, Abbott charged that "we have need to beware lest the devil, having been cast out of the South . . . return."[27] Abbott reiterated the idea in his Home Missionary Society address: "Out of the Southern country God has cast the devil."[28] Abbott did not believe that Southerners were fellow Christians differing in their social and political views. Instead, God justly condemned such people because of their unlawful, blasphemous rebellion against the United States. In his celebration of

American victories, speculation about the millennial age, and demonization of the Confederacy, Abbott used American Providentialist reasoning to urge his listeners to support the Union's crusade for sacred liberty.

American Providentialism: Henry Ward Beecher

What Abbott said to a smaller audience in Terre Haute was echoed by some of the North's leading Protestants ministers. At the time of the war, Henry Ward Beecher (1813–87) had already established a national reputation. As the son of the famous revivalist Lyman Beecher, Henry Ward had some natural career advantages. These were multiplied by his own extraordinary oratorical gifts and powers of self-promotion. After beginning his ministry in Indianapolis, the younger Beecher in 1847 became the founding pastor of Plymouth Church (Congregationalist) in Brooklyn. The architecture of Plymouth itself was designed to showcase its pastor's speaking abilities; instead of the traditional pulpit at the front of the sanctuary, Beecher stood in the middle with the audience seated in a wide circle around him. Services at Plymouth could be quite an occasion given the church's seating capacity of 2,100 with standing room for hundreds more.[29] When Beecher hosted mock slave auctions to showcase the villainy of human bondage, the rest of the country took notice.

To be sure, Plymouth's pastor was not a consistent or profound thinker. As William G. McLoughlin harshly put it, "Beecher felt obliged to say something about almost everything that happened in the world about him, and he was such an intellectual sponge that he picked up every cliché and catch-phrase of the moment and spewed them out at random."[30] Still, despite his lack of consistency and originality, Beecher served as the preeminent voice of Northern Protestantism in the mid-Victorian era. As such, his perspective matters to those seeking to understand religious support for the Civil War. To quote McLoughlin again: "For at least three decades, Beecher was the high priest of American religion. His pulpit was the nation's spiritual center—at least for that vast body of solid, middle-class Protestant citizens who were the heart of the nation. By his sermons, his publications, and his public lectures he kept in constant touch with the public. Millions read him, millions heard him, millions believed in him."[31] Or, as his biographers have said, Beecher was "the most famous man in America"—a "popular prophet."[32] The Brooklyn minister held a position of considerable social privilege by virtue of his ethnicity, religion, gender, geographical location, and vocation, even though such privilege was not what it had been even several decades before.[33] Although Beecher could

FIGURE 1. Henry Ward Beecher, c. 1860. Library of Congress, Prints & Photographs Division, LC-DIG-cwpbh-03065.

be critical of the United States, he too employed American Providentialism as he mostly conflated the North's fortunes with God's purposes during the Civil War years.

Beecher proved most willing to confront the United States' sins in a Fast Day sermon preached at Plymouth in January 1861, three months before the war began. In "Our Blameworthiness," Beecher spoke frankly about national wrongs and divine judgment. Unsurprisingly, the antislavery Beecher portrayed human bondage as the nation's chief scandal. He argued that 1620 witnessed the arrival of two opposing systems on the American continent: Puritanism and slavery.[34] Both had grown together over the following two centuries, leaving the nation in a deserved crisis. Even though present-day Northerners did not condone slavery, they still participated in the problem and needed to repent.[35]

Although Beecher did not get all the details of colonial history correct in his analysis, his sincere condemnation of the nation's sins reflected a rare moment of humility.[36] He also took the occasion to chastise Americans for their treatment of Native Americans and their conduct of the Mexican-American War a decade and a half before. Beecher decried Americans' "provocations, the grinding intrusions, and the misunderstood interpretations of [Indians'] policies" as evidence of their mistreatment of the natives. The Mexican situation was not much different: "The Mexicans have felt the same rude foot. This nation has employed its gigantic strength with almost no moral restriction."[37] On this day of fasting, Beecher took national repentance seriously.

"Our Blameworthiness" proved to be an anomaly. Perhaps the existence of actual warfare—of shots fired and lives lost—compelled the Brooklyn minister to adopt more stridently patriotic attitudes. Regardless, throughout the rest of the conflict Beecher talked in grandiose terms about the divine, messianic nature of the Union and God's providential work in it. Beecher first outlined the messianic quality of the nation in an address to a regiment of Brooklyn soldiers whose equipment had in large part been paid for by Plymouth Church.[38] He took for his text Psalm 60:4: "Thou has given a banner to them that fear thee, that it may be displayed because of the truth." Instead of exploring what this verse might have meant to the Old Testament Hebrews, Beecher launched into a paean to the American flag. For most of its history, he argued, the flag had been to other nations "like the bright morning stars of God"—an allusion to Jesus' description of himself in Revelation 22:16. With a reference to the prophet Isaiah's prediction of Christ's birth, Beecher elaborated what the United States meant to the rest of the world: "the galley-slave, the poor, oppressed conscript, the trodden-down creature of foreign despotism, sees in the American flag that very promise and prediction of God,—'The people which sat in darkness saw a great light; and to them which sat in the region and shadow of death light is sprung up.'"[39]

As the war was ending in the spring of 1865, President Lincoln requested that Beecher give an address on the momentous occasion of the raising of the flag at Fort Sumter, where it had been lowered in humiliation four years earlier. This invitation afforded Beecher another opportunity to speak of the flag in sacred terms. Rejoicing that the national emblem had only once touched the ground during the famous inaugural battle in 1861, Beecher referred to it as "cast down but not destroyed"—a phrase employed by the Apostle Paul in 2 Corinthians 4:9 to describe the Christian's difficult life. As Beecher continued, he compared the flag to the gospel message of liberty that Christ preached in Luke 4:18–19. Beecher imagined patriotic Americans' reaction to the raising of the flag: "Hark! they murmur. It is the Gospel that they recite in sacred words: 'It is a Gospel to the poor, it heals our broken hearts, it preaches deliverance to the captives, it gives sight to the blind, it sets at liberty them that are bruised.' Rise up, then, glorious Gospel banner, and roll out these messages of God." Just as the stricken Israelites had looked upon the brazen serpent in the desert for healing, just as Jesus had instructed his listeners to look upon the cross for salvation, so now victims of oppression around the world should do the same toward the American flag, Beecher said: "look upon this sign lifted up, and live!"[40] Beecher's biblically knowledgeable audience could not have missed the point regarding the messianic character of the United States.

This messianic perspective gave Beecher confidence that God's Providence favored the Union. In his address to the Brooklyn regiment, he assured the soldiers that the Almighty had commissioned their cause: "And now God speaks by the voice of his providence, saying 'Lift again that banner! Advance it full and high!' To your hand, and to yours, God and your country commit that imperishable trust." The soldiers themselves were "called by the Spirit of your God" to raise once again the American flag in rebel territory.[41] Beecher was equally clear on other occasions that God was the ultimate commander of the Union Army and the ultimate source of its victories. "The God of justice is the God of battles," he affirmed in 1863, and since the Emancipation Proclamation had now been proclaimed, "may we not believe that now He that leads the armies of the heaven and of the earth will give us victory?"[42]

Such convictions allowed Beecher to be nearly unrestrained in his language condemning the South. As with Abbott, the belief that God backed the Union invited Beecher to portray the South as the province of Satan. In his address on the flag, Beecher found at least one cause for rejoicing at the Southern rebellion: the rebels had had the decency to create a new flag to symbolize their godless cause. "I thank them that they took another flag to do the Devil's work, and left our flag to do the work of God!" Beecher declared to resounding applause.[43] On another occasion, with regard to slavery, he could assert that "the Devil educated" Southerners, but "the Lord educated us!"[44] Only one proper destination awaited the devilish men who had led the rebellion. At Fort Sumter in 1865, Beecher envisioned what Judgment Day held for Jefferson Davis, Robert E. Lee, and other Confederate leaders:

> And, then, these guiltiest and most remorseless traitors, these high and cultured men with might and wisdom, used for the destruction of their country; these most accursed and detested of all criminals, that have drenched a continent in needless blood, and moved the foundations of their times with hideous crimes and cruelty, caught up in black clouds full of voices and vengeance and lurid with punishment, shall be whirled aloft and plunged downward forever and forever in an endless retribution; while God shall say, "Thus shall it be to all who betray their country;" and all in heaven and upon the earth will say, "Amen!"[45]

Even for the nearly abolitionist Beecher, blasphemous rebellion against the United States, not human bondage, ranked as the South's greatest crime. Through his portrayal of the Union in messianic terms, the South in diabolical terms, and his confidence that God would give victory in the Manichaean struggle, Beecher encouraged support for the war by investing earthly concerns with sacred significance.

American Providentialism: Horace Bushnell

A figure not far removed from Beecher's theological orbit was the Connecticut Congregationalist Horace Bushnell (1802–76). Bushnell was a graduate of Yale College (1827), Yale Divinity School (1833), and a longtime minister in Hartford. An intellectual pioneer, he took the modified Calvinism he had learned under N.W. Taylor at Yale and added a good helping of Romanticism via his reading of Samuel Taylor Coleridge. Ultimately, through works such as *Discourses on Christian Nurture* (1847), he abandoned the evangelical stress on revivals and dramatic conversions in favor of more gradual moral improvement in Christian living.[46] Given his intellectual background, Bushnell might have been expected to provide a more learned, moderate voice to the public discourse concerning the war. His erudition certainly did affect his interpretation of the conflict, as did his ethnic status as a New England Brahmin. Yet in two major addresses—one at the beginning and the other at the end of the war—Bushnell exploited theological language only to stoke Northern pride and sacralize the Union.[47]

On July 28, 1861, a few days after the First Battle of Bull Run, Bushnell preached a sermon titled "Reverses Needed," which would become one of the most prominent sermons of the war. The Union had suffered almost 3,000 casualties at Bull Run, shocking those who had predicted a quick, decisive victory for the North.[48] Trying to make sense of these losses, Bushnell told his Hartford congregation that he would attempt to illuminate the deeper meaning of the war, especially its "moral and religious ideas." He began doing so with an American history lesson whose principles did not depart all that much from the ones Beecher had laid out in "Our Blameworthiness." Like Beecher, Bushnell believed that two philosophical strains had been competing for supremacy in American political life. On the one hand was a religious element embodied by New England. Colonial New Englanders believed that God was the source of government; voters might elect individual men, but since God had established the government, the basis of its authority must not be questioned. On the other hand, Bushnell maintained, Thomas Jefferson and the French philosophes had advocated a "social contract" view of government at odds with the godly New England perspective. In Jefferson's view, according to Bushnell, human beings created governments and could make and unmake them at will. Tragically, this "atheistic" doctrine had hindered Americans from fully realizing their nationality. Now, Bushnell concluded, the nation was witnessing the result of the conflict between these two incompatible theories.[49]

Despite the war's human cost, all was not lost. Indeed, the war could serve a purgative function by cleansing the nation from Jefferson's godless principles while founding a truer American nationality on the sovereignty of God. Violence and blood sacrifice would be the means. Americans would have to undergo a "bloody baptism," Bushnell warned, because "without shedding of blood there is no such grace prepared" (a reference to Hebrews 9:22). Ultimately, Bushnell said, the final Union victory would produce "a kind of religious crowning of our nationality," making all the sacrifice worthwhile. Just as in the Old Testament, God was purifying his chosen people through the trials of war. "Any thing," Bushnell pleaded, "that we may have a nationality."[50]

Four years after Bull Run, at the war's end, Bushnell returned to these themes. On July 26, 1865, almost four years to the day after he had preached "Reverses Needed," Bushnell addressed a Yale College commencement ceremony honoring the alumni who had died in the war. Complementing the view of Abbott and Beecher, Bushnell argued in his speech, titled "Our Obligations to the Dead," that the Southern insurrection was not simply a misguided effort based on incorrect presuppositions; instead, it was a clear rebellion against God. Bushnell praised the fallen Northern soldiers because they had died to "vindicate the law as [God's] ordinance."[51] For Bushnell, the American government was ordained by God; it was not a "merely human creation." Waxing poetic, the Congregationalist theologian rejoiced that the war had finally purged godless elements from the United States, just as he had predicted four years earlier: "[National unity] will be no more thought of as a mere human compact, or composition, always to be debated by the letter, but it will be that bond of common life which God had touched with blood; a sacredly heroic, Providentially tragic unity, where God's cherubim stand guard over grudges and hates and remembered jealousies, and the sense of nationality becomes even a kind of religion."[52]

In this address Bushnell continued to use the religious imagery of baptism and atonement to describe the Union sacrifice.[53] Although it had become common to employ the language of atonement to describe the war, few elaborated the concept to the extent that Bushnell did.[54] Union soldiers, he claimed, had left "martyr testimonies." As sacred heroes, they had "bled for us; and by this simple sacrifice of blood they have opened for us a new great chapter of life."[55] Here Bushnell echoed sentiments he had expressed a year earlier. In an essay titled "The Doctrine of Loyalty," the Hartford pastor averred that loyalty "offers body, and blood, and life, on the altar of its devotion." Moreover, "it is, in fact, a political worship, offering to seal itself by a martyrdom in the field."[56] Here all distinctions between sacred and secular realities vanished. For Bushnell, American sacrifices were akin to those of Christ's upon the cross. The dead Union soldiers had made effectual atonement for the sins of the nation. The war's survivors, in turn, had been "baptized for the dead" and had been commissioned to begin the work of Reconstruction.[57] The judgment of Bushnell's biographer Barbara M. Cross is astute: "Interpreted through Christian sacrifice and redemption, the war became for Bushnell a decisive, even a final, moment of America's history, lifting the nation forever beyond secularism. For men of the next generation like [Washington] Gladden and Abbott, the Civil War would be the first blow in the long battle for social perfection; to Bushnell, it revealed the eternal necessity for tragedy and bloodshed and pointed away from history to Christ's eternal sacrifice."[58]

The following year, one of Bushnell's most important theological works shed additional light on his views concerning death, sacrifice, and atonement. In *The Vicarious Sacrifice* (1866), he argued against the traditional view of Christ's atonement as penal substitution. Developed from the writings of Anselm of Canterbury (1033–1109), the substitutionary position interpreted Jesus' death as a sacrifice necessary to propitiate the wrath of God the Father and provide forensic justification to human beings. In contrast, Bushnell

advocated the "moral view" of the atonement—that is, that the chief significance of Christ's death lay in its example of self-sacrificing love. Penal substitution, Bushnell insisted, "offends every strongest sentiment of our nature.
[Christ] cannot become guilty for us."[59]

At first glance, this argument might seem to reduce the sanguinary nature
of atonement, limiting its importance for Christian doctrine. Christ's death,
after all, might be like any other noble sacrifice with no special sacred significance. But that is precisely the point. When Bushnell took the atonement out
of the supernatural realm, he allowed all kinds of ordinary sacrifices to be associated even more closely with Christ's death. In fact, in *The Vicarious Sacrifice* he explicitly compared the love of patriots for their country with the love
and agony of Jesus at Gethsemane.[60] Through such emotionally charged associations and through his combination of nationality and spiritual cleansing,
Bushnell elevated the Civil War to a holy crusade whose martyrs purchased
redemption for the nation.

As supercharged as their rhetoric was, the three ministers' points of view
reflected rather than contrasted with religious feelings in the North as a whole.
Quotations from ministers associated with a variety of denominations and locations demonstrate this point. The pastor of Park Street Congregational
Church in Boston, A.L. Stone, for instance, maintained that "If war is a duty,
it is a Christian duty, as sacred as prayer—as solemn as sacraments." Likewise,
T.M. Clark, a bishop in the Episcopal Church in Rhode Island, expressed equal
confidence in the nobility of the war: "It is a holy and righteous cause in which
you are enlisted . . . God is with us . . . the Lord of Hosts is on our side." Putting the American Providentialist attitude simply, S.W. Lynd, a Methodist minister in Ohio, advised his listeners that "Our beloved Union is the offspring of
special Providence." One of his superiors in the Methodist church, Bishop Matthew Simpson, agreed: "We will take the glorious flag—the flag of our country—
and nail it just below that of the cross!" Of these sorts of sentiments, none was
more famous than those of Unitarian Julia Ward Howe's "Battle Hymn of the
Republic," composed in 1862. Its close linkages between religion and nationalism elevated the American nation to sacred status in ways that were thoroughly
in keeping with the temper of the times.[61]

Compared to Beecher and Howe, Matthew Simpson was modest in claiming that the flag held a place "just below" that of the cross. For Protestant ministers across the North, it was commonplace to equate the Union and the
Kingdom of Heaven, the City of Man and the City of God, and the Southern
state and the Devil. These rhetorical tropes reflected deep immersion in the
American Providentialist tradition.

Democratic Christian Republicanism: Lyman Abbott

American Providentialism, with its combination of confidence in God's favor, hope for the millennium, condemnations of the South, and elevation of the American nation-state to messianic and martyr status, provided only one of the ideological motivations for Northern ministerial support of the war. Lyman Abbott also supported the North using vociferous rhetoric because he subscribed to the principles of democratic Christian republicanism.[62] In *America's God* (2002), the historian Mark Noll defined this term as "the patterns of thought . . . that joined Real Whig political thought to Protestant theology." That is to say, British Enlightenment ideas concerning liberty, tyranny, and civic humanism became blended with traditional conceptions of the Christian faith. The result was a distinctively American theology articulated most extensively by antebellum evangelicals.[63] In a later work, *The Civil War as a Theological Crisis* (2006), Noll elucidated three implications of Christian republicanism, two of which are relevant here.[64] First, Americans influenced by Christian republicanism—following especially the Enlightenment context—believed that they could reliably discern the cause-and-effect relationship between human behavior and divine actions.[65] Second, the character of America's citizenry mattered: virtuous citizens would preserve the nation's liberty while vice would lead to tyranny.[66] Finally, another implication of Christian republicanism (which Noll did not explicitly discuss at length) is simply the notion that Protestant Christianity and political freedom are inseparably connected. For Abbott, this often meant making close connections between Christianity as a religion and democracy as a form of government.[67] In his writings concerning the Civil War, Abbott advocated all three components of what might be called democratic Christian republicanism.

First, Abbott expressed unbounded confidence in his ability to connect earthly concerns with divine favor or displeasure. Although Southern clergy spilled much ink in justifying slavery from the pages of the Bible, Abbott declared in 1861 that the slave system was "antagonistic to the plainest principles of humanity and the simplest precepts of the Gospel."[68] Those who demurred on this question had evidently deafened their ears to the divine voice. Beecher likewise could write in 1863 concerning slavery, "Never before was there an issue so clear on both sides."[69] Abbott placed confidence in the Union because he believed God undoubtedly favored the American cause.

Second, Abbott promoted the second tenet of Christian republicanism: the principle that immoral citizens could not maintain true freedom. Abbott denied the sincerity of Southerners' religious convictions, insisting that they lacked true Christianity. An editorial in the *Weekly Wabash Express* put the sentiment well when it commented that almost all American Christians supported the Union while the "large majority" of the rebels were "defamers of God and the Christian religion."[70]

Abbott thought in this way for several years before the war broke out. In 1856 the twenty-year-old took a trip to Georgia on behalf of his brothers' law firm and cataloged his impressions of Southerners in a letter to Abby Hamlin. He reported first that "as we left Washington City I began to get into a rather dubious-looking company" as evidenced by his companions' use of tobacco and their unwashed clothes. In addition, one Southerner, like Coleridge's Ancient Mariner, casually killed a beautiful bird simply for sport, an incident that horrified the young traveler. Abbott also singled out Southerners' foul language for condemnation. "I scarcely talked with any one from the time I left New York who did not swear habitually," the future minister recorded. After discussing Southerners' immoral habits, Abbott launched into an issue apparently related: their toleration of the "accursed system" of slavery.[71] Clearly, for Abbott, Southerners' personal immorality was related to their toleration of slavery (the antithesis of political freedom). In other words, Southerners' failure to promote virtue led to slavery, speaking condemnation on their society.

Abbott also expounded a philosophy that Christian republicanism implied. This notion posited that Protestant Christianity and political freedom inevitably went together. Accordingly, throughout his article on "Southern Evangelization" Abbott explicitly argued that republicanism depended on Christianity. "In truth," he asserted, "the principles of religion underlie republicanism. Religion teaches man that he is a son of God, and thus makes him unwilling to be a slave of man." He scoffed at the notion that republican government could be maintained without Christianity, citing the collapse of ancient Greece and Rome as examples. It was no coincidence that, prior to the diffusion of religious knowledge through the printing press, oligarchies prevailed. Until a society had free churches, Abbott believed, it could not sustain a free government: "Men fought for religious liberty first, for civil liberty afterwards. First came the battles of conscience, afterwards the battles of the States. The Reformation came before the civil war in the Netherlands, and the Revolution in England, and America. Protestantism paved the way for republicanism."[72] In this scheme, because the North rejected slavery and embraced democracy, Northerners must also be practicing true religion.

By contrast, Abbott demonized the South for failing to adhere to the democratic Christian republican framework. First, in writing about the South, Abbott returned to the correlation between "true Christianity" and political freedom, arguing that the South lacked both. The thesis of his 1864 article, "Southern Evangelization," was that military victory was not enough; rather, the victorious North must now teach the rebellious states to govern themselves correctly. "We have not only to conquer the South," Abbott declared, "we have also to convert it. We have not only to occupy it by bayonets and bullets,— but also by ideas and institutions." To do this, common schools and churches must be established. Those who thought the South Christian made a grave mistake; according to Abbott, the South needed missionaries as desperately as the western frontier. The land of the Confederacy had proven even more resistant to "a full and free gospel" than "Roman Catholic Italy, Mohammedan Turkey, heathen India, or barbaric Africa."[73] Fifty years later, as Americans fought Germans in Europe, Abbott returned to this line of thinking, arguing that Germans worshiped the Norse god Odin. In Abbott's ideology, Southern slaveholders and German autocrats alike proved that they were not true Christians because they concentrated power in the hands of a few. Abbott's wild claims about his enemies' lack of true religion illustrate just how much he allowed his democratic Christian republicanism to influence his views on America's wars.

From this ideological vantage point, one statement of Abbott's quoted earlier makes even more sense. When Abbott declared, "America will either remain in God's service, an exponent of individual freedom, or it will go over to Satan's, and relapse into oligarchy and thence into monarchy," he was emphasizing America's divine origin.[74] But he was doing more than that. Using the language of democratic Christian republicanism, Abbott was connecting Christianity with political freedom while he associated the undemocratic concentration of power (oligarchy and monarchy) with the forces of evil. Such a rubric sometimes made for strange historical bedfellows. In "Southern Evangelization" he compared the work of the Union Army to that of the Protestant Reformation: Martin Luther "wielded a battle-axe that clave asunder the doctrines and oppressions of the Church of Rome" while John Calvin's ideas provided "the world's nursery of freedom in church and State"—exactly, in Abbott's view, what Reconstruction was designed to accomplish. What did the Protestant Reformers have in common with the Union army? Both fought "for liberty."[75] While the North practiced true religion and maintained a free society, the South's slaveholding system implied that its Christianity was not legitimate. Southern society, therefore, stood condemned and was in need of spiritual as well as political Reconstruction. Abbott minimized any distinctions between Christianity as a religion and republicanism as a political philosophy, lending sacred significance to the latter.

Democratic Christian Republicanism: Henry Ward Beecher

Beecher's adoption of the democratic Christian republican paradigm also motivated his support for the North in the war. Like Abbott, he regularly connected Christian belief and political freedom while denying the Christianity of Southerners. In particular, at various stages in the conflict Beecher argued that God was a democrat, that Christian democracy was the goal toward which political history was heading, and that the triumph of the Union vindicated republicanism.

In November 1862 Beecher preached a sermon titled "The Ground and Forms of Government," in which he laid out some of these ideas. His text was the thirty-fourth chapter of Job, where Job's friend Elihu contends that God makes no distinction between the rich and poor. Based on this passage, Beecher exclaimed, "God is the greatest democrat in the universe" because He treats all of his creatures equally. Indeed, "as you go toward heaven, you go toward the true divine democracy." This trajectory seemed to be the pattern of the nineteenth century, he maintained, given the gradual disintegration of absolute governments around the world. The democratic movement was divinely sanctioned, if not ordained: "God's hand, like a sign-board, is pointing toward democracy, and saying to the nations of the earth, 'This is the way: walk ye in it.'"[76] Ultimately, he said in another sermon during the war, "the history of the preaching of the Gospel has been a history of the development of democratic ideas."[77]

With these premises about the purposes of God and the progressive direction of history, Beecher entertained the obvious question: to what extent was the United States embodying the democratic ideal? On the one hand, things did not look good. Beecher powerfully lambasted the race prejudice that ran unchecked in the North, reminding his listeners of the irony of enjoying the blessings of liberty while denying those blessings to others.[78] The nation did have sins of which it needed to repent. On the other hand, Beecher undermined his words of chastisement by claiming that the United States was doing better "than any other nation." Judged on the Christian republican scale, where "the ripest fruits of Christian culture" mingled with "our democratic institutions," the nation as a whole treated its most vulnerable citizens fairly well.[79] Beecher's listeners might easily have concluded that an even more thorough application of democratic Christian republicanism would heal whatever ailed American society.

Beecher applied these convictions directly to the war. Civil wars were to be lamented, he asserted in a sermon titled "The Southern Babylon," but hope bloomed in this one: "For there is just now a conflict for the government of this continent between two giant forces—the spirit of Christian liberty and democracy, and the spirit of aristocratic oppression." One side stood for "the elevation of the ignorant and the poor" and the other for crushing the same. Thus, Beecher could conclude, Americans were "witnessing the illustrious parts of the conflict between the great cause of God in modern civilization and the cause of the Devil."[80]

When victory finally came, only one interpretation was possible. Demonstrating the ways that American Providentialism and Christian republicanism reinforced each other, Beecher sounded a triumphant note even during the sad occasion of a service memorializing President Lincoln after his assassination. The Union's victory taught those who questioned the American experiment to stop doubting and believe: "Republican institutions have been vindicated in this experience as they never were before." The Almighty, moreover, had ordained this result: "God, I think, has said, by the voice of this event, to all nations of the earth, 'Republican liberty, based upon true Christianity, is firm as the foundations of the globe.'"[81]

If the North was imperfectly fulfilling the Christian republican mission, the South was entirely derelict. Because Protestantism provided the foundation for republican life, Beecher sought to prove that Southern clergy were not authentically Christian. As the war was beginning, Beecher declared from his Plymouth pulpit that the Southern churches held the "diabolical principle" that some men were born to govern and others to be governed. Therefore, they were "sound on the question of the Bible" but "infidel on the question of its contents!"[82] Slavery had corrupted the religion of white Southerners, "drugg[ing] the priests at the altar" and causing them to "read God's word backward." Truly, Beecher maintained, "the apostasy of the Southern churches is one of the most extraordinary that ever took place." The ministers were most culpable, guilty of "utter apostasy" and even of forswearing "the Lord that bought them"—a reference to 2 Peter 2:1.[83] Although Beecher certainly had grounds for criticizing a ministry integrally involved in slavery, the point is that, as a Christian republican, he had to attack the moral and religious character of his political opponents.

Accordingly, since only virtuous citizens could maintain a republic, Beecher took pains to highlight the backwardness of the South. First, slavery had made whites as well as Blacks ignorant. It was "impossible" that intelligence could flourish in the South so long as the slaves lacked access to basic education. The general lack of knowledge, in turn, had led to the rebellion: poor whites were easily cowed by their leaders because ignorance prevented them from fully understanding the political issues at stake.[84] Ignorance was only one Southern defect; immorality was another. Beecher stated with confidence in 1862 that when the war ended, Union soldiers would return home, declaring: "Southern men do not know anything; they are ignorant, wasteful, shiftless, miserable fellows."[85] Indeed, he remarked elsewhere, Southerners lacked civilization altogether. Slavery promoted the "duels, riots, assassinations, and bloody broils" endemic to Southern society; the lower states were not truly "civilized communities."[86]

Beecher followed this reasoning by explicitly denying the democratic or republican nature of the Confederate States, even when the specific charges were rather wild. "The South have set themselves free from democracy and republicanism," he proclaimed in "National Injustice and Penalty" (1862), "They are neither republican nor democratic. They are aristocratic, and are verging close upon monarchy."[87] In his address at Fort Sumter, Beecher again charged that the South had given up republicanism for rule by an aristocracy who only deluded the people with words such as "Democracy." Confederate leaders would have accepted a war "twice as bloody" if only they might rule unrestrained by the hindrances of elections and the popular will.[88] For Beecher, Christian Republicanism combined with American Providentialism to justify and sacralize the Union and the war.

Democratic Christian Republicanism: Horace Bushnell

In general, Horace Bushnell did not tie his religiously inflected rhetoric and enthusiasm for the Union as directly to Christian republicanism as did Abbott and Beecher. His support stemmed chiefly from his mystical conception of American nationality and the martyrdom of Northern soldiers. In the end, although Bushnell used different reasoning to arrive at Christian republican conclusions, he also argued that God had ordained American democracy and that immorality ran rampant in the South.

In "Reverses Needed," Bushnell explained at some length the organic conception of nationality that he would reiterate in "Our Obligations to the Dead." Specifically, in "Reverses Needed," he included an intriguing passage on the inherently democratic nature of American government. People could not simply create governments ex nihilo, he maintained; rather, "we are born into government as we are into the atmosphere, and when we assume to make a government or a constitution, we only draw out one that was providentially in before us." In the American case, he went on, it was impossible for a monarchy or aristocracy to arise because God had not fitted the American people for such a government. Instead, "the church life and order was democratic" and the English constitution—which Bushnell saw as democratic—necessarily determined the democratic or republican character of the United States, at least its Northern portion. Bushnell attributed these developments to God. "We did not make them," he declared, "We only sketched them, and God put them in us to be sketched. And when that is done, they are His, clothed with His divine sanction as the Founder and Protector of States."[89] For Bushnell, like his German contemporary Leopold Von Ranke, nations were thoughts of God. Since God had ordained the democratic nature of American government, other forms of government could never work.

Bushnell also advocated the corollary that Southerners were immoral for resisting the divine plan. He predicted a bad end for states like the Confederacy that sought artificially to create a government without God's approval. Where there was no religious sanction upholding the laws, people would simply ignore the ones they did not like. Southern slavery made the situation even worse. Echoing Jefferson's famous warning in *Notes on the State of Virginia* (1781) (an affinity Bushnell would not have appreciated), the Hartford minister argued that those reared in a slaveholding society did not "live in law" but grew up "into their will, into self-assertion, into force and bloody passion, and all the murderous barbarities." Southerners despised "obedience to God," while vicious habits were eventually "bred into the stock" until the people would be both "unfit to be rulers" and "incapable of being ruled."[90] Although he did not explicitly say so, perhaps one of the reasons Southerners dangerously followed this path was that they had not accepted the Christian democracy that God had ordained from the start. In his argument for the divine origins of American democracy and his characterization of Southerners as vice-ridden and unfit for government, Bushnell also advocated the principles of Christian republicanism.

As with American Providentialism, the figures under consideration here stated at more length what many ministers across the North were proclaiming. As early as January 1861, Henry Whitney Bellows, the minister at All Souls' Unitarian Church in New York City, contrasted the "Christian civilization" of the free labor North with the "domestic slavery" dominating the South. The Baptist minister James T. Robinson, from North Adams, Massachusetts, offered historical lessons like those taught by Bushnell. In 1865 Robinson rejoiced that "the Barbarism of the Plantation kneels to the Christian civilization of the Puritans." If Massachusetts Baptists could demonize the South, so could New York Episcopalians. The *Churchman*, one of that denomination's organs, suggested the immoral Southern culture of violence was connected to its toleration of slaveholding.[91] The kind of Christian Republican rhetoric offered by Abbott,

Beecher, and Bushnell could be found in ample supply among white Protestant clergy from most traditions and in most locations during the war years. To be sure, some religious spokesmen resisted the providentialist and Christian republican tropes; their voices, however, proved less popular during wartime than the confident, reassuring proclamations that joined God and country.[92]

Melody and Counterpoint

The application of theological language to political situations primarily explains why Abbott, Beecher, and Bushnell supported the Union so vehemently in the war. The twentieth-century German theologian Dietrich Bonhoeffer once wrote that in the battle between the forces of darkness and the forces of light, there could be "no rusty swords"; the nature of the battle was too important to admit of reluctant or timid soldiers.[93] The trio of ministers featured in this chapter put such ideas into practice when they elevated the Civil War to a holy conflict.

Social status played an important role too. By virtue of their race, gender, location, and calling, the Congregationalist trio felt a particular investment in the Union. In their minds, it was their noble Pilgrim and Puritan ancestors who had built up the edifice of the United States. By implication, they were now the custodians of the nation, tasked with its preservation. The Union must not fall on their watch. Of the three, Bushnell adopted the most explicitly racialist tones in his rehearsal of American history. Decades before the Civil War, he was adamant that Anglo-Saxons were responsible for the prosperous condition of the United States. The historian Reginald Horsman goes so far as to say, "For Bushnell, God had reserved America for a special people of Saxon blood."[94] Bushnell's investment in the American nation was social and racial as well as ideological. Likewise, Abbott and Beecher could advocate emancipation as a humanitarian, even Christian, policy, or as a pragmatic military move, but their ethnic and class privilege would not allow them to stomach social equality between the races. Chandra Manning illustrated how white Northern opinions on slavery and race changed over the course of the war, but also how the advocacy of true racial equality was tenuous.[95]

Tragically, the American state that emerged in the aftermath of the Civil War was mostly to follow Bushnell's vision of a white Protestant nation. Although ex-slaves briefly benefited during Reconstruction, more troubling developments occurred in this period as well. Specifically, the "greater reconstruction" that followed on the heels of Appomattox Courthouse involved transformations in the west as well as the south. The same Union soldiers who had pacified the Southern rebellion—most famously George Armstrong Custer and William Tecumseh Sherman—now went west to pacify Native Americans. They brought pious schoolmasters and earnest missionaries in their train, whose attempts at benevolent evangelization among the natives often fell flat. Where the spiritual mission failed, however, the political one too often succeeded. With the support of Congress and President Ulysses S. Grant—another Union soldier who had headed west after the war—religious bodies, especially Quakers, were given free rein to mold natives in their image. The Quaker solution, permanent reservations, would be part of the domestic colonialism the American government gained experience practicing decades before the Spanish-American War. When natives resisted federal direction, the authorities were there to persuade them with guns, as occurred repeatedly between 1865 and 1898. Ironically, this willingness and ability to stamp out Indian "rebels" in the service of (white) nationalism was also part of the legacy of the Civil War.[96]

During the war, before bullets began flying, it was at least conceivable for humility and nuance to carry the day. Beecher could speak gravely of national sins in January 1861, and Abbott could remark in December 1860 that the South was "full of noble, christian patriots, lovers of their country, lovers of their fellow men, lovers of liberty, lovers of God."[97] Armed conflict in April 1861 changed all that. Thereafter, the Congregationalists brooked no compromise with the devilish foe. The atmosphere of war gave voice to full-fledged Christian nationalism in a way that peacetime could not. Advocates of humility and nuance found it hard for their voices to prevail when their neighbors were dying around them.

After Appomattox Courthouse, Northerners tended to remember the conflict for the fresh national feelings it engendered. In a development Bushnell especially would have appreciated, sectionalism gave way to national unity. As the United States sought to heal after four years of bloody conflict and a contentious period of Reconstruction, it became much more palatable to celebrate the nationalist or reconciliationist outcome of the war than to remember its emancipationist legacy. For most of the nation, this is precisely what happened in the late nineteenth century.[98] Some fear that this interpretation still prevails in contemporary American popular culture.[99]

One group that refused to adopt this view was the nation's African Americans. As David Blight shows, Black heroes kept the abolition of slavery front and center in their communities' memory.[100] Northern Black Christians often advocated a different point of view on the war than that offered by their white counterparts. Why African American Methodists often thought like white Protestants but sounded important notes of dissent is the subject of chapter 2.

CHAPTER 2

"Heavy Is the Guilt That Hangs upon the Neck of This Nation"

The African Methodist Episcopal Church
and the Civil War

If Lyman Abbott had walked about a mile to the southwest from First Congregational in Terre Haute, he would have encountered an unassuming white house on Crawford Avenue. The home's modest exterior belied its importance. During the antebellum era, from the safety of a tunnel located beneath its first floor, runaway slaves escaped to the bank of the Wabash River, which they subsequently crossed as part of their journey to Canada. The house had religious significance as well. In addition to being a stop on the Underground Railroad, it also served as the meeting place of Allen Chapel, Terre Haute's African Methodist Episcopal (AME) congregation.[1]

The pastor of Allen Chapel, who signed his name "T. Strother," sometimes contributed to the *Christian Recorder*, published in Philadelphia. Begun in 1852, the *Recorder* served as the official organ of the AME Church.[2] The paper struggled during the 1850s, but by the time of Elisha Weaver's editorship during the Civil War, the *Recorder* made enough money for Weaver to print every week.[3] Although based in Philadelphia and reliant on local subscriptions, in the 1860s the paper commanded a national audience, reaching some readers as far away as California and Louisiana. Although ministers made up a good percentage of the paper's readers, subscribers represented a diverse socioeconomic and vocational background. A few readers were middle- or upper-class, but most of *Recorder* subscribers probably owned no property at all.

Subscriptions in 1864–65 totaled somewhere around 1,000, about the same number as the Congregationalist journal *The New Englander*.[4]

As the AME's organ, the *Recorder* was entirely free from outside control; it was the only specifically Christian newspaper published by free Blacks without any supervision by whites.[5] The publication thus offered one of the few forums where African Americans could speak to each other directly about intellectual matters and practice self-representation freely.[6] The AME Church itself surpassed other Black denominations in its organization and "sense of mission," exercising great influence within the Black community through the twentieth century and beyond.[7] Although the church's leadership in the 1860s did not speak for all American Blacks (some of whom rejected Christianity entirely), the denomination did claim at least 70,000 of the nation's African Americans as members.[8] For these reasons, the *Recorder* serves as an exceptional lens into the thinking of Northern Black Christians.

As a church paper, the *Recorder* was often preoccupied with denominational matters—accounts of bishops' meetings, revivals, and the like. However, from 1861 to 1865, it also commented at length on the Civil War. Weaver (c. 1830–c. 1871) often wrote about the righteousness of the war, the desirability of African Americans serving in it, and God's hand in the outcome of specific battles. In addition, Weaver printed dozens of letters on these subjects from ordinary readers. Beginning in 1863 the *Recorder* included a plethora of commentary from Black soldiers.[9]

This chapter uses these types of writings to analyze the stance of the AME Church toward the Civil War and the American nation. On some occasions, the *Recorder* sounded very much like the elite Northern ministry. Like Lyman Abbott, Henry Ward Beecher, and Horace Bushnell, writers in the *Recorder* supported the war by deploying theological language; they traced God's providential actions throughout the crisis, assured their readers of President Lincoln's Christianity, and doubted the sincerity of white Southerners' religious convictions. Close analysis, however, also reveals significant differences. Unlike the elite Northerners, the *Recorder* often printed dissent on each of the foregoing matters. Some AME writers cautioned readers not to conflate church and state so easily, urged patience in interpreting God's designs, critiqued the Union and its very foundations bitterly, and wondered if the United States would ever be a fit place for African Americans to dwell peacefully.

In the main, AME debates did not reveal two distinct camps advocating radically different and internally consistent perspectives on these questions. Instead, the fortunes of the war and the evolving status of Blacks during four short years meant that sometimes writers changed their minds or advocated views not entirely in keeping with what they had said earlier. The first half of this chapter illustrates how the AME could sound like the elite white ministry. The second half shows the more interesting counterpoint perspective that revealed significant differences between mainline white Protestants, on the one hand, and the AME, on the other.

Ultimately, writers to the *Christian Recorder* interpreted the war and the nation in contrasting ways. At the time of the war, after centuries of racialized oppression, it appeared to many African Americans, on the one hand, that the egalitarian impulses in the Declaration of Independence and the Constitution might finally be realized. White men, after all, were killing each other over the issue of Black slavery (implicitly before January 1863 and explicitly afterward). After a long struggle, "colored troops" were finally receiving the same pay as their white counterparts. "The wheels of time continue to revolve in our behalf," one of the *Recorder*'s regular contributors, Lizzie Hart, wrote hopefully in April 1865. "The building of American liberty is being accomplished."[10] On the other hand, racism remained entrenched. President Lincoln had considered colonization for African Americans, Blacks had not been immediately welcomed into the Union Army, and when admitted they did not at first receive full wages. Could America live up to its founding promises? Would Blacks ever achieve full equality in a nation built on the foundation of racial inequality?[11] The answers to such questions were not obvious in 1861, and they remained uncertain in 1865. But in the intervening years, due to the war itself, African Americans witnessed momentous developments in their legal and political position that forced them to grapple in a new way with the question of the American nation and their place in it.

This chapter argues that just as they did for white Protestant leaders, ideology and social station determined AME writers' outlook on the war and the nation. In this case, the *Recorder* and a substantial number of its writers refused to deploy theology for Christian nationalist ends. Sometimes their conservative theological assumptions would not allow them to absorb the City of God into the City of Man. Likewise, by virtue of their race and class, they occupied a vastly different social station. AME members could never assume the inherent virtues of the United States in the way that a figure like Beecher could. As a result, Black Methodist opinions on the war never reflected the brand of Christian-inflected patriotism promoted by celebratory white clergy. Grappling with AME perspectives sheds light on debates within the communion that would prove foundational for African Americans' understanding of their place in the nation.

New Contributions

From the civil rights era forward, there has been an explosion of scholarship on African American history. In their work on the Civil War, scholars attempted to recapture the perceptions of the conflict held by free and enslaved Blacks.[12] Fewer attempts were made to understand the war from the standpoint of specifically Christian African Americans.[13] A few studies used the *Christian Recorder* for this purpose, however. Hazel Dicken-Garcia and Linus Abraham analyzed the *Recorder*'s commentary on the war during the conflict's first year.[14] Eric Gardner's 2015 study of the *Recorder, Black Print Unbound* covers the war years but does not give sustained attention to the conflict itself.[15] More helpfully, Sandy Dwayne Martin argues that Black Methodists saw the war as a "new Exodus" and an opportunity to affirm the need for specifically Black churches.[16] The most thorough account of the meaning of the war for Black Methodists comes from Clarence E. Walker's *A Rock in a Weary Land* (1982), which contextualizes the *Recorder*'s opinions concerning the war within African American thought as a whole, tracing changes over time in the *Recorder*'s editorial stance.[17] This chapter asks some of the same questions Walker addresses but employs different analytical categories to answer them.

We need more research on this topic because histories of Black Methodism specifically have tended not to study the debates over the war in that communion. When Daniel Alexander Payne (1811–93), one of the AME Church's most important bishops, wrote his *History of the African Methodist Episcopal Church* in 1891, he said very little about the subject.[18] Likewise, when Charles S. Smith updated Payne's *History* in 1922, he too spent little time on the war, confining his attention to denominational politics and church developments.[19] Other studies show no greater interest. Gilbert Anthony Williams's history of the *Christian Recorder* disregards almost entirely what Weaver and the periodical said about the armed conflict, as does Julius Bailey's study of print culture in the AME Church.[20] Nelson Strobert's recent biography of Bishop Payne also ignores the conflict, as do two recent studies of Black Methodists' social thought and theological rhetoric.[21]

This chapter engages the arguments and debates that occurred in the *Recorder* for the entire war. It also contextualizes that commentary with the better-known views of elite white Northern ministers. When historians see the similarities and differences between the two groups' rhetoric surrounding the war, they can better assess the factors that led some northern Christians to support the Union and others to denounce it. Such clearer vision will also allow scholars to grasp more completely how each group thought of itself in relation to the nation-state—and how the experience of civil war solidified, challenged, or remade that relationship.

Ideological Reasons to Support the Union

We have already seen in detail how white Northern ministers based their justification of the Civil War on ideological or theological reasons. They were
not alone. Especially at the beginning of the conflict, but extending throughout it, writers in the *Christian Recorder* also echoed this perspective. Their means
of doing so took at least five forms: enlisting God on the side of the North;
stating that northern soldiers' death had atoning power; tracing God's providential hand in victory and defeat; eulogizing President Lincoln as a saint; and
questioning whether white Southerners were true Christians.

From the beginning of the war, the *Recorder's* editorial page assured its readers that God favored the Union. Although in general peace was preferable,
"there are times when humanity, Christianity and the Gospel of Christ impel
us to war," Weaver argued in April 1861. Despite the grievous inequalities
under which northern Blacks labored, the *Recorder* still affirmed that "the support of a government like ours" and "the maintenance of the majesty of a
Constitution and laws the freest and most beneficent the world ever saw" justified "this most righteous war."[22] Considering the nation's racism, Weaver
thought it unwise for Blacks to offer themselves for military service. Still, he
urged his readers that "God calls you *now* to make intercession for the United
States," reminding them that "by your prayer of faith, the God of battles may
strengthen, defend, and perpetuate the Government at Washington, causing
it to triumph over all its enemies." Prayer would be good preparation for the
day that the government would finally call upon Blacks for military aid.[23]

Sometimes the *Recorder* appealed directly to the Bible to link the Union's
military efforts with the cause of God. In June 1861, Weaver criticized "those
most pious presses" that objected to the religious coloring that some Christian organs (like the *Recorder*) gave to the Northern cause. He sarcastically in-
quired, "Why don't they find fault with David for having carried on military
operations, to drive the usurper Absalom from the throne of Israel?" Indeed,
Weaver went on, they must quarrel with God, for had the Almighty not inspired David's imprecations against his enemies? He quoted the following
verses from Psalm 55 to prove that God sanctioned bloodshed in a just cause:

> Destroy, O Lord! and divide their tongues.
> Let death seize upon them.
> Let them go down quick into hell.

Although Weaver did not directly invoke this curse on the South, it was not
hard to read between the lines. Just as Absalom's revolt against a godly ruler

had ended in destruction, so the Confederacy's secession also deserved divine condemnation.[24] A few weeks later, Weaver recommended the Old Testament's martial histories as appropriate material for wartime study. The Bible, he maintained, was written by "hard-fisted working men"—the "Garibaldis, Cromwells, Washingtons and Lincolns of their day." Holding up Joshua, David, and Daniel for special admiration, Weaver suggested that piety and soldiering fit together easily. There was no doubt about the application to the present day: those who knew they would go to heaven if they fell in battle made better soldiers than those unsure of their eternal state.[25]

Ordinary correspondents to the *Recorder* expressed similar sentiments. From Pittsburgh, Pennsylvania, a man named Samuel Watts wrote in July 1864 of "our brave and patriotic soldiers . . . fighting to sustain the cause of God and liberty." With clear references to John 15:1–6 and Romans 11:17–24, Watts warned that "those who are not grafted in the root of the Federal Constitution, will be burned up, so that they will be left without root or branch."[26] Joseph E. Williams, writing from Nashville, Tennessee, stated it even more directly. In September 1863, Williams wrote an eloquent letter to the *Recorder* to explain his enlistment. His linkage between his Christian faith and his military character is best revealed when quoted at length:

> This is my watchword; let us rally to the cry of freedom and liberty forever, at the point of the sword and the bayonet. We shall have enlisted in a glorious cause, that is sacred to God and to man. I contend that men are not afraid to die in a cause like this. It is Christian-like to war for truth and justice; for liberty of soul and body; for equal rights with the rest of mankind. The Lord has promised to aid us as He did Joshua, when he commanded the sun to stand still until Joshua had won the victory. I am for Union, and I am for the liberty of our race at all hazards, though our blood may flow like rivers.[27]

Through the editorial page and letters written by ordinary subscribers, AME writers regularly rehearsed the argument that God favored the Northern cause.

In addition to generic "God and country" rhetoric, the *Recorder* occasionally dragooned specific theological ideas into the service of war-making. One correspondent used the imagery of atonement and sacrifice to buttress support for the Union. In August 1863, Thomas H.C. Hinton wrote to the *Recorder* to urge African Americans to do their patriotic duty and fight. He acknowledged that Blacks bore no responsibility for the war but argued that it was a divine principle that the innocent must suffer with the guilty. In making this point, Hinton echoed Horace Bushnell's use of the Bible by alluding to Hebrews 9:22: "precious must be the blood that's spilt, the most costly the sacrifice made for the remission of sin." Hinton argued that Black soldiers who died in the conflict would imitate Christ, laying down their innocent lives for a sinful people.[28]

Providential reasoning also characterized the *Recorder*'s reading of the war. Tracing the hand of God in governmental affairs had been a common feature of American Protestantism in the colonial and early national periods, but even in the age of the railroad and telegraph the practice continued to thrive. Throughout the war, the *Recorder* and its correspondents strove to interpret God's actions in the conflict.

That the Lord had ordained the war to destroy American slavery was the common refrain. In Weaver's view, the Almighty had waited until the Confederacy had "fill[ed] up the cup of its iniquity" by making slavery its cornerstone, to "bare his arm in the sight of all the people."[29] Now, in the proper time, God would unleash his wrath. Strother echoed this idea in July 1864. For Strother, "the existence of American Slavery was the sole cause of the great present Southern rebellion." Anticipating the sentiments of Lincoln's Second Inaugural Address, Strother declared that the Almighty would not permit slavery to disappear without bloodshed. Anyone who denied this, he charged, in less Lincolnian language, proved himself "the most stupid jackass that the earth ever produced." Strother implied that God would allow the awful war to go on indefinitely until the federal government recognized the full civil rights of African Americans.[30]

In making the fate of the nation dependent upon its promotion of God's will, Strother adopted what historian Nicholas Guyatt has termed "judicial providentialism." In contrast with "historical providentialists"—who believe that God predestines the behavior of certain nations for certain purposes—and "apocalyptic providentialists"—who focus on divining the current manifestations of events depicted in the biblical book of Revelation—"judicial providentialists" believe that God rewards and punishes nations based on their behavior.[31] Voices in the *Recorder* usually advocated the "judicial providentialist" position. "Right and truth are dear to Him," the *Recorder*'s editorial page declared in a typical statement of the position, "and if a nation is unrighteous and false, it matters not to Him what nation it is. He would smite ours, as readily as he would smite any other."[32] Such reasoning characterized the *Recorder*'s attempt to understand the meaning of the war and the Union's initial setbacks.

The *Recorder*'s providentialism came through most clearly in response to particular battles. The loss of the First Battle of Bull Run in July 1861 shocked Northerners who expected the Army of the Potomac to rout a ragtag band of rebel miscreants. In an attempt to explain what had gone wrong, the *Re-*

corder employed providentialist reasoning. The argument went like this: since the Union attack occurred on a Sabbath, since a Northern general was alleged to have been intoxicated at the time of the battle, and since Northern leaders were arrogant in general, God was punishing the nation through its habitual sins of Sabbath-breaking, drunkenness, and pride. Weaver strongly implied that the battle would have been won if Americans had not been guilty of those sins.[33]

A month later, the *Recorder* grew even more explicit as it continued to reflect on the loss at Bull Run. The editors dismissed purely naturalistic explanations of why the Union had been defeated (the Confederacy's fine cavalry and its fresh reinforcements) in favor of a providential one. The periodical laid the blame squarely at the feet of its readers: "You did it." Everyone who boasted of the North's superior resources, everyone who operated a saloon, everyone who broke the Sabbath invited God's judgment on the nation. "This war is from the hand of the Almighty," the editorial page intoned, "for a punishment to all the people of the land, North as well as South. Every man of us must suffer one way or another, for every one of us has sinned against God." The *Recorder* concluded by advising its readers to humble themselves and repent. If they would do so, the newspaper promised, "we shall have no more such disaster."[34] Clearly, for the *Recorder*, battlefield victories and losses directly correlated to the righteousness of the people. Yet, it is important to see something else here as well. In laying the blame for military losses at the feet of his readers, Weaver reckoned Blacks as full-fledged members of American society. They bore equal culpability for the nation's sins because they too counted as members of American society, with all the honor and dishonor that status implied.

Despite the imperfections in the North, AME spokesmen believed Providence favored the Union in its just war. "Our country is right," the editors flatly declared in November 1861, "therefore, God is with her."[35] Likewise, "E.W.D." of the Fifty-Fourth Massachusetts thanked God in 1864 for preserving many of his outfit, noting at the same time that "God has fought our battles for us." E.W.D. credited God for Northern victories.[36] Another writer, "J.P.C.," felt it necessary to defend the legitimacy of the war as late as October 1864. He had few kind words for the nation as a whole because it had sinned repeatedly "under the full blaze of gospel light." The present conflict, however, he thought a "holy war" because God had brought it to deliver the slave. Adopting a theme that would recur in later American wars, J.P.C. said that soldiers could fight with a good conscience so long as they gave God the glory and resisted the impulse to hate their enemies: "It is the Lord's doing, and marvellous in our eyes," he concluded, invoking Psalm 118:23.[37] For some in the AME, God had ordained the war. If Northerners would repent, the Lord would see them to victory.

The nation's present sins notwithstanding, the *Recorder* and its writers also generally held a high view of the United States. In addition, they showed increasing respect for President Lincoln, sometimes even highlighting the Christian character of both the nation and its president. Just after the war broke out, Weaver editorialized that the nation was worth preserving. He maintained that the United States had been influenced by Greek, Roman, and biblical sources. The noble government must be defended because "Moses, Joshua, Jeremiah, Isaiah, Christ and his apostles . . . wrought at [sic] principles which have been framed into the structure of our Government."[38] In this view, the United States had at least a partially Christian origin. In 1863 another writer seized on the Declaration of Independence's guarantee of equality as the nation's unrealized potential. Universal equality, inherent in a core founding document, he called "God's own truth." Now the Almighty was bringing such equality through the fearful mechanism of war.[39]

Like most other Northerners, the *Recorder* also published hagiographical portraits of President Lincoln after his assassination in April 1865. As we will see, AME writers had expressed ambivalence about Lincoln throughout his presidency. Yet at his death they universally pictured him as a Christian martyr despite Lincoln's own lack of orthodox Christian faith.[40] One letter to the editor referenced John 5:24 in its confidence that Lincoln had "passed away from death unto life, where he will enjoy the communion with hosts of other immortal patriots, and statesmen who have gone before him."[41] Lizzie Hart also spoke of Lincoln's "eternal gain," while a soldier, W.B. Johnson, felt sure that the late president "to-day sings the song of redeeming love" and "sleeps in Jesus."[42]

Finally, like the white Protestants, the *Recorder* sometimes cast aspersions on Southerners' Christianity and morality. In February 1865 one writer sent his reflections on the South to Weaver. "Junius Albus" began by comparing Southerners to pagans of the Old Testament who worshiped Baal. Although he admitted that Confederates diligently observed fast days, he thought this would gain them very little favor with God because "they seem to have overlooked the only fast that God has appointed, and the only fast that God will approve: 'that they break every yoke, and let the oppressed go free.'" Characterizing Southerners as only "nominally Christians," the writer concluded his article by comparing the fate of the South to that of Sodom and Gomorrah.[43]

Other correspondence written around the same time further illustrates that the *Recorder* connected Southern oppression with moral depravity. In the same issue where "Junius Albus" doubted Southerners' Christianity, Henry McNeal Turner (1834–1915)—the first African American chaplain appointed by the federal government and a regular contributor to the *Recorder*—also employed this line of reasoning. Stationed in Smithville, North Carolina in February 1865,

Turner provided a colorful account of the vice he had encountered among the local white population. On his second day in the town, he found a Black woman and a group of aristocratic white women arguing over the ownership of some wood. When the Black woman stood up for her rights, one of the white women "called her a liar, with another expression too vulgar to mention." The Black woman then retorted that "I am no more a liar than you are," which sent the whites into a paroxysm of rage. They "grabbed up several clubs, and leaped at the door, using the most filthy language in the vocabulary of indecency." All in all, Turner described the white women as "a gang of fice [sic] dogs."[44] Another letter, from Commissary Sergeant John C. Brock, in May 1864 confirmed the impression of a barbarian South. Writing from a camp near Milford Station, Virginia, Brock compared the Northern "energy, thrift, and the spirit of improvement" with the "desolation and destruction" that characterized the South. "There are marks of civilization, nowhere," he reported. "We very often see white children, and even men and women, that cannot read a word. Surely, this is a land of darkness, and gross darkness covers the people thereof."[45]

The *Christian Recorder* did not portray Southerners as true Christians mistaken concerning what the Bible taught about slavery. Instead, the publication often depicted them as beyond the pale of Christian civilization. These ideas had consequences for AME commentary about what was morally permissible in wartime. When negative attitudes about Southern Christians were combined with convictions regarding the holiness of the war and its atoning power, perhaps it became easier to justify some of the war's outrages. One might have some sympathy for fellow Christians mixed up in a conflict no one wanted, but who could have mercy on a pagan, immoral enemy still seeking to persecute the helpless?

Perhaps because of such perceptions, Turner could describe a Virginia skirmish where Confederate troops were "unmercifully slaughtered" as "the grandest sight I ever beheld."[46] On another occasion, the chaplain even laughed at an atrocity when the victim was an impudent rebel.[47] Other writers also justified lawless violence and crimes against humanity in the name of anti-Southernism. On several occasions the *Recorder* hailed John Brown as a hero, even as "freedom's martyr."[48] When rebels were said to be unchristian and the Union cause divinely sanctioned, it became much easier for Christians in the North—Black or white—to make war against the South.

The preceding paragraphs represent only a small sampling of the *Recorder*'s Christian nationalism during the Civil War. Like their elite, white counterparts, AME writers instinctively applied theological categories to the Union and the fate of its armies. Still, even more interesting than the ways they mirrored commonplace Yankee rhetoric are the dissenting notes that the *Recorder* and its contributors struck throughout the conflict. The remainder of the chapter will analyze how resistance to combining church and state, interest in colonization, and distrust of President Lincoln made up an important counterpoint to the majority views expressed above.

Counterpoint

Although patriotism and Christianity almost always went hand-in-hand during the Civil War years for both Unionists and Confederates, sometimes dissenting voices could be heard in the pages of the *Christian Recorder*. Throughout the war, indignant writers strongly disagreed with the godly patriotism that often characterized views like Weaver's and Beecher's. These men and women did not necessarily oppose the war outright, but they rejected the brew of Christian nationalism in greater measure than most *Recorder* writers did. Instead, they offered a revealing critique of what they perceived as the arrogant, unchristian American nation.

The boldest opposition to enlisting religion in the service of the nation came from the pen of Mrs. Mary A. Williams in September 1864. Writing from Louisville, Kentucky in highly ornamental language that sometimes obscured her argument, Williams succeeded in making her main point clear enough: "The blessed and sublime Author of our creed never meant it to be the channel of the courtly influence or the source of a corrupt ascendancy." Even more strongly, she warned against "polluting the purity of heaven with the abominations of the earth, and hanging the tatters of a political piety upon the cross of an insulted Saviour."[49] Political and spiritual realms must be kept separate.

Sometimes Weaver also gave more thought to the nature of God's Providence and the character of the enemy than his rhetoric quoted above would suggest. The occasion of a Confederate fast day in 1862 prompted reflection on precisely how God worked in human affairs. "We should always be careful and not interpret the designs of Providence too fast," Weaver urged. "First appearances are often deceptive. The wicked are frequently permitted to prosper greatly, so that, when their end shall come, their ruin and destruction may be the more complete." Moreover, the North might learn a lesson from the piety of the South. The highest levels of Confederate leadership regularly praised God for victories, and Weaver allowed that many of their leaders honestly believed in the Southern cause. After all, were not Jefferson Davis, Robert E. Lee, Stonewall Jackson, James Longstreet, and many others faithful Christians? Where Abbott and some *Recorder* writers denied the Christianity of Southerners, Weaver worried that "the prayers of these men are to be feared even more than their swords."[50]

Resistance to dissolving the differences between church and state appeared in other contexts in the *Recorder* as well. In August 1861 a trenchant editorial demonstrated the limits of the *Recorder's* willingness to conflate the church and the nation. "Spiritual interests and eternal realities are in danger of being forgotten in view of the absorbing question of the times," the article argued. To be sure, this amounted to more than a brief for the doctrine of the "spirituality of the church," the idea that churches should not comment at all on secular matters. AME leaders would be unlikely to advocate that teaching since it had been precisely such doctrine that prompted Southern Presbyterians to portray slavery as beyond the bounds of legitimate ecclesiastical concern.[51] Instead, the editorial objected that wartime zeal too often led religious writers to absorb the City of God in the City of Man. In its complaint, the editorial named Beecher specifically. It claimed that Beecher had preached a sermon suggesting that slain Union soldiers would go straight to heaven on the merits of their service to the government. For the *Recorder*, such a doctrine eviscerated "the value of the great atoning sacrifice and the new birth" not to speak of "the merits of Christ's death and the renewing work of God's Spirit." The paper worried that another "gentleman who is esteemed a Christian" had made false promises to unregenerate Northern soldiers by assuring them that *"if they fell on the field of battle, in such a cause, heaven was open to receive them."* Those who truly cared about the troops, the article said, should "beseech them to seek salvation and heaven only through faith in the merits of the Saviour's blood, and righteousness."[52]

The controversy seen here as early as 1861 would surface again in later American wars, where "salvation by khaki" became a source of contention in Christian communities. Then, as here, those who opposed the teaching did so because they maintained a conservative theology that refused to jettison traditional understandings of salvation, even during wartime. As much as the *Recorder* believed in the worthiness of the struggle, the earthly cause of the Union could never equal the eternal cause of the Kingdom of God. Conservatives maintained a belief in the supernatural work of God, which remained distinct from any secular salvation.

Other correspondents echoed the same general position. A letter written by "J.K.P." also worried in November 1861 that Christians too often neglected spiritual duties due to the extraordinary nature of the war. Unlike much commentary on the conflict, white or Black, J.K.P.'s letter sharply distinguished earthly affairs from the Kingdom of God:

> But God's people ought not, by any means, to forget their high and holy calling, or to remit their Christian duties, because of the agitation without. They ought not to suffer the temporal things to crowd aside those which are spiritual. They ought not to become so occupied with the earthly circumstances, the course of events, as to find neither time, place nor inclination for spiritual exercises—for the duties which they owe to God, to their souls, to the Church and to the world. They are citizens of a "kingdom" which is "not of this world"; their citizenship in this kingdom takes precedence of their citizenship in the earthly country: and no interest in the affairs of the earthly country - dear to the heart though that country be - ought to be suffered so to occupy and distract their minds as to take off their devout attention from the things of that kingdom of which Christ is the head, and with which they are so closely identified.[53]

Christians could be patriots, but they must not allow their civic duties to trump their spiritual ones.

Some opinions in the *Recorder* also militated against the godly patriotism that prevailed most of the time. Crucially, in these cases criticism of the American nation overwhelmed expressions of loyalty. Before the war began, Weaver maintained that African Americans should be indifferent to the outcome of the nation's impending internecine conflict. True, the *Recorder's* home state of Pennsylvania had provided relatively beneficent laws, so Blacks had a duty to protect the state should it be invaded by rebels. Nevertheless, since *Dred Scott v. Sanford* had taken away their claims to citizenship, "we, in turn, are absolved from any *allegiance* to the *federal* government. Every State that refuses to grant us the rights and privileges of citizenship, is to us a *foreign government.*" Consequently, "with the Union as it is, we enter no claim, nor have we any *special pleadings for its preservation.* It belongs to those who created it."[54] Although the war's events led him to a growing interest in preserving the nation, here Weaver expressed indifference to its fate.

The following year, AME bishop Daniel Alexander Payne echoed this perspective. In a sermon in Baltimore celebrating the abolition of slavery in the District of Columbia, Payne distanced his church from the American nation. Although his main point was that Black Christians should pray fervently for their leaders and country, he also made sure to get in a few words about the war itself. The bishop was "glad" that the government forbade African American service at this point in the war, characterizing the struggle as "a kind of family quarrel." "Therefore," he went on, "let a stranger take heed how he meddles, lest both parties unite to drive him out of the house." By praying for the government and its soldiers, "we can accomplish what we could not if we were leading the van of battle; for conquering armies are preceded and succeeded by anguish, misery, and death, but our service brings down nothing but blessings upon all."[55] Payne had no sympathy for the slaveholding South, but he also hesitated to identify his community entirely with the Union.

A year and a half later, even harsher sentiments appeared in a letter to the editor. The author became one of the *Recorder*'s most interesting contributors and eventually a bishop in the AME Church. Irascible, mercurial, egotistical, prophetic, Turner could usually be counted on to provide a controversial point of view and express it in colorful language. Born free in South Carolina in 1834, Turner became an itinerant Methodist minister, traveling across the South in the 1850s. From 1858 to 1863 he pastored several congregations successively in the Baltimore Conference before becoming the Union's first Black chaplain in 1863. As a bishop (1880–1915), he denounced Jim Crow laws and advocated the return of Blacks to Africa.[56]

During his pastorate of Israel Church in Washington, DC, in 1862 he launched an attack on the nation in the pages of the *Recorder*. The article made extended comparisons of the United States with biblical Egypt (enslavers of the Israelites), and it employed apocalyptic themes. Turner believed the millennialist prophet William Miller was not that far off when he predicted the end of the world in 1842. For Turner, God was preparing the world "for some dreadful issue"; Miller's mistake had only been to declare exactly what would happen and precisely when it would occur. With this backdrop, Turner interpreted the sufferings of the Union Army as plagues sent by God, warning the nation to *"let my people go."* Combining the plagues with the vials described in the book of Revelation, Turner concluded that five judgments had already occurred and predicted the sixth one could come any day. He foresaw catastrophic warfare between the United States and European nations unless the South's slaves were immediately freed and granted full civil rights. If the nation persisted in its stubbornness, then "the inexpressible tortures inflicted upon ancient Egypt, the cruelties of Antiochus to the Jews, the devastation of Jerusalem by the Roman Generals Titus and Vespasian, the bloody streets of France in 1792, will all hardly bear a comparison to what will befall this nation."[57] Writing his letter from the nation's capital two days before the Fourth of July, Turner revealed a perspective on the character of the United States sharply at odds with that prevalent in mainstream Northern religious culture.

Ironically, Northern white Protestants and Turner in one sense agreed: both thought that the war was being fought for millennial stakes. Where Lyman

FIGURE 2.   Henry McNeal Turner, 1863. Library of Congress, Prints & Photographs Division, LC-USZ62-138376.

Abbott optimistically hoped that Christ's reign might begin in the United States, Turner drew on the same biblical imagery to predict apocalyptic destruction. To be sure, neither Turner nor Abbott much liked their experiences in the ante-bellum South. Yet Turner's status as a Black man allowed him to see the meaning and consequences of slavery in a way that Abbott never could. Like nearly all white Republicans, Abbott's racial privilege permitted him to view the preservation of the Union as a greater priority than abolition. Turner's racial experiences, by contrast, caused him to see little value in maintaining a slaveholding nation. In these cases, ideology, race, and class blended to determine one's outlook on the war and the meaning of the United States. They also remind us just how pervasive millennialist interpretations remained in the mid-nineteenth century.

Ordinary readers echoed Turner's critical sentiments, albeit in a milder way. An anonymous writer in June 1862, for example, doubted the Christianity of America's white citizens. Using biblical language, the writer condemned both Northerners and Southerners, speaking of "their utter disregard of righteousness, justice, love, and mercy." Truly, white Americans had brought the war on themselves: "they have strenuously disregarded the plain teachings of the Bible; they have not loved justice, nor done righteously; they have not had compassion on the stranger within their land when they have seen him standing ready to perish; but in the pride of their hearts have oppressed them, and provoked Heaven's displeasure."[58] Where "Junius Albus" had leveled a similar critique at white Southerners, this author made the judgment national.

The poet and abolitionist Frances E. Watkins Harper, writing the following week, also argued that God had brought the war on an unrepentant land. The United States was hardly the Christian nation it supposed itself to be; instead, "heavy is the guilt that hangs upon the neck of this nation, and where is the first sign of national repentance? The least signs of contrition for the wrongs of the Indian or the outrages of the negro?" America could have been a beacon to the rest of the earth, she affirmed, but "instead of that she has dwarfed herself to slavery's base and ignoble ends," becoming a story and a by-word to the watching world. Like Beecher, Harper pointed to the United States' criminal mistreatment of Native Americans and African Americans. Unlike Beecher, Harper interpreted such treatment as part of a pattern of national white supremacy rather than as a regrettable aberration or a mere sectional problem.[59]

Negative views of the nation could impinge on the question of Black military service, once such service became an option in late 1862.[60] In August of that year, "M.S.D." wrote in this vein to discourage fellow African Americans from volunteering. The paltry wages Black soldiers received hardly sufficed to entice him into a Confederate line of fire. Moreover, lack of promotion removed any sense of honor one might derive from military service: "I do not see as it is any honor for a colored man to go to war, for they are not allowed to command, and it is not much honor to fight and gain no laurels."[61] If M.S.D. won no awards for his altruism, African Americans who had enlisted also wrote to the *Recorder* to voice their frustrations at the unequal conditions

FIGURE 3.   The Fifty-Fourth Massachusetts (Colored) Regiment (Currier & Ives Lithograph). Library of Congress, Prints & Photographs Division, LC-DIG-ppmsca-35357.

they faced. Orderly Sergeant John H.W.N. Collins of the Fifty-Fourth Massachusetts pointed out the well-known heroism of his particular regiment before complaining about Congress's slow allocation of wages. Although he loved the Union, it was a "disgrace" that Black men "should be compelled to fight and toil without receiving their stipulated remuneration." They could not, after all, live day-to-day on the pathetic "hackneyed expressions" intended to compare them favorably with white soldiers; if the government wanted to show its gratitude, he implied, it should pay them promptly.[62] His perspective echoed that of Weaver, who wrote in April 1864 that God would never allow the nation to prosper until it treated all races equally.[63]

At least Collins held out some hope for the future; another soldier experiencing mistreatment, Orderly Sergeant G.W. Hatton, abandoned his faith in the country altogether as a result of his war experiences. Hatton had been wounded at Petersburg on June 15, 1864, leading to a period of convalescence in Hampton Hospital near Fortress Monroe. It was bad enough, he reported, that he had been forced to accept his reduced army wage, "the degrading sum of $7 per month, that no man but the poor, down-trodden, uneducated, patriotic black man would be willing to fight for." But the final straw consisted in the racial discrimination he could not escape even at the hospital. The institution denied his father the right to take him home to recover while a white man who came for the same object carried his own wounded son away immediately. This painful experience led him to exclaim, "Mr. Editor, when, oh! when can one of my color, and in my position, at this time, find a comforter? When will my people be a nation? I fear, never upon the American soil; though we may crush this cursed rebellion."[64] Printed alongside the *Recorder's* regular patriotic utterances, letters like these blasted the government and questioned the righteousness of the United States.

Hatton's doubts about the future of Blacks in the United States found a ready audience among some other disgruntled *Recorder* writers: those who advocated Black colonization.[65] The prevalence of debates in the *Recorder* over emigration also illustrates the hostility to the United States that some of the paper's correspondents harbored. In August 1862, President Lincoln met with a group of Black leaders, proposing that African Americans populate a colony in Central America. The president reasoned that Blacks and whites "suffer from each other," while entrenched racial prejudice would militate against Black equality even after the abolition of slavery.[66]

The scheme came to nothing, but colonization nevertheless recurred as a frequent topic of discussion in the *Recorder* during the war years.[67] Foreshadowing his later advocacy of Black Americans' migration to Africa, Turner provided some of the earliest support for the emigration movement. In doing so, he anticipated and refuted the objections of those who wished all Blacks to stay in America. If many whites advocated colonization out of racist motives, what did it matter? "God has often made use of the devil and his instrumentalities, to work out for his people ineffable blessings." If whites wanted Blacks to go so that there would be no danger of interracial marriage, all the better: "we should fear and tremble for our daughters and sisters," Turner warned, lest they pollute themselves by marrying whites. Liberia had proven itself a competent nation-state operated by Black men and would be a haven for African Americans who chose to migrate there.[68]

Turner found that other Blacks echoed his belief that colonization would be a good alternative for African Americans. "West Jersey," writing from Canada in May 1863, urged colonization on the twin grounds of evangelism and self-improvement. In his view, Black Americans had a duty to take the gospel back to Africa if they truly meant what they said about converting that continent. Fortuitously, such migration would also result in better lives for themselves. Had African Americans returned to Africa earlier, he stated, "my impression is, that today would have found us in a position far more elevated than any we shall occupy for a much longer time to come" in America.[69] Another letter, written in the fall of 1862, affirmed that colonization would improve the lives of self-respecting African Americans. In this case, the writer employed gendered appeals to manliness and racial uplift to convince reluctant readers that the moment for colonization had arrived. "W.C.D." of Newport, Rhode Island acknowledged that not everyone would make a good colonist; he only wanted "men that have become tired of being foot-balls for the white man . . . those who feel themselves degraded, and are sick of hearing their wives and daughters slandered . . . those who are willing to sacrifice their lives for a better home, if such can be found." Currently, American Blacks amounted to "nothing, not even respected by our own people," but colonization could allow them to "join heart and hands in building up a country where we can enjoy liberty to the utmost extent."[70]

The *Recorder*'s regular correspondent in Brooklyn, "Junius," who would have been aware of Henry Ward Beecher's work at Plymouth Church, also expressed pessimism regarding the long-term fate of Blacks in the United States. Sounding like Lincoln, Junius argued that "the deep seated prejudice which has taken hold of this nation in consequence of slavery and the condition of the Black man, will require more years than . . . I have to live, to give permanence to our rights in the affairs of the nation." Indeed, Junius proved prophetic in his prediction of the tragic fate of Blacks in the postwar United States: "They may possess a few acres of land, but no political rights; their sons may never look forward to any office of emolument, or trust in the government of this country." Therefore, he thought, African Americans must act now and leave. God helps those who help themselves, Junius concluded, enjoining his readers to "colonize, migrate, emigrate, turn the physical world upside down . . . 'The world is my country.'"[71] Even though he lived near an antislavery church like Plymouth, Junius could not believe that Blacks had a promising future in the United States. Procolonization writers never gained a majority among writers to the *Recorder* (although they almost certainly numbered more than Turner's estimate of 5%); still, their viewpoints illustrate the extent to which deep-seated (and eminently understandable) distrust of the United States permeated the thought of some in the AME.[72] While Weaver and many other writers spoke in more hopeful terms of the nation, a vocal minority resisted such claims. Those advocating colonization rejected the commonplace conflation of Christianity and American democracy.

Finally, in contrast to those who used religious language to bless President Lincoln, many *Recorder* correspondents openly criticized him, especially early in the conflict. "J.P.C." used the occasion of a national fast day in October 1861 to attack the president and his alleged racism. His litany was basically accurate: Lincoln did not support abolition; he had "no quarrel whatever with the south, upon the slavery question"; he desired to preserve the *status quo ante-bellum* Union, with its "corner-stone," slavery; he was pledged to uphold the

Dred Scott decision; and he opposed admitting African Americans to the military. For these reasons, J.P.C. argued, Lincoln could not have intended to include Blacks in his call for a day of fasting because he did not recognize African Americans as "part and parcel of this nation." Indeed, he warned, acts of piety such as national fasts would not succeed so long as racial discrimination continued. "If the President and his people would be heard and accepted," he chided, "they must take their Black brothers with them to the throne of grace."[73]

Such charges foreshadowed some of Frederick Douglass's complaints about the president, which he included in a January 1862 speech reprinted (with explicit approval) in the *Recorder*. According to Douglass, the administration failed to provide "anything like a frank and full statement of the real causes which have plunged us into the whirlpool of civil war." Just as Jefferson Davis would not admit that the Confederacy was devoted to maintaining racial oppression, Douglass implied, so Lincoln was too "ashamed" to say explicitly that the contest concerned slavery above all. Attempts to blame geographical variations, demographic differences, or Southern ambitions for the conflict only obscured the war's real cause.[74]

While Douglass eventually mended relations with Lincoln, Turner proved one of the president's most acerbic critics in the AME.[75] In March 1862 Lincoln sent a message to Congress proposing a plan of compensated emancipation whereby the federal government would provide financial aid to any state willing to free its slaves. Even the president acknowledged that the idea was mainly a ploy to keep the Border States from joining the Confederacy.[76] About two weeks after the proposal came to public attention, Turner wrote to the *Recorder* to dampen the enthusiasm that some of his friends had expressed. He began by mocking the president's ambiguous language, noting that "both Houses of Congress were thrown into a mazy wonder, as to how they would unwind the intricate strata of its apparent preternatural syllabication." "Collegiate sons, who had been reared on the bread of literature," he went on, would join newspapermen in the conclusion *"I don't know what it means."* African Americans hoped to hear an abolitionist message in the president's plan, but Turner thought he understood the real import of Lincoln's proclamation: "I look at it as one of the most ingenious subterfuges, to pacify the humane and philanthropic hearts of the country, that was ever produced." Ultimately toothless, the plan required state initiation and cooperation to secure emancipation.[77]

Even harsher criticism appeared in the following months. In the same article where he speculated on the apocalyptic future of the nation, Turner offered a scathing critique of the president. Although Lincoln would ultimately come to be identified with Moses, at this stage the president reminded Turner of another Old Testament character. Turner left no doubt about whom he had in mind: "Abraham Lincoln and not Jeff. Davis becomes the Pharaoh of the mystic Egypt (American slavery)." Fort Sumter and Bull Run had announced God's displeasure, but Lincoln would still not heed the call to *"let my people go."*[78] When John C. Frémont attempted to free some of the slaves in the border state of Missouri, "the presidential Pharaoh hardened his heart and made void all his proceedings."[79] Likewise, when a general acted on his own authority to free slaves in several Southern states, "the presidential Pharaoh hardened his heart, and in one grum mutter, furious enough to make hell grumble, precipitately hurled them back into the darkest caverns of oppression." As long as inequality continued, Turner thundered, "mystic Egypt" and "mystic Pharaoh" would suffer unbearably.[80]

Ordinary writers also described their dissatisfaction with the president. In an article published in September 1862, the same writer who questioned the Christian character of the American people mocked the motives behind Lincoln's flirtation with colonization. The anonymous author also compared the present situation with the circumstances of the Israelites in ancient Egypt. Then, he wrote, God raised up a prophet to deliver his people so that they could worship Him freely. "But how changed the scene now! The chief of the nation calls the poor despised to offer them means of emancipation, and prays them to depart that his brothers may stop cutting each others [sic] throats."[81] Another writer, William Steward of Bridgeton, New Jersey, considered the admittance of African Americans to the military a pragmatic, rather than principled, decision by the president: "Abraham Lincoln and his practical associates, when they found it necessary, when they found that white men sticking to their party were becoming scarce, saw fit to heap a burden upon" African Americans "and call upon them to show their patriotism to a country which has always denied them the right to be men." He implied that Blacks should fight, but for him the maintenance of the Union or loyalty to the president took a decided backseat to the more immediate goal of demanding civil rights.[82]

Some of the *Recorder's* writers resisted the common habit of interpreting the preservation of the Union as a crusade. Theologically, AME dissenters emphasized distinctions between sacred and secular affairs more than elite white Protestants did. In addition, the experience of severe racial oppression allowed AME writers to see through the blind patriotism and canting hypocrisy that sometimes characterized Northern views of the war, the Union, and the president. African American Methodists' social position, combined with their greater hesitancy in using ideology in the service of nationalism, enabled some of them to resist the Christian jingoism that often justified the war.

AME Opinion Compared with Northern White Protestants

The experience of the Civil War had tremendous consequences for the AME's northern members. Indeed, the conflict became both a promise and a crucible for free Blacks in the north. It was a promise because the conflict provided the occasion for marked advancements for African Americans—emancipation, participation in military service, and equal pay for soldiers, to name a few. Some Blacks held out hope that other progressive measures would follow in the wake of peace. At the same time, the war was a crucible because it helped to form Blacks' conception of the nation as a whole. None of the achievements listed above happened immediately—emancipation (and then only for slaves in the Confederacy) had to wait until 1863; the administration initially forbade Blacks from military service; and pay failed to be equal or forthcoming for most of the war. The result was that, as the war and its effects on African Americans unfolded, the *Christian Recorder* provided an arena for debate about the meaning of the conflict and the character of the nation.

"Junius," who wrote to the *Recorder* from Brooklyn, illustrated most clearly how the war prompted sustained reflection on the place of Blacks in the nation. In the fall of 1863, Junius had forecast a pessimistic future for African Americans in the United States and advocated colonization. A year and a half later, intervening events had made him change his mind. "We never intend to leave this country while a white man remains in it," he stated in February 1865. "We intend to stay and enjoy all the luxury and pleasures of this lovely climate and beautiful country." Although he still worried about the fate of African Americans after the war, he resolved that "we will never leave these shores while others live to enjoy the blessings of a free government here."[83] The rapidly changing circumstances caused by the fortunes of war prompted evolving views of the nation.

The war had different stakes for elite white Protestants. When the majority of the white Northern clergy interpreted the war, they rarely disagreed to the extent found among the contributors to the *Christian Recorder*. Elite ministers like Abbott, Beecher, and Bushnell especially had no reason for such disagreement; they were heavily invested in the American project by virtue of their race, class privilege, northeastern background, and theological outlook. They thought of themselves as the custodians of the Northern civilization they and their ancestors had helped to create. Republican institutions, free labor, and a flexible theological orientation rooted in New England Calvinism represented to them the pinnacle of Christian civilization. Simply too much was at stake in the survival of the North's Christian republic for self-questioning or theological humility to prevail.

African American Christians in the North, by contrast, interpreted the situation differently. Some of them sincerely appreciated the generally Christian orientation of American society with many advocating the Northern cause based on familiar Christian nationalist reasoning. However, all of the *Recorder's* writers, regardless of their wartime perspective, saw the baleful ways that American society had failed to uphold its professed values. This perception fueled a critique (sometimes polite, sometimes raucous) of the United States as a whole that made it impossible for the communion unambiguously to conflate God and nation.

Another minority group in America, Roman Catholics, also help illuminate the broader points of this chapter. While plenty of Catholics fought in the war and some used it as an opportunity to showcase their patriotism, the communion in the North remained divided over the war's righteousness. Several times, Catholic editors blasted Beecher by name in their critique of the Protestant ministry. The *New-York Freeman's Journal and Catholic Register*, edited by the volatile Catholic convert James McMaster, denounced "the polluted pulpits of the Beechers" in a November 1860 editorial. Baltimore's *Catholic Mirror* offered a more specific condemnation in March 1861 when it compared "sensation literature" to "sensation sermons"—pulpit messages that addressed topics ranging from "women's rights" to "Free-love" to "Abolitionism, politics, [and] Sharp's rifles." Too many Protestant clergymen, the paper lamented, "attract and delude the people" with wild schemes. Lest readers wonder whom the *Catholic Mirror* had in mind, the editorial stated directly that "Ward Beecher is . . . a sensation preacher." Here, a Catholic periodical denounced Beecher for his penchant for preaching on secular topics and political liberalism.[84]

At the time of the Civil War, Catholics usually remained on the margins of American life in terms of public power and influence. As with other groups, their theological distinctiveness and social position influenced the way they evaluated the war. In their case, their ideological outlook and social station set them apart from most white Protestants. The New York draft riots of 1863 (carried out mostly by Irish Catholics), the jailing of James McMaster in 1861, traditional Catholic loyalty to the Democratic Party, almost universal opposition to abolition, and general antipathy toward Protestants of all kinds illustrated the extent of Catholics' removal from the world of Abbott, Beecher, and Bushnell. As a result, Catholics offered searing cultural critiques of the United States, criticized Beecher by name, rejected the United States as a Bible civilization, and blamed schismatic Protestants for bringing on the fratricidal war.[85] In doing so, their perspectives resembled those of the AME communion more than they did the common outlook among their white Protestant counterparts.

Catholics also offered an alternative point of view on another American conflict: the Spanish-American War of 1898. As with African American Methodists in the Civil War, plenty of Catholic nationalists eagerly conflated God and country in their support for what they perceived as a crusade. At the same time, a vocal minority of Catholics critiqued American society and its war of choice based on their ideology and social position. Before examining these points of view, we will first see how mainline white Protestants used their influence to champion the war with Spain using the same Christian nationalist rhetoric employed in the Civil War.

CHAPTER 3

"A War of Mercy"

White Mainline Protestants and the
Spanish-American War

At the end of the Spanish-American War, President William McKinley's Secretary of State John Hay famously remarked that the conflict had been "a splendid little war." From the American military perspective, the facts bore him out. The United States suffered a mere 385 battle deaths during the struggle, which lasted only from April to August of 1898.[1] Still, despite its short duration, the war was a watershed moment for the nation. For the first time since the War of 1812, Americans fought against a European power. Moreover, for the first time in the nation's history an officially declared war resulted in the acquisition of imperial territory outside of North America.[2] How contemporary Americans viewed the conflict bears further investigation.

Important studies of the Spanish-American War highlight various reasons why Americans supported the conflict and how they justified it. In an influential book, Kristin L. Hoganson emphasizes the gendered discourse that helped "provoke" the conflict; in her view, cultural ideas about manliness underlay the rush to battle.[3] She writes that "because jingoes had anxieties about gender they thought war would address and because gender beliefs served as a powerful political tool, it comes as no surprise that they drew on gender convictions in their efforts to convince less martial Americans to support the prospect of war."[4] Alternatively, Louis A. Pérez, Jr. argues that the United States had long desired to expand southward and that Cuba's central role in the conflict has been overlooked.[5] While these studies emphasize important factors shaping American involvement in the conflict, they do not fully appreciate the centrality of religious actors in promoting it.[6]

In particular, from April to August of 1898, Anglo-Saxon Protestant clergy consistently portrayed the war as righteous, using theology to interpret the war and justify it. More specifically, they supported the war for three reasons: through American providentialism, ministers closely identified American military fortunes and divine blessing; through democratic Christian republicanism, they promoted the idea that the United States was free and virtuous while Spain was tyrannical and immoral; and through the Social Gospel, clergy sanctified fighting on behalf of the less fortunate. In these ways, white Protestants adapted some of the language and ideas that they had used to justify the Northern cause in the Civil War thirty-five years before. As in that conflict, they elevated the war with Spain to a crusade. Subsequently, ideology and social position also revealed religious justification for and opposition to American imperialism, which proved much more controversial than the war itself. Foregrounding religious perspectives, especially since they reflected viewpoints common among the Anglo-Protestant ministry, deepens insight into the Spanish-American War and the imperial America it midwived.

The Crisis of 1898

To understand support for the war, it is necessary first to examine the background of the Cuban crisis. By 1898, a substantial portion of the Cuban population had been dissatisfied for several decades with Spanish rule over the island. Despite the failure of an 1868–78 rebellion, Cuban insurgents tried again in 1895 to overthrow their European rulers.[7] Spain, less successful this time in suppressing the revolt, sent the notoriously brutal general Valeriano Weyler to pacify the island. Weyler, in turn, ordered the entire population of several cities into camps near military headquarters, where the hapless Cubans were practically held as prisoners. By 1898, some observers estimated that 400,000 Cubans had died in these camps.[8] In January President McKinley deployed the battleship USS *Maine* to Havana harbor to protect Americans in that city.[9] One of the key factors prompting American support of the war was the longstanding perception of Spanish tyranny ninety miles south of the border.

Several weeks after the deployment of the *Maine*, an indiscreet letter from the Spanish ambassador Enrique Dupuy de Lôme exacerbated tensions between the two nations. On February 9, the *New York Journal* printed an offensive private letter from Dupuy de Lôme, in which he referred to President

McKinley as "weak and a bidder for the admiration of the crowd, besides be-ing a would-be politician."[10] Dupuy de Lôme almost immediately resigned his post, but the damage to the Spanish image in the United States had been done. Then, only a week later, the *Maine* exploded in Havana harbor.

The destruction of the *Maine* set off an avalanche of opinion concerning the proper American response; viewpoints ranged from hesitation and patience to jingoistic calls for reprisals. When Congress declared war only two months later, however, almost all opposition to the conflict vanished from influential white Protestants. Analyzing how and why prominent clerical spokesmen and officially Christian publications backed the war effort helps further uncover the ideological and social motivations for war.

American Providentialism

First, perhaps the most important motivation for vociferous support of the Spanish-American War lay in the belief that God directed American affairs. Whether or not traditional views of Providence were fading for ordinary Americans in the Gilded Age, the nation's Protestant clergy enlisted providen-tial interpretations frequently during the Spanish-American War.[11] No one captured this attitude better than Lyman Abbott.

By 1898, because of his writing and preaching, Abbott had become one of America's most well-known spiritual guides. Sixty-two years old, in the prime of his career, he had been for the past decade the successor to none other than Henry Ward Beecher as pastor of Plymouth Church in Brooklyn, a location at the center of American power. His sermons were often excerpted or re-printed in the New York press.[12] At the same time he served as editor-in-chief of the *Outlook*, whose weekly circulation of 100,000 was about twice as great as the Methodist *Christian Advocate* (New York) and roughly comparable to the 150,000 of the secular monthly *Century Magazine*.[13] Abbott gained enough rec-ognition to become the victim of Mr. Dooley's satirical pen in 1899 and around the same time began an extensive correspondence with Theodore Roo-sevelt.[14] Abbott's justification of the war, then, mattered for his audience of prosperous white Protestants since his sermons and editorials reached a vast and influential group.

For the *Outlook* editor, the United States amounted to more than an ordinary nation in the divine scheme. Espousing what historian Nicholas Guyatt calls "historical providentialism," Abbott identified the United States as the New Is-rael, a nation chosen by God to accomplish certain purposes in history.[15] Abbott proclaimed this view most explicitly in a sermon he preached to his Plymouth congregation on May 15, about a month into the war. He began this message by recounting how God had chosen the Old Testament Hebrews to be his "favored people." God had protected and guided them, he said, and had given them productive land on which to live. Yet, "more even than the Hebrew people," Abbott asserted, "have the American people been favored of God." He lauded the beautiful land of the United States, celebrating the population growth and accompanying "civilization" that made America the envy of the world.[16]

To account for the nation's remarkable success, Abbott turned to the Reformed concept of divine election. Although Abbott and his generation of liberal Protestants had long since abandoned the traditional Calvinist doctrine of individual salvation by predestination, Abbott in this sermon employed the concept to describe the United States.[17] "We are," Abbott proclaimed, speaking of Americans, "an elect people of God. We have received, pre-eminently, His blessing, His gifts, and shone with His glory." Just as God had chosen the Hebrew nation under the Old Covenant, Abbott believed, so He had now chosen the United States in these latter days to accomplish his purposes.[18] The *Outlook* reiterated this assessment three weeks later. As the journal outlined the rationale for colonizing the Philippines, it reflected upon "the great trust" that God placed upon the American people. After all, the periodical stated, God had "called them from all nationalities" to accomplish His purposes.[19]

Abbott also expressed strong confidence that he knew the nature of these purposes. Most important, God had chosen the United States to shine as a beacon of freedom to the world. In his May 15 sermon, Abbott applied the language of the prophet Isaiah to America's messianic mission: "He has elected us . . . to be a light to the nations of the world and a salvation for all humanity." Since the nation's founding, Abbott claimed, the United States had attracted attention from other countries: "From the very beginning of the American Revolution, the eyes of the European nations have been turned hitherward." The successful history of the United States vindicated its role as the divine ambassador of freedom.[20] Now, Abbott believed God was calling the nation to continue its godly mission by spreading liberty and justice to other parts of the world.

Because the nation was fulfilling divine purposes, God himself would guarantee the success of American arms. When President McKinley proclaimed a day of Thanksgiving in June, Abbott rejoiced that "America is permitted to fight God's battles for him." He was especially exuberant over what seemed to be providential victories in Cuba (Santiago) and the Philippines (Manila). The *Outlook* thanked God because He had "thought [America] worthy to execute his commission of justice and liberty."[21] To Abbott, Commodore George

Dewey's victory at Manila Bay resounded with messianic meaning: "To this American nation, whose light of intelligence, of liberty, of humanity has been the distinguishing characteristic of its life . . . there comes to-day from the guns of Dewey's fleet across the sea this prophetic call: 'Arise, shine, for thy light has come, and nations shall come to thy light, and bring to the lightness of thy rising.'"[22] According to the *Outlook*, Commodore Dewey's fleets had simply been on "God's errands of justice and liberty."[23]

This conception of America, in turn, led to a particular interpretation of the war. According to Abbott, the United States had not initiated the conflict; instead, God ordained the war, simply using America as His means to accomplish a predestined end. Abbott explained this way of thinking in a letter to his brother Edward Abbott: "steadily, it seems to me, events have forced us forward; events which are Gods [*sic*] way of teaching men their duty."[24] Even before the conflict began, Abbott assured his readers that "It is . . . a Christian duty to accept the sword Excalibur, when divine providence puts it into our hands."[25] Using the same metaphor in a sermon at Plymouth, Abbott emphasized the disinterested, benevolent character of America intervention: "When God puts the sword in our hands let us use it, and when we have used it throw it into the sea."[26] After the decisive conquest of Manila in May, the *Outlook* reiterated the United States' passive role in the divine plan. American arms would inevitably triumph because "the Nation is simply the hand of Providence; its task was made for it by its history, and they who fall in the doing of that task fall in a noble cause."[27]

Similar justifications for the war were offered by articles in the theological journal *Bibliotheca Sacra*. The journal had historically enjoyed a close relationship with the Congregationalist Andover Theological Seminary under the editorship of Edwards A. Park. In the early 1880s, however, Park correctly perceived theological drift at Andover and moved the journal out from under the seminary's auspices to preserve its orthodox character. By the time of the Spanish-American War, *Bibliotheca Sacra* offered mostly conservative but not reactionary views on issues relating to textual biblical criticism while proffering slightly more liberal ones on theistic evolution. Yet the editors also found space in the fall of 1898 for a few reflections on the Spanish-American War.[28]

Although the editor G. Frederick White held more conservative theological positions than did Abbott, he reached nearly identical conclusions about the scrap with Spain. He too believed that the conflict had been nothing short of a religious duty: it "would have been unchristian," he said, to ignore the plight of the Cubans. Moreover, it fell to the United States to perform the liberating work since America was especially worthy. "With all their faults," White solemnly averred, "the institutions of America are the hope of the world." Such greatness entitled, or even required, the United States to show global leadership: "a nation as great as the United States should make the weight of her influence felt throughout the world, all the more because her aims are so high and her institutions so worthy of imitation." The argument would not have been complete without a religious coloring: "the glory of a nation, like the glory of God, is not a thing to be lightly esteemed."[29]

Such prowar attitudes fit the times perfectly; only a handful of Protestant clergy publicly opposed the war. One of those who did so was Lyman Abbott's brother Edward, a conservative Episcopalian priest in Boston. Not only did the two Abbotts diverge on theology, they also faced off on the question of American politics. When the Episcopalian clergy of Massachusetts passed resolutions endorsing the war, Edward Abbott protested that Spain and the United States had not exhausted peaceful solutions to the conflict. Therefore, endorsement of the war was "contrary to the teaching of our Lord Jesus Christ." Likewise, Edward Abbott's Episcopalian colleague C.W. Duane wrote to affirm his antiwar position. Duane blamed the war on "the papers who want to make a market for their 'Extra' lies, & the politicians who are willing to sacrifice thousands of lives" for reelection.[30]

Such opponents of the war, however, remained a decided minority. Their arguments fell flat among Americans who saw the United States as virtuous and progressive (especially in contrast with allegedly corrupt Spain). The well-known New York Congregationalist Josiah Strong (1847–1916), for example, agreed that the United States was specially chosen. In an apology for a greater role in the world for the nation, Strong rehearsed similar themes of divine blessing. In his view, "God had winnowed Europe for the seeds of civil and religious liberty" before planting them in America.[31] Strong could thus confidently speak of "the place in the world which God has given us."[32] Similarly, the Canadian American minister Robert Stuart MacArthur of New York's Calvary Baptist Church made God's supposed involvement in the conflict equally clear. Addressing the American Baptist Publication Society, MacArthur imagined "the voice of God" speaking to the hero of Manila, Commodore Dewey: "As I was with Moses, so shall I be with thee, O heroic Commodore Dewey. No Spanish ship shall long stand before thee, thou leader of victorious Americans, in this triumph of humanity, of liberty, and of true Christianity."[33] As in many such instances, confidence in God's favor toward the United States contributed to national chest-thumping. Such sentiments were simply more appealing than the more pessimistic or critical ones offered by Edward Abbott or C.W. Duane.

On July 10 Reverend Frank Bristol of Washington's Metropolitan Methodist Episcopal Church offered an even grander vision of America and its present war. Preaching to a standing-room-only crowd that included President McKinley, Bristol brought the house down: "Were the guns of Dewey and Sampson less providential than the ram's horns of Joshua, the lamps and pitchers of Gideon, or the rod of Moses? Were Manila and Santiago less providential in the history of human freedom than Jericho and Ai?" In his view, those who had died in the war had "offered their lives on Liberty's holy altar." Indeed, fallen American soldiers composed the latest links in an unbroken chain of martyrs to liberty and conscience stretching back from the Civil War to the Revolution, the Pilgrims, the Protestant Reformers, the first-century martyrs, the apostles, and even Christ. The *New York Times* reported the president "deeply impressed" by this discourse that drew on biblical language and ideas to celebrate American victory.[34]

The Chicago Baptist P.S. Henson agreed with Bristol. "Never was the hand of God more manifestly visible" than in American military victories, he declared. The Unitarian minister F.C. Southworth also echoed the providential interpretation. Across the nation, he exulted, men were responding to McKinley's call to arms in the words of the prophet Isaiah: "Here am I; send me." Because the war was a humanitarian one, he stated, it took on a "unique and sacred" character. Baptists and Unitarians did not normally agree about much, but here they joined forces to identify and celebrate God's providential blessing of America.[35]

A year and a half after the conclusion of the war, Lyman Abbott continued to advocate a providentialist interpretation. In discussing the duties of Americans toward their new colonial possessions, the *Outlook* looked back on the war with Spain. The analysis first offered in 1898 had not changed much: "We have believed and we still believe that the war against Spain was a most just and necessary war; that on it we had the right to invoke 'the considerate judgment of mankind and the gracious favor of Almighty God,' and that by both it has been sanctioned; [and] that if by his providence God ever signified his approval of war, he did so by the unparalleled successes of our navy at Manila and Santiago."[36] This was said, not in the medieval crusades or the Thirty Years War, but in 1900 by a progressive American Protestant leader. To adequately understand the Spanish-American War, we must reckon with the otherworldly sanction with which some of its proponents invested it.

Christian Republicanism

Abbott also justified American participation in the war through observations associated with democratic Christian republicanism, a constellation of ideas defined in chapter 1. One implication of Christian republicanism Abbott frequently articulated was the assumption that political liberty and true Christianity were connected. Echoing statements he had made during the Civil War, Abbott argued in July 1898 that a free religion (Protestantism) was a prerequisite for democracy. "The foundations of self-government," the *Outlook* thought, "must first be laid in a free religion and a universal education."[37] As the *Outlook* weighed the United States' options in governing the territories acquired in the war, it reflected on the responsibilities of American Christians. Since permitting an established church in the Philippines was unthinkable, American Catholics needed to show Filipinos how to practice Catholicism without the benefit of the state. Yet, "here, too," Abbott argued, "is a field for Protestants, in no sectarian or polemical spirit, but as preachers of the liberty wherewith Christ makes us free. The Protestant sects ought to lay aside their sectarianism and unite in a common effort to teach the Gospel of liberty which they have inherited from Luther and from Paul."[38] What exactly did Abbott mean by the phrase "Gospel of liberty"? Most likely he did not strictly mean a disestablished church (the appeal to Luther would not make sense in that reading). Instead, by "Gospel of liberty," it seems likely he meant simply the traditions of political freedom that, in his view, inevitably grew out of a free, Protestant religion.[39] For Abbott (as for Frank Bristol), a direct intellectual path led from the Apostle Paul to the Magna Carta to the Protestant Reformation to the Founding Fathers. By discussing political liberty in the context of disestablishment and by using the term "Gospel," Abbott drew from the well of democratic Christian republicanism to justify American actions.

Another aspect of Christian republicanism is that the character of a nation's citizenry matters. Virtuous leaders and citizens will preserve the nation's liberty while widespread vice will lead to tyranny.[40] In keeping with this line of thinking, Abbott endeavored to show the moral corruption of the Spanish colonial state and its agents while he beatified the character of the United States and its soldiers. In doing so, Abbott implied that undemocratic political structures produced immoral Spanish soldiers while free institutions produced virtuous American citizens.

To illustrate the connection between vice and tyranny, he first associated the present Spanish government with the backward religious and political systems of pre-Reformation Europe. In a May 14 article titled "An Irrepressible Conflict," the *Outlook* contrasted the achievements of the Anglo-Saxon nations with those of Spain. While the Anglo-Saxon countries had welcomed the Protestant Reformation, Spain had "stood for merciless and arbitrary suppression of freedom of faith, worship, action, and thought." Abbott trotted out the archetype of the "implacable Spanish priest" and reminded readers that Spain had wasted most of its economic gain from its New World colonies in the "futile attempt to annihilate Protestantism." Spaniards, he said, opposed "civil and religious liberty." Continuing in this vein, Abbott went on to accuse Spain (with some justification) of the "systematic robbery" of Cuba, arguing that "history can show no more appalling chapter of greed, cruelty, and incompetence than the government of Spain on this continent."[41] Two months later, Abbott invoked the memory of the Inquisition to demonize his Spanish foes.[42] He also accused the Spanish government of inadequately educating its people, attributing American military success to the United States' well-educated, disciplined fighting forces. "The conflict at Manila and that at Santiago," he averred, "were between the Public School and the Inquisition; between a century which teaches the common people to think, and one which forbids them to think."[43] In his view, viciousness characterized the backward Spanish nation.

"An Irrepressible Conflict" revealed other dimensions of Abbott's thought as well. First was the allusion to the Civil War in the article's title. Just as conflict between North and South could not have been avoided, the *Outlook* declared, "for the same reason, the war between Spain and this country was inevitable." Backward, repressive Spanish Catholicism was locked in a duel to the death with progressive Anglo-Saxon Protestantism. Second, in keeping with his penchant for world-historical interpretations, Abbott argued that the present struggle merely continued a conflict "between Anglo-Saxon and Spanish civilization" persisting since the British victory over the Spanish Armada in 1588. Abbott underlined what the outcome of that battle meant for his readers: "For the fate of America hung in the balance when the Armada sailed; if [Spanish emperor Philip II] had crushed England, no English-speaking colony would have been planted in the Western world."[44] This analysis, with its combination of religious antagonism and ethnic nationalism, elevated the stakes of the conflict to stratospheric importance.

In addition to governmental tyranny, the *Outlook* alleged, vice ran rampant among ordinary Spanish soldiers. Abbott had it "on good authority" that Spanish privates were actually selling their weapons to their enemies, the Cuban insurgents. The soldiers needed money, in turn, because of rampant bribery and corruption among the Spanish military brass.[45] The moral debauchery of the Spanish soldiers also extended to their ostensible alcohol abuse. Abbott reported that before the battle of Santiago, the Spanish soldiers had been "filled with liquor," in consequence of which they had "fired so rapidly that they had neither the brains nor the time to take aim."[46] The *Outlook* the following week further detailed Spanish dependence on alcohol. According to Abbott and his editorial colleagues, the Spanish officers had mandated that "extra grog should be served to the sailors to fortify them" for battle.[47] The Spanish were not worthy opponents in Abbott's Christian republican scheme; instead, they were moral degenerates. Although the *Outlook* did not directly say so, it was reasonable to conclude, in Christian republican fashion, that such personal immorality stemmed from the oppressive combination of church and state exemplified in Spanish Catholicism. National tyranny and personal immorality at least partially explained Spanish defeat.

If the Catholic Spanish were immoral and tyrannical, Americans presented a marked contrast. The *Outlook*'s coverage of the war chronicled in depth the virtue of both the American nation and particular individuals. As to national righteousness, the American military had long abandoned daily alcohol rations for its soldiers while the navy was treating its Spanish prisoners of war with remarkable humanity. The *Outlook* reported that the prisoners of war received "excellent treatment" en route to the United States and that "every provision [would] be made for their comfort."[48] In an article celebrating the Fourth of July, Abbott maintained that even the war itself was being prosecuted with remarkable uprightness. "So far," he wrote, "not a false note has been struck, not an ignoble deed done; at every point there has been unostentatious but splendid courage."[49] In contrast to Spanish despotism, Abbott believed, the United States was a virtuous republic.

The *Outlook* happily reported as well on the promising spiritual state of the American military forces as individuals. On July 30, Abbott recounted the work

FIGURE 4.   Images of the Spanish-American War. Library of Congress, Prints & Photographs Division, LC-DIG-pga-01623.

being done with American troops by the Young Men's Christian Association (YMCA). At Camp Alger, Virginia, for instance, 130 soldiers attended Bible classes, 2,686 showed up for "Gospel meetings," and 57 were converted. The staff of the YMCA had even better success at Camp Lee, Virginia, where over 100 soldiers professed Christ for the first time.[50] Lieutenant Richmond Hobson, who had instantly become an American celebrity for his daring actions at Santiago harbor, had served as a YMCA chapter president in 1888.[51]

Abbott was hardly alone in these interpretations. In July 1898, William B. Millar, the secretary of the Army and Navy Christian Commission (ANCC), used the *Independent*—a New York weekly once associated with Beecher—as a forum to showcase the successes of his organization, which aimed to inspire Christian conduct among American soldiers. Sponsored by the YMCA, the ANCC's advisors included the evangelist Dwight L. Moody, the Civil War general O.O. Howard, the philanthropist William E. Dodge, and other luminaries. The ANCC did all it could to promote moral living among the enlisted men. It furnished wholesome reading material, supplied ice water buckets (as opposed to alcoholic beverages), provided "innocent games" like chess and checkers, and pitched large tents for religious services. Cooperating with the military chaplains, Moody and his music minister Ira Sankey oversaw revival services in the camps; Millar reported that these were evidently successful since "scarcely a service passes without definite decisions for Christ."[52]

White, writing in *Bibliotheca Sacra*, was pleased to hear of such developments. "To a remarkable extent the officers both of the navy and the army are men of positive Christian character," he maintained. "Recruits have come from the most intelligent and prosperous classes, representing in an unusual degree the colleges, the high schools, the Sabbath-schools, and the Christian Endeavor Societies of the country." White argued that American soldiers' bravery was due to the free society from which they came. In Christian republican fashion, he also offered a warning that Americans must be sure to maintain the virtuous nature of their society.[53] By chronicling the virtue and piety of the American nation and its soldiers, supporters of the war upheld a key tenet of democratic Christian republicanism. That ideology helped justify the war and explain American military success.

Others stood with figures like Abbott, Millar, and White as they too used anti-Catholic or Christian republican language to justify the conflict. Although all nations had some incidents to be ashamed of, observed the Methodist *Christian Advocate* in May 1898, "Spain unquestionably is the worst among those who use an alphabet of twenty-six letters." Spain's immorality, the *Advocate* thought, could be attributed to its Catholicism. Whereas other nations such as Switzerland, England, and the United States had gradually made moral progress as a result of the Reformation, Spain was still mired in the bog of popish tyranny. Accordingly, it was not surprising that that nation exhibited sixteenth-century morality.[54]

For his part, the Social Gospel leader Washington Gladden of Columbus, Ohio, showed no surprise that Spain was losing its grip on Cuba. Gladden ascribed Spain's current woes to the legacy of the Inquisition, which he characterized as "an attempt to exterminate independent thought and rational leadership." He added that "the history of Spanish decay and misrule shows how deplorably successful the attempt has been."[55] Expanding on this religious theme, Gladden also thought that Catholicism had contributed to the inability of Cubans to create and maintain a free government. Distinguishing between American Catholics and Cuban Catholics, Gladden praised the former but argued that the latter "follow Spanish ideas, and the type of intellect and character which they are producing there is a very different thing" from the positive social contributions of American Catholics.[56] The backward version of Catholicism practiced by the Spanish and their hapless subjects, Gladden implied, was inimical to the traditions of republicanism. The widespread anti-Catholic attitudes in American society likely also factored into antiwar Americans' voices being drowned out.

Yet no one put the Christian republican thesis as succinctly (or as baldly) as Frank Bristol, the Methodist pastor in Washington, DC. "Do you look toward Manila and Santiago and say superior guns did the business?" Bristol asked rhetorically. "I say superior men stood behind the guns, superior schools stood behind the men, the superior religion stood behind the schools, and God, the Supreme, stood behind the religion." This was no surprise since Americans were "the rich, consummate flower of the ages, the highest evolution of history."[57] Though such assertions certainly smacked of ethnocentrism and more than a little arrogance, they were firmly rooted in the Christian republican synthesis that connected Protestantism and democracy. Many white Protestant ministers invoked religious ideas to justify American participation in the Spanish-American War, explain American victories, and demonize their foes.

The Social Gospel

Leading Protestants also justified the war on Social Gospel grounds.[58] Variously labeled "the Social Gospel," "social Christianity," and "applied Christianity," this theology meant, in Abbott's words, that Christians must "carry religion into daily life, not . . . keep it for the closet and the church."[59] Behind this rather basic evangelical principle, however, lurked the idea that, as Josiah Strong put it, Christians should construct "the organization of society on a Christian basis."[60] Social Gospelers, therefore, advocated a plethora of political measures such as greater rights for labor, city reform, and racial reform, all of which championed the cause of society's downtrodden.[61]

At the heart of social Christianity lay the notion that the strong should serve the weak. When Abbott discussed America's special place in the divine plan, he noted that God had "elected us *for a service.*" Americans must not "merely . . . enjoy wealth and culture and liberty for ourselves" when God called the United States to spread these blessings "to the nations of the world."[62] In making the case for the war, Abbott called on his congregants to apply their Christian principles abroad: "And now a third question has been presented to us, by the providence of God: Are you a selfish nation? Do you care only for your own liberty? Do you care only for the freedom of men oppressed and enslaved within your borders, or have you ears that are open to the cry of oppressed humanity everywhere? Dare you hazard something; dare you endure something for a people for whom you have no national responsibility and with whose welfare your own is not intertangled?"[63]

In addition, Abbott also employed Social Gospel ideas about the brotherhood of man to urge his readers to support the war. In a May 7 editorial titled "To the Front," the *Outlook* explained that "a common humanity" was the only factor that bound Cuba and the United States. Indeed, the war simply amounted to "a crusade of brotherhood. It is the answer of America to the question of its own conscience: 'Am I my brother's keeper?'"[64] The mere fact that all men were brothers made America's duty clear. The United States must answer the question of the Old Testament character Cain—"Am I my brother's keeper?"— in the affirmative.[65] Not to do so would be to betray the most basic principles of the Social Gospel.

With this theological basis, Abbott insisted that the United States would fight the war only for humanitarian, altruistic motives. In the wake of the *Maine*'s destruction, yellow journals such as William Randolph Hearst's *New York Journal* demanded immediate revenge.[66] The *Outlook*, by contrast, rejected the idea that the United States would engage in a war of vengeance. The journal maintained that if war came at all, it would only be undertaken in the name of humanity.[67] Senator Redfield Proctor's report, released on March 17, amplified Abbott's humanitarian concerns about the situation in Cuba. Proctor's testimony drew public attention to what the *Outlook* called "the terrible barbarism of this [Cuban] civil war, and the indescribable suffering which has followed upon the policy pursued by the Spanish government." The *Outlook* also seized upon Proctor's conclusion that nearly all Cubans (1.4 million) favored independence while only the Spanish military and creoles (approximately

200,000) wished to continue Spanish rule.[68] In short, the Proctor Report solidified Abbott's view that a corrupt minority was tyrannically suppressing the rights of a majority. Although as of March 26 he favored simple recognition of independence rather than immediate armed intervention, he recognized that the former policy could produce the latter result.[69] One month later Abbott reiterated that America would not seek revenge for the destruction of the *Maine*. The nation would fight only to relieve Cubans of a corrupt government and to put an end to Spanish barbarism. For the *Outlook*, if interference came, it would be because of "honor, conscience, and humanity."[70]

Once war was declared, Abbott underscored the humanitarian motivations prompting American action. In contrast to those hoping to gain strategic territory and economic advantage from the war, Abbott pleaded that those goals would "both belie our public professions and convert a war which in its origin was one for humanity into one for National aggrandizement."[71] In a June 15 sermon, he reinforced the Social Gospel, humanitarian reasons for war. "A Christian nation," he argued, "is one which seeks not its own glory, its own prestige and power, but seeks the welfare of the human race."[72] The conflict would only be "a Christian war," he declared in another sermon, "if we are forced and driven into it in order that we may set a people free for their own Christian development."[73]

Others agreed with the Social Gospel sentiments offered by the *Outlook*. The *Independent* published a poem about the war in July 1898, which explained in threefold fashion why the United States was at war: "In our hatred of the falseness and the tyranny of Spain / In the passion of our pity for her famished and her slain / In our horror of the slaughter of our brothers of the 'Maine.'" The poem went on to reject the idea that the United States should "fight for self-protection only," declaring that "to wage a war of mercy is our Heaven-appointed part." In this formulation, a "war of mercy" had nothing less than a divine sanction.[74]

The editors of the *Independent* echoed these social gospel justifications with specifically biblical admonitions. "There can be no doubt that the impulse to the present war with Spain has been a distinctly moral one, and an unselfish one," they declared in July. Indeed, it was a Christian duty since "power is a trust from God." Unlike Cain, Americans in the war had been acting on "the principle that every man is his brother's keeper." In case readers missed the point, the *Independent* also appealed to the parable of the Good Samaritan in the New Testament. Unlike the priest and Levite, who ignored a victim of assault and robbery, the Samaritan in Jesus' parable rescued the helpless man and saw to his needs. The *Independent* applauded Americans for not acting "the part of the Levite" in the present case of Spain and Cuba.[75]

Washington Gladden also supported Cuban intervention based on Social Gospel reasoning. Gladden asserted that fighting the war was simply another form of humanitarian aid for a downtrodden people. "We know that all men are children of the Father," he wrote, "and the same impulse that prompts us to send food to the starving in India or China prompts us to smite the misgovernment that is starving to death hundreds of thousands of helpless Cubans." Gladden went on to emphasize that faith was not merely an individual matter: "Nations as well as men have relations and obligations to others which they must own and fulfill in the fear of God."[76]

The Texas Episcopalian Edgar Gardner Murphy expressed similar sentiments. Murphy called upon American clergymen to remind their congregants of the "real reasons" that America was fighting the war. He wrote of the "considerations of humanity and those sentiments of international compassion which have moved us to intervene." Yellow journals could not be relied upon to emphasize this motivation, so it fell to the clergy, among other institutions, to remind Americans that "this war is a war in the interest of peace."[77] Adherents of Applied Christianity accepted no boundaries in their social work: the world was their parish.

Social Location

As much as theological and ideological factors influenced these leaders to support the conflict with Spain, more earthly factors like race and gender also mattered. Kristin L. Hoganson, T. J. Jackson Lears, and Gail Bederman write accounts of the anxieties that elite white men experienced in the late nineteenth century. Concerns such as neurasthenia, "race suicide," decadence, feminization, and over-civilization prompted some to believe that war and imperialism would add a tonic of "manliness and civilization" to a weakening American body politic. "For the late-Victorian bourgeoisie," Lears writes, "intense experience—whether physical or emotional—seemed a lost possibility." Theodore Roosevelt's well-known 1899 speech, "The Strenuous Life," epitomized the expression of these concerns and the desirability of the imperial remedy. The United States would restore itself and raise up other nationalities, the argument went, when it accepted greater world responsibilities.

Doing so meant war and conquest, which would revitalize American (male) civilization. Although the figures in this chapter like Abbott, Strong, and Gladden did not normally couch their support for the Spanish-American War and its imperialism using these terms, gendered concerns were certainly lurking

FIGURE 5.   Congregationalist minister Washington Gladden. Library of Congress, Prints &
Photographs Division, LC-DIG-bellcm-00111.

in the background for them. All three supported the "muscular Christianity"
movement, for example, while Gladden and Strong wrote books on the subject of Christian masculinity. The historian Clifford Putney maintained that
"the issue of unmanliness in religion was not peripheral to the Social Gospel;
it was central." For these upper-class white men, gendered considerations likely
factored into their enthusiasm for the struggle.[78]

If gender played a role in the advocacy of war, so did race. "Anglo-Saxon Protestant racial superiority," Susan K. Harris writes in her study of American religion and colonialism, "appear[ed] routinely in arguments both for and against annexation of the Philippines."[79] Abbott's support of imperialism was tinged with the racial views he held as a white man; the *Outlook* hoped that establishing an American protectorate in the Philippines would allow the native population some freedom while American workers would have time to instill "the Anglo-Saxon spirit" in the islanders.[80] Like many of his class, he considered Anglo-Saxon civilization more advanced than others.[81] Abbott also supported close relations with Great Britain based on their common Anglo-Saxon heritage while insisting as late as 1907 that Filipinos (whom he characterized as "children") were not yet ready to govern themselves.[82] Scholars have shown at length just how racialized the discourses concerning colonialism in the Philippines became. As much as American providentialism, Christian republicanism, and the Social Gospel prompted support for the war, ugly racial supremacy and turn-of-the-century anxieties about gender played a role as well.[83]

Postscript: The Religious Debate Over Empire

Even before the war was over, religious leaders debated what should be done with the colonial possessions American forces had captured from the Spanish. The responses ranged widely, with some strongly opposing the acquisition of any overseas territory while others welcomed imperialism as another gift from God.

In one sense, the American empire was nothing new. In the previous decades, as Walter LaFeber and others have argued, the American government assiduously went about extending its authority over the American West. The means it used to do so were violent ones: conflicts with the Sioux and Cheyenne at Little Big Horn in 1876, the Apache in 1886, and the Lakota at Wounded Knee in 1890 serve as only the most well-known of the violent encounters between American forces and Native American groups in the decades following the Civil War. The process of subduing and governing the west required an increase in federal authority in the late nineteenth century.[84]

Religion played an integral role in this earlier manifestation of the American empire as well. Protestants who considered themselves "friends of the Indian" sought to achieve the Christianization and Americanization of Native Americans by peaceful means. Many denominations sent missionaries to the west to evangelize and educate local native groups. These Protestants, however, thought nothing of overturning natives' cultural ways and considered their own civilization vastly superior. Some were implicated in imperial designs since they reported to the federal government as well as to their denominational backers. Catholics also sought to convert natives and rescue them from the twin evils of heathenism and Protestantism. Indians themselves turned to religious practices to combat the intruders, practicing rituals like the Ghost Dance to defend their cultures from outside intervention. The political and military conquest of the American west cannot be understood apart from religious forces.[85]

Once again Abbott fit the pattern well. The Congregationalist editor thought of himself as benevolently interested in natives' welfare and could be quite critical of widespread governmental corruption and mistreatment in Indian affairs.[86] In 1884 the *Christian Union* (the original name of the *Outlook*) serialized Helen Hunt Jackson's novel *Ramona*, which depicted the wicked ways white pioneers had treated American Indians. Abbott believed keeping Indians as permanent wards of the state, stuck on reservations, profited neither the nation nor the Indians themselves. Instead, he argued that tribal ownership of reservation land ought to be transferred to Native Americans as individuals so they could assimilate into American society and gain the benefits of "civilization." More controversially, he maintained that Congress ought to compel natives to accept this policy, even if it meant abrogating previous treaties. In addition to editorials in the *Christian Union*, Abbott promoted these measures through consistent participation in the "Friends of the Indians" conferences organized by the Quaker philanthropists Albert and Alfred Smiley at their scenic property in Lake Mohonk, New York.[87]

Abbott also became involved in practical politics to achieve his goal. After persuading the Lake Mohonk committee to adopt something close to his original plan regarding the reservations, Abbott and others met with President Grover Cleveland at the White House in November 1885 to advocate their idea. Two years later, Senator Henry L. Dawes (with whom Abbott had previously corresponded) sponsored the landmark legislation that "substantially" reflected the Lake Mohonk committee's proposal. Abbott's penchant for trusting the American government to solve other people's problems was illustrated here as well as in foreign conflicts. Abbott's advocacy of imperialism abroad was very much in keeping with his role in establishing imperialism at home.[88]

Although religious groups differed concerning the means necessary to pacify the west, most assumed that it was necessary and did not think that what they were doing constituted "colonialism." Assuming colonial territory outside of North America in the wake of the Spanish-American War proved more controversial. Still, whether they realized it or not, white Protestants who championed an imperial role for the United States overseas were simply following in the well-worn tracks of domestic imperialism. The same impulses that told them they were governing American Indians for their good also assured them that the Philippines would be better off with American rule. The Philippine-American War was thus not an anomaly in an otherwise peaceful Gilded Age; instead, it can be seen as another step in the growth of America's empire.[89]

While Americans debated the question of imperialism, specifically religious arguments were brought to bear on both sides. For his part, Abbott emerged as the chief ministerial champion of imperialism. In July 1898, Abbott laid out concretely the policy the United States should adopt toward the captured colonies of Spain. America must establish "in every such colony . . . a government which will secure to the inhabitants justice, liberty, and popular education." The *Outlook* editor-in-chief believed the United States must "create, and for a time control, educational systems in Cuba and the Philippines for their interests." These goals, he said, could be accomplished by establishing territories, colonies, or protectorates. Abbott favored the last of these three options because the first two granted too much autonomy to the Filipinos.[90]

At the heart of Abbott's support for imperialism and the war lay his ideological commitment to the Social Gospel emphasis on uplifting the oppressed around the world. At the same time, racialized assumptions about Filipinos' present incapacity for self-government undermined this goal. As a result, over the next months and years Abbott found himself defending the humanitarian mission to the Philippines while simultaneously denying that Filipinos were ready for autonomy. More than once, as when he famously referred to "an imperialism of liberty," his positions led simply to cognitive dissonance.[91]

But the nation's best known Christian advocate for imperialism was not Abbott but President William McKinley himself. A devout Methodist who had experienced a conversion as a young man, served as president of the Canton, Ohio, YMCA, and read the Bible daily, McKinley based his foreign policy on what he thought was God's leading. Famously, McKinley paced the White House floor, imploring the Almighty's guidance on what to do with the Philippines. At the end of his reflections, he decided that God was calling the United States to govern the islands, a conclusion that meshed well with his convictions about America as a providential nation. McKinley's resolve to "educate the Filipinos, and uplift and civilize and Christianize them, and by God's grace to do the very best we could by them" fit perfectly with Social Gospel ideas.[92]

By contrast, another camp of religious leaders spoke out against the imperialistic policies pursued by the McKinley administration. The *Independent* heartily supported the war, but it shrunk from endorsing the acquisition of colonial territory. The Filipinos "have been fighting valiantly for their freedom," it asserted in late July 1898, "and those who fight for freedom are too good to be slaves." The paper considered the Filipino leader Emilio Aguinaldo and his associates to be American allies: "we cannot break our agreement; we cannot betray the insurgents." A week later, the *Independent* put forward a complementary position, rejecting the idea that the United States sell Spain's imperial possession in an international auction.[93]

William Jennings Bryan, who was a devout Presbyterian in addition to being a free-silver Democrat, used biblical reasoning to come to the same conclusion in January 1899. Bryan considered it gross hypocrisy to celebrate democracy at home while subjugating foreign nationals abroad. "The Bible teaches us that it is more blessed to give than to receive," he maintained, "while the colonial policy is based upon the doctrine that it is more blessed to take than to leave." What really irked the Nebraskan were the religiously tinged arguments like the ones Abbott and McKinley were formulating: "to defend forcible annexation on the ground that we are carrying out a religious duty is worse than absurd."[94]

At the Broadway Tabernacle in New York, Charles E. Jefferson added his voice to those who opposed imperialism on religious grounds. In a powerful biblical reference, Jefferson compared the siren songs of the imperialists to the Devil's temptation of Christ on the mountaintop (Luke 4:1–14). "The avarice for domain, finely cloaked under religious and patriotic phrases, appeals to us with all the subtlety and persuasiveness of a devil," Jefferson complained, insisting that "we must not be imposed on by phrases such as 'Manifold Destiny,' 'Providential openings,' [or] 'God's manifest decrees.'" Imperialism would only lead to decay and destruction, he argued, rattling off several ancient empires (like Rome) that had overreached. Jefferson concluded that he stood not for "Imperial America" but for "Christian America."[95] The Spanish-American War generally received strong support from white mainline Protestants, whereas imperialism provoked much sharper debate. Although some religious voices used the same "God and country" arguments to support both war and imperialism, others drew on religious arguments to oppose colonialism.

The Spanish-American War was hardly the last time that white Protestants would give divine sanction to national warfare. Many of America's religious leaders would repeat similar themes twenty years later as the United States fought another ostensibly humanitarian war—this one to "make the world safe for democracy."[96] In the age of the motor car and airplane—even more than in the Civil War and Spanish-American War—armed conflict became a means to redeem godly civilization from barbarians bent on its destruction. As Abbott would put it, the struggle was nothing less than a "twentieth century crusade."[97] World War I would witness the most extreme outbursts in the service of Christian nationalism, but the foundations for such thinking were laid much earlier. The Civil War and the Spanish-American War were training grounds for the more consequential conflict to come.[98]

Although a breadth of perspectives on the righteousness of the war with Spain existed among white mainline Protestants, the loudest and most influential writers and pastors trumpeted a God-ordained, democracy-serving, humanity-uplifting mission to deliver Cubans from oppression. Most white Protestant Americans simply did not have eyes to see that the American government did not invariably champion freedom. The discordant voices, like those of Edward Abbott and C. W. Duane, were lost in the chorus of Protestant-inflected patriotism.

Yet, even as confident ministers published their convictions about the Spanish-American War, others resisted the urge to deploy theological language to justify the conflict. A few perceptive critics pointed out the irony of two Christian nations warring against each other. The Irish Catholic satirist Finley Peter Dunne, writing in the voice of his fictitious barkeeper Mr. Dooley, memorably satirized the easy connection between Christianity and war:

> Th' Lord knows how it'll come out. First wan side prays that th' wrath iv Hiven'll descind on th' other, an' thin th' other side returns th' compliment with inthrest. Th' Spanish bishop says we're a lot iv murdherin', irreligious thieves, an' ought to be swept fr'm th' face iv th' earth. We say his people ar-re th' same, an' many iv thim. He wishes Hivin to sink our ships an' desthroy our men; an' we hope he'll injye th' same gr-reat blessin'. We have a shade th' best iv him, f'r his fleets ar-re all iv th' same class an' ol' style, an' we have some iv th' most modhern prayin' machines in the warruld; but he prays har-rd, an' 'tis no aisy wurruk to silence him.[99]

American Catholics, in particular, had specific reasons to hesitate to support the conflict. Chapter 4 will explore the ways that American Catholic leaders often echoed Protestant jingoism, but it will also illuminate an important antiwar counterpoint that reveals much about how ideology and social position influenced Christians' views of America's wars.

CHAPTER 4

"I Look upon This War
as an Impudent Crime"

Roman Catholicism, Americanization,
and the Spanish-American War

The Catholic Dilemma in 1898

On May 4, 1898, hundreds of Roman Catholic bishops and priests assembled at St. Patrick's Cathedral in New York. Joined by thousands of laypeople who packed the capacious church, the clergy had gathered to mark the twenty-fifth anniversary of Archbishop Michael Corrigan's episcopate. The morning's elaborate high mass provided a spectacle for the faithful, but the afternoon banquet supplied even greater excitement for the more earthly-minded. After the Auxiliary Bishop John Farley relayed the Vatican's congratulations and listed Corrigan's accomplishments, he introduced a nationalistic note to the proceedings. Reflecting on the recent outbreak of hostilities with Spain, Farley sounded a lot like Josiah Strong when he declared the United States "the greatest country that man ever lived for, bled for, or died for." Moreover, he proclaimed, "now that it is engaged in a deadly struggle, the Catholics of the country will be the first to risk their lives in its defense." In response, Philadelphia's Archbishop Patrick John Ryan leaped to his feet and led the assembly in a spontaneous rendition of "The Red, White, and Blue." When the singing died down, Rochester's Bishop Bernard McQuaid, usually a fierce opponent of American innovations within the church, added his own patriotic word: "When we find that the principles underlying our government are those which make people great and noble, have we not cause to be proud of this country of ours? The nations of Europe have again and again pointed at us the finger of scorn, and have taken pains to blazon our failings to the world. But we are not looking for lessons from Europe. We want a country unshackled by the chains of European customs."[1] Despite the fact that the United States was then at war "with a Catholic country," he went on, "we will stand with [America], ready to shed our blood, and the Catholics of the United States will be the first in the struggle." At this, the prelates and priests were on their feet again— "wav[ing] their napkins and shout[ing] at the top of their voices," the Boston Catholic newspaper *Pilot* reported—ready for another round of patriotic songs.[2]

To some extent, the actions of the Catholic hierarchy that afternoon in New York should not be surprising. Only a week and a half before, the United States had launched an ostensibly humanitarian war in response to the brutal Spanish suppression of a rebellion in Catholic Cuba and the allegedly unprovoked destruction of the USS *Maine* in Havana harbor. Spurred on by the yellow journalism of newspapers like William Randolph Hearst's *New York Journal* and Joseph Pulitzer's *New York World*, war fever swept the nation, including its Catholic citizens. Yet the Catholic clergy's enthusiasm for the war should also give us pause. Still outsiders looking in at the Protestant establishment, reliably Democratic in voting behavior, and theoretically loyal to an international church that counted Spain among its most prominent members, American Catholics might also have been expected to oppose a war launched by Protestant Republicans wary of popery.

American Catholics stood on both sides of the question. Many joined the bishops at New York in national wartime enthusiasm, but a significant minority resisted the force of public opinion by consistently criticizing the conflict. This chapter examines how and why American Catholics reacted in vastly disparate ways to the war of 1898. Doing so will illustrate how the atmosphere of a popular American war contributed to a fierce debate within American Catholicism and will also allow us to see more clearly the assumptions and ideology of the mainline Protestant world.

Catholic attitudes toward the conflict have not received sufficient attention, and on the occasions where historians have noticed Catholic commentary on the war, they have been practically unanimous in maintaining that the American church lent its crucial support to the war effort.[3] James Hennesey's *American Catholics* (1981) states: "American Catholics supported the war."[4] Matthew McCullough's *The Cross of War* (2014) likewise leaves the impression that Catholic dissenters did not exist.[5] Even Andrew Preston's magisterial study of religion and foreign policy fails to appreciate the antiwar position some Catholics adopted during the Spanish-American War.[6] Preston acknowledges the existence of a "thoughtful debate" within the American Catholic Church on the question but examines only the "measured yet patriotic response" of the war's supporters.[7] It is significant that, in contrast to the providentialism that characterized much of the prowar lobby (both secular and religious), a minority of Catholics opposed the war. They did so because they refused to equate American military victory with divine favor, rejected the idea of America as a Christian nation, and evinced sympathy for the Spanish foe. Even as military triumphs piled up and victory became imminent, these Catholic critics persisted in decrying the war.

Examining the American Catholic reaction to the Spanish-American War provides new insights on several fronts. First, a greater understanding of Catholic experiences of the war offers a fresh perspective on domestic debates. Mapping Catholic commentary onto our larger interpretation of this conflict demonstrates that an understanding of the antiwar protests in 1898 remains incomplete without acknowledgment of significant Catholic contributions. The dearth of scholarly material on Catholics and the war is especially surprising since by 1890 Catholics comprised the nation's largest religious communion.[8] Paying greater attention to the religious motivations for and against the war with Spain adds another dimension to our understanding of national debates about the justice of the conflict.

Second, this chapter sheds light on the important debate concerning how the American Catholic church became "Americanized"—that is, the ways that it incorporated patterns of thinking common in the dominant political culture.[9] Because Catholics differed theologically from Protestants, often possessed an immigrant background, and ostensibly pledged first loyalty to the Vatican, suspicious Anglo-Protestant gatekeepers regarded them with hostility that could rise to ferocity.[10] Conflicts over Bible reading in Cincinnati public schools (1869–70); the ruckus over Republicans' "Rum, Romanism, and Rebellion" remarks (1884); Strong's warning about the dangers of immigrant Catholicism in his popular book *Our Country* (1885); and the founding of the anti-Catholic American Protective Association in 1887 illustrate only in part the extent to which anti-Catholicism still haunted the nation in the late nineteenth century.[11] In response, leading Catholics in this period strove to prove that American Protestants had nothing to fear. Catholics seized on Christopher Columbus (an Italian Catholic) as a national saint, while Archbishop James Gibbons and the 1889 Catholic Congress both stressed the compatibility of Catholicism and American ways.[12]

In this context, the Spanish-American War was another revealing moment for the church in its process of Americanization. The patriotic response of the Catholic majority allowed the church to be seen more widely as fully American. Catholic periodicals of all kinds took delight in recounting the heroism and loyalty of Catholic soldiers. While dissenting Catholics provided an insightful counterpoint perspective that illuminates the assumptions of the dominant religious culture, the war allowed Catholics to become more culturally mainstream. When American Catholics volunteered to fight against a Catholic Spanish empire, few critics could persuasively claim that they were secretly loyal to a foreign power.

Third, although the perspectives of prowar Catholics often revealed a remarkable absorption of mainstream American opinions about national righteousness, antiwar Catholics fought back against such assumptions. Conscious of their identity as Catholics first and Americans second, they commented on the war and the nation with more critical distance. As in other conflicts, a combination of ideological commitments and social position shaped Catholic Americans' responses. In this case, religion itself influenced social location; when Catholics practiced a marginalized religion (especially in its more conservative varieties), they found themselves pushed to the margins of American cultural and political life. In short, when war came in 1898, Catholics responded along a wide spectrum that needs to be grasped for a fuller understanding of how Americans at the turn of the century debated ideas of war, patriotism, and America's world role.

American Catholic Support for the War

Many Catholics who supported the war did so for religious reasons. Just as it did to many (but not all) Protestants, the struggle appeared providential to some prominent Catholics.[13] Confident that they could discern the hand of God in current events, these interpreters consistently saw the Almighty intervening on behalf of the United States. The St. Paul, Minnesota *Northwestern Chronicle*, owned by Archbishop John Ireland (1838–1918), was an early advocate of war, frequently criticizing President William McKinley's attempts at a diplomatic solution. The *Chronicle* believed that God had appointed the United States to avenge the *Maine*, whose destruction it ascribed to Spanish treachery. Using apocalyptic rhetoric, the *Chronicle* editorialized that in response to the explosion of the *Maine*, "God's hand will be heavy upon that sinful nation which has become an abomination of desolation, and the instrument for divine vengeance has been chosen." Unlike most Catholic publications, the newspaper's enthusiasm for American war-making extended to an endorsement of imperialism. Rejecting the Founding Fathers' isolationist advice as outdated, the *Chronicle* maintained that American rule would bring "liberty, peace and prosperity" to "benighted nations." This argument also adopted a providentialist coloring when the *Chronicle* asserted in May that "destiny" required the United States to take its rightful place among the world powers. In August the Paulist *Catholic World* (New York) also attributed American military success to divine favor, crediting "the hand of some superhuman power" for a particularly dramatic naval victory.[14]

Catholics also had a more self-interested reason to promote the war. As Gary Gerstle argued, American military conflicts have often provided opportunities for marginalized groups to join mainstream national culture.[15] In their case, Catholic periodicals backed the conflict to rebut the charge of nativists that Catholics made untrustworthy citizens. "The names of Catholic American citizens are plenty on the rolls of volunteers," the *Northwestern Chronicle* boasted. "Where now is the patriot of the A.P.A. stamp?" Farther east, the Boston *Pilot* announced in a headline that Catholics were "Volunteering in Large Numbers" and "Proving Their Patriotism." Likewise, in Philadelphia, Archbishop Patrick John Ryan assured the local press that "The Catholic Church in America is patriotic" and that the Pope did not secretly favor the Spanish.[16] In the same vein, the *Catholic World* eulogized a Catholic captain who had died at the battle of Santiago, declaring him to be "a true American, a true Catholic, a true man." Even the antiwar *Ave Maria*, operated by Holy Cross priests in Notre Dame, Indiana, reported that "Catholics have not been lacking in patriotism," drawing attention to a Toledo, Ohio, newspaper's comment that a Catholic private was "only one of many who are showing some people how to be real Americans." "Remembering that Toledo used to be a hotbed of A.P.A.-ism," the *Ave Maria* observed, "there is much significance in these words."[17] Under assault from a Protestant nation still distrustful of "Romanism," Catholics supported the war in part to prove their loyalty.

Yet the widespread adoption of American Providentialism suggests that religion provided an even stronger basis for the prowar sentiment. In San Francisco, Father William D. McKinnon, who would serve as a chaplain in the war, told a group of young men in April that "religion and patriotism are one and inseparable." On the other side of the country, Bostonians listened to Father Denis O'Callahan celebrate the providential history of the United States in a Fourth of July oration. The events of the past year, O'Callahan maintained, tell "us again how the providential hand of God led our fathers from the land of bondage, from the narrowness and contentions, the prohibitions, civil and ecclesiastical, of the old world." With Spain and Cuba in mind, O'Callahan reiterated that the Declaration of Independence was "the handwriting on the wall to tyranny everywhere: because it was and is the Magna Charta, not of one nation, but of humanity, and of universal and triumphant democracy." Keeping perfect time with the providentialist chorus, O'Callahan exclaimed, "Surely there is a providence which shapes man's ends." In the South, Bishop Anthony Durier of Natchitoches, Louisiana even echoed ideas of Manifest Destiny in a pastoral letter: "By his Monroe Doctrine and his army of free men, Uncle Sam rules from ocean to ocean, from pole to pole, and shapes the destinies of the New World under Divine Providence."[18] Where some Catholics like Baltimore's Archbishop James Gibbons supported the war only reluctantly, others such as O'Callahan and Durier trumpeted the spiritual significance of American military victories.[19] Influential white Protestants did not stand alone in investing the secular conflict with sacred meaning; quite a few Catholic leaders propounded a providentialist interpretation of the war as well.

No one did this more effectively than Minneapolis-St. Paul archbishop John Ireland. The archbishop was born in Ireland in 1838, immigrating with his family to the United States in 1849. He served as a Union chaplain in the Civil War before working his way through the Catholic hierarchy in the subsequent decades.[20] Ireland advocated a progressive theology that saw God as especially immanent in human affairs. Where conservative popes like Pius IX (r. 1846–78) saw quite a bit of danger in the modern world, Ireland embraced the democratic spirit of the United States. His most famous phrase—"Church and Age! Unite them in the name of humanity, in the name of God!"—expressed his outlook. Although he, along with most American Catholics, retained an interest in Italian politics and was never reconciled to Pius IX's loss of temporal power in the 1870 risorgimento, as an "Americanist" bishop Ireland accepted the United States' democratic arrangements and praised the First Amendment.[21]

Surprisingly, Ireland did not immediately advocate a military response to the destruction of the *Maine*. Instead, in the spring of 1898, he traveled to Washington at the request of Pope Leo XIII in a secret attempt to broker a peace settlement between the United States and Spain.[22] When his negotiations failed, however, Ireland became (in public) the most prominent Catholic champion of the war.[23] In July, for example, Ireland argued that "The ideals of America are in God's designs," portraying wars as "one of those mysterious agencies through which Providence works in shaping the destinies of nations." Immediately after military action began, the archbishop asserted that the war had "a providential purpose," going so far as to compare the conflict to the medieval Crusades.[24]

Ireland's providentialism was most clearly on display in an October 1898 address in Chicago. As one of the keynote speakers for the city's "Peace Jubilee," the archbishop found himself addressing over 4,000 guests, including President McKinley, cabinet members, and military officials. He began by connecting the "jubilee of peace" with the "jubilee of victory," instructing Americans to "be glad and rejoice; for the Lord hath done great things."[25] Although warfare must not be commended for its own sake, Ireland maintained, "[a] just and necessary war is holy." Indeed, soldiers who died in such conflicts heroically laid down their lives on the altar of their nation: "The sword in their hands is the emblem of self-sacrifice and of valor: the flag which leads them betokens their country, and bids them pour out in oblation to purest patriotism the life-blood of their hearts."[26] Warming to his theme, Ireland noted that the United States was taking its "proper place among the other nations of the earth" and gaining the respect of the rest of the world. "All this does not happen by chance or accident," the archbishop reminded his audience. Instead, "an all-ruling Providence directs the movements of humanity. What we witness is a momentous dispensation from the Master of men." Echoing Virgil's tribute to the beginning of the Augustan age (as well as biblical imagery), Ireland announced that "to-day, we proclaim a new order of things." In words (coincidentally) evocative of John Winthrop's famous sermon, "A Modell of Christian Charity" (1630), Ireland began his peroration by noting, "America, the eyes of the world are upon thee."[27]

Ireland's 1898 address expressed an American Providentialism that grew out of sentiments he had voiced four years before. In 1894 in New York, the archbishop affirmed that the Almighty exercised sovereign rule over all nations; national destiny depended on God's providence. In the divine scheme, however, nations were not necessarily equal: "The [national] limits are widened according to the measures of the destinies which the great Ruler allots to peoples and the importance of their part in the mighty work of the cycles of years, the ever-advancing tide of humanity's evolution." A few paragraphs later, Ireland explained where the United States fit into God's plan: "America . . . is the highest billow of humanity's evolution, the crowning effort of ages in the aggrandizement of man. Unless we view her in this altitude we do not comprehend her; we belittle her towering stature, and hide from ourselves the singular design of Providence in creating her."[28] From this perspective, then, Ireland seemed to espouse historical providentialism in seeing a special role for the United States. In his public addresses, Ireland rushed to equate American victory with God's favor and providence. For both the Minneapolis archbishop and elite white Protestants, nations were simply tools in God's hands; in this case, the Almighty was using the war to raise America to its proper place in the world.

For some Catholic supporters of the war, providential interpretations of the conflict led naturally to demonization of the Spanish foe, which took two forms: denying that Spain was a legitimately Catholic country and hoping for the empire's extermination. Unlike Lyman Abbott, these Catholic writers did not directly attribute battlefield defeats to Spanish vice; instead, they attacked

Spain because they doubted the nation's orthodoxy. The *Northwestern Chronicle*, for example, argued that everyone knew "the influences which surround and have surrounded and governed Spain are not Catholic, but Masonic." The periodical declared that Spain was "the most un-Catholic nation on God's earth." In August, the *Catholic World* also picked up the charge of Masonry. Although in May the journal had expressed confidence that "Spain is a Catholic country," by the war's end it had switched positions, denying Spain was "the real Catholic country she is represented to be." Instead, the publication asserted that Masonry ran "rampant" among Spain's "fast-living officials." "The lodges," in turn, had brought on the war to maintain the extravagances of this corrupt class. Continuing the condemnation of Spain, Archbishop William Gross of Oregon cataloged Spanish vices (bullfighting, Sabbath-breaking, and insubordination to the Pope) before concluding that among the governments of Spain, Italy and France, "there are no greater enemies of the Catholic church." As if to prove his point, next to its account of Gross's speech, the *Northwestern Chronicle* printed a column describing Spain's rebuff of Leo XIII's peace overtures. Across the country in Brooklyn, Father Sylvester Malone used his May 1 homily to denounce the Spanish government. Its policies and "tyrannical reign" were "in direct opposition to the teachings of the Catholic faith," he concluded. American Catholics would never show "any sympathy" for such a nation.[29]

Sometimes this condemnation of Spanish Catholicism went hand-in-hand with a desire for the elimination of the Spanish empire altogether. On April 1, the *Northwestern Chronicle* editorialized that war "will come, and be short and decisive. The issue will see Spain's flag disappearing forever from the western continent." A few weeks later the newspaper elaborated on this theme: "It is war only which will bring peace to us. Spain is behind a hundred years or more of the world that surrounds it. A rotten un-Catholic government with an arch-Mason as its head, proclaiming Catholicity. A nation professedly Christian, while in voice and deed defying all the doctrines of Christ. Let fate fall on it. It has been a disgrace to the Catholic Church and to civilization throughout many patient ages. Its hour has come."[30] In the *Chronicle's* view, the empire's sins rendered it unfit to exist any longer.

Such providentialist rhetoric echoed to an unusual extent the sentiments of the nation's leading Anglo-Protestant clergy. Despite substantial antagonism between Catholics and Protestants, the war provided an occasion for both groups to celebrate God's special guidance of the United States. When they reasoned providentially and spoke about the character of the nation, enthusiastic Catholic supporters of the war differed little from the nation's leading Protestant voices.

Thus, whether they realized it or not, Catholics who adopted the rhetoric of American Providentialism internalized and passed on some of the political and intellectual assumptions common to the dominant culture. Although "Americanization" encompasses several processes, one of its aspects involves what historian Philip Gleason calls "a basic intellectual reorientation." According to Gleason, outsiders of any kind can become Americanized if they pledge allegiance to "the abstract ideals of liberty, equality, and republicanism."[31] Although that might sound easy enough in theory, to do so in 1898, American Catholics needed to erase the stigma of antirepublicanism that had long marked the church. Indeed, liabilities such as the church's opposition to the 1848 European revolutions, Pius IX's Syllabus of Errors (1864), and the conservative political views of Leo XIII caused Protestant Americans to view Catholicism with suspicion.[32] While the war afforded Catholics an opportunity to showcase their patriotism to a skeptical nation, it also revealed the extent to which many had absorbed typical American intellectual habits in doing so. American Catholics breathed in the dominant political and religious assumptions in the air, and those assumptions had consequences for the way they viewed the war with Spain. Catholic support displayed the extent to which some had adopted or modified mainstream American ideas while jettisoning traditional Catholic reservations about the United States. The war of 1898 was a key moment for Catholics in their quest to be seen as fully American.

Opposition to the War

Historians have long recognized that the Spanish-American War did not garner unanimous support. Even after the explosion of the *Maine* in February 1898, many Americans resisted the fervent calls to arms. E.L. Godkin, the editor of *The Nation*, defended the character of the Spanish government and implied that Spain had just as much right to rule Cuba as the United States did Florida. Harvard University professor Charles Eliot Norton took a more unusual course when he spoke out against the conflict after the fighting had begun. In a June 7 address to the Men's Club of the Prospect Street Congregational Church in Cambridge, Massachusetts, Norton excoriated the war as "unrighteous" and "the way of barbarism," going so far as to advise his listeners not to enlist. From the world of humor, Finley Peter Dunne's Mr. Dooley joined those skewering American leaders. Ever a keen observer of American life, Dunne used Mr. Dooley to satirize such otherwise untouchable war heroes as Admiral George Dewey and Lieutenant Richmond Hobson. When Dooley's friend Mr. Hennessey expressed the opinion that "a man ought to stop fightin' whin th' war is ended," Mr. Dooley replied that Dewey had "started without askin' our lave, an' I don't see what we've got to do with th' way he finishes."[33] Although the struggle with Spain proved to be one of the nation's most popular wars, dissenting voices could be heard as well.

These well-known antiimperialists based their antagonism to the conflict on various factors. Norton feared that the United States had unjustly "hurried into war" against a nation that did not want it, departing from its old republican traditions.[34] Another opponent of the war, the journalist Oswald Garrison Villard, decried the conflict on doctrinaire pacifist grounds.[35] To these motivations for antiwar sentiment, Catholic opponents added another: skepticism about the inherent virtues of the American nation.[36] Although antiwar Catholics expressed multiple reasons for their opposition to the war, an unwillingness to view the United States as especially praiseworthy played a central role in their thinking.

To be sure, very few American Catholics actually declared for Spain or tried to subvert the war effort. Those who did were quickly punished. When a western priest named Father Weber instructed a group of New York Catholics that, if war came, their duty would require them to enlist on the Spanish side, Archbishop Michael Corrigan promptly expelled him from the diocese. If that were not enough, in the aftermath of the incident someone attempted to kill Weber by mailing him a package designed to explode when opened.[37] Disloyalty rarely occurred in a communion whose members were taught to obey the laws of their nation regardless of their personal political feelings. Despite their substantial distance from the American mainstream, even the German-language *Katholische Rundschau* (San Antonio, Texas), reminded its readers that "America is our fatherland, be it through birth or free choice," and stated that all Catholics should obey the government's demands.[38] Dissent was only permissible within certain bounds.

What then separated antiwar Catholics from their militant brethren? Catholics mostly opposed the Spanish-American War because of their perception of the nature of the United States. Whereas Ireland based his support to a significant extent on the positive character of the American government and its people, dissenting Catholics rejected such a perspective. Where Ireland interpreted military victory as a sign of providential favor, antiwar Catholics deployed theology in a different way. Specifically, they doubted the unique righteousness of the United States, did not equate the progress of the Kingdom of God with the good fortunes of the nation, and defended Spain as authentically Catholic. Furthermore, their position as religious outsiders prompted a different assessment of the nation. Where Ireland and other prowar bishops exercised at least some political and social power, the lower social status of antiwar Catholics afforded them a vantage point from which to critique mainstream American assumptions.

First, some Catholics opposed the war on the grounds that the United States was an unrighteous nation and therefore not to be trusted. This group included Arthur Preuss (1871–1934), the editor of the St. Louis *Review* and son of *Die Amerika* editor Edward Preuss. As a serious Lutheran, the elder Preuss had earned doctorates in both philosophy and theology, tutored at the University of Berlin, and launched an attack on the dogma of the Immaculate Conception of Mary in 1865. Three years later, conflicts with the theologically liberal elements in German Lutheranism impelled Preuss to resign his position and immigrate to the United States, where he accepted a position at St. Louis's Concordia Lutheran Seminary. Eventually Preuss came to believe that traditional Lutheran theology amounted to little more than a half-way house between Roman Catholicism and theological modernism; in 1871 he resigned from Concordia and entered the Catholic Church.[39]

Arthur Preuss was his father's son. Beginning in 1894, the twenty-three-year-old editor used the *Review* as an organ to attack sectarian Protestantism and the Americanist developments within Catholicism. Unsurprisingly, he also questioned the righteousness of the United States. Shortly after the war began, he printed a letter to the *Review* that scoffed at the notion of the United States as the earth's most Christian nation. The letter began by acknowledging that "even high dignitaries of the Church have ventured the assertion that ours is 'the most Christian country' in the world." In the writer's opinion, this notion was ridiculous: although Americans discussed religion incessantly, this phenomenon could be attributed to the "multiplicity of sects with which we are cursed" rather than to genuine religious feeling. Moreover, the absence of prayer, and the "crimes that are daily committed" militated against the notion of the United States as especially righteous. "In the face of facts," the writer concluded, "it is but a hollow phrase—with little substance to it—to say that this is the most Christian country." In August the *Review* continued this attack on the uniquely Christian character of the United States. Quoting a writer in *Scribner's* who described the world of business as dishonest, unfair, and unprincipled, Preuss concluded sadly, "We are a nation of 'business-men,' and some of us claim, forsooth, that we are 'a Christian nation.'"[40]

Other antiwar Catholic publications, like the *Globe* and the *Ave Maria*, echoed these sentiments. Published in New York by a Catholic convert, William Henry Thorne (1839–1907), the *Globe* provided consistent, colorful criticism of the United States. In December 1898, one of its writers, quoting Luke 18:11, mocked those concerned about cruelties in Cuba but oblivious to the legacy of slavery and the mistreatment of Native Americans in the United States. Also challenging its readers to question the character of the nation was the *Ave Maria* (subscription: 20,000), a newspaper edited by the Holy Cross priest Daniel E. Hudson (1849–1934) in Notre Dame, Indiana. Raised in a cross-confessional family (his father was a Methodist and his mother a Catholic), Hudson became a zealous Catholic strongly opposed to Protestant notions of American exceptionalism. On June 25 a hostile "anonymous correspondent" attempted to bait the *Ave Maria* into condemning Spain by asking, "What do you think of Spanish ladies attending bull-fights? Does this indicate high civilization? Did you ever know Americans to be guilty of such atrocities as the Spaniards have committed in Cuba?" In response, the newspaper did not miss a beat: "Bullfights are not to our liking," it admitted, but neither were American "prizefights nor football matches." Spanish women, moreover, were wrong to attend the bullfights, but American women were wrong to "wear in their head-gear feathers and wings which they have often been informed are torn from living birds." As for atrocities, Hudson pointed to the lack of racial justice in America: "As a good American, we blush to say that a man was burned at the stake by a mob in the city of Dallas, Texas on the very day our anonymous friend was inditing his queries. The crime was a heinous one, but that does not matter; nor does it matter, in our opinion, that the criminal was a negro. His skin was not blacker, perhaps, than the hearts of his murderers."[41] Unlike many, the *Ave Maria*, *Globe*, and *Review* objected to characterizations of the United States as an especially Christian nation.

These antiwar publications did not compartmentalize their views concerning the sins of the nation but applied them specifically to the war. In July, the *Review* correspondent George T. Angell (himself a Protestant) lamented the outrageous dishonesty of American newspapers. Predicting that the lies the newspapers had told about the Spanish-American War would eventually fill several volumes, Angell concluded sarcastically, "If our war (as has been represented) is a 'holy war,' it is a terrible pity that it has given rise to so much lying." In other words, Angell could doubt the justice of the war because he distrusted the virtuousness of the American press. In addition, the *Ave Maria* opposed the war in part because it did not believe the testimony of Redfield Proctor, the senator whose investigative mission in Cuba had been the source of Americans' knowledge of alleged Spanish atrocities there. The *Ave Maria* had "not the slightest" respect for Proctor's findings, it maintained, because the senator "went to Cuba in the yacht of a yellow journal. His hands were tied: he had to see what little he saw through the goggles of the proprietor. It was a decidedly undignified thing for a United States Senator to do."[42] In questioning the righteousness of their own nation and its leaders, the writers of the *Review* and the *Ave Maria* resisted the popular tendency to view the United

States as especially godly. These sentiments were reflected in negative attitudes about the war.

Second, in addition to criticizing the righteousness of the United States, antiwar Catholics also opposed the conflict because they refused to see the church and the nation as interchangeable categories. This temptation was great, especially when American military victories appeared providential, as they did to John Ireland and like-minded Catholics. But to the *Ave Maria*, American victories did not mean God favored the national cause. When the New York *Observer* expressed pious outrage that the Spanish had attacked American soldiers on a Sunday morning, and attributed the subsequent American victory to Spanish sacrilege, the *Ave Maria* jeered that "this would make a lovely story for a certain sort of Sunday-school paper, if it were dressed up a little." Making clear that he did not condone Sunday morning attacks either, editor Daniel Hudson nevertheless noted that "There is danger . . . that the little Ingersolls produced by such religion as the *Observer* professes will ask themselves why the crews of the American ships didn't keep on with their devotions instead of immediately pursuing the wicked Spaniards and breaking the Sabbath." The *Catholic Record* (Indianapolis) also mocked the idea that military success signaled divine favor. If this were true, the *Record* argued, then "Bonaparte was very much approved, for no commander ever gained so many victories."[43] With their sardonic commentary, the *Ave Maria* and *Catholic Record* showed rare boldness among American religious periodicals in resisting a providential reading of American military victories.

The *Ave Maria*'s opposition to this kind of providentialism also appeared in its response to a suggestion of the Presbyterian Board of Missions that God had allowed the war in order to Christianize the Philippines. "We cannot ignore the fact," the Presbyterians had maintained, "that God has given into the hands of American Christians the Philippine Islands, opened a wide door to their populations, and has by the very guns of our battleships summoned us to go up and possess the land." Hudson criticized this self-assured attitude by drawing attention to American Protestant failings in other lands: "When Hawaii was opened up to the Protestant missionaries, they also went up and possessed the land, thereby robbing a poor 'widow woman' [Queen Lili'uokalani] of her ancestral lands and throne. Since that time any chance reference to 'missionaries' sons' provokes a sneer from the ungodly and calls a blush to the cheek of every decent Protestant." Filipinos would remember the defeat of Manila as a "restful holiday," he predicted, compared to the moral and doctrinal evils that Protestant missionaries would bring.[44] In this case, specifically Catholic convictions prompted the *Ave Maria* to resist the urge to identify secular military victories with the progress of the sacred Kingdom of God.

Catholic periodicals such as the *Review* and the *Ave Maria* rarely missed a chance to lampoon Protestants on any topic. Their frequent critiques of "the sects" and their "bishops"—a title always set in quotation marks to distinguish it from authentic Catholic bishops—revealed divisions in American Christianity still stark at the turn of the twentieth century. This attitude also manifested itself in criticism of Protestant ministers' jingoism. "Many" Protestant ministers, the *Ave Maria* declared on May 7, "preferred war to peace." The periodical then unfavorably compared such jingoes to the Pope—"the Vicar of the Prince of Peace"—who had done his best to prevent conflict.[45] In Preuss's *Review*, a writer who signed himself "C. Ch." accused Protestant clerics of hypocrisy. Those striving for war, he said, ignored Jesus' command to turn the other cheek when insulted. Although Christ had taught, "blessed are the peacemakers," "representatives of the Protestant pulpit see in war greater national blessings." "C.Ch." proposed a practical course of action for such militant clerics: "These warlike divines might have the courage of consistency and go to the front."[46]

The St. Louis *Review* likewise took a stand against the war based in part on its skepticism that God uniquely guided and blessed America. A few weeks into the war, the *Review*'s editors learned that St. Patrick's Cathedral had installed a gigantic American flag—"the largest in the city"—between the church's two spires as a demonstration of its patriotism. In a signed article, Preuss deplored this display as "ostentatious and bombastic." Regular readers of the *Review* would not have been surprised. Four weeks before, Preuss had reprinted an editorial from the New York (Methodist) *Christian Advocate* disapproving of the placement of flags in church sanctuaries. The *Advocate* had written that "nothing should be exhibited in a church except what relates directly to the worship of Almighty God as superior to every human institution, to the human race itself and to the universe." Indicating its sympathy for this view, the *Review* noted that this position "might be profitably pondered" by Catholics eagerly aligning their patriotism and their faith. The *Review* argued that patriotism should "be restricted in its methods of expression" and criticized a telegram sent by a group of young women to President McKinley before the war, which simply stated, "To h—with diplomacy!"[47] Antiwar Catholics' refusal to equate patriotism with Christianity and their reluctance to invest the conflict with theological significance contributed in no small measure to their opposition to the Spanish-American War.

Third, some Catholics opposed military action because they refused to demonize the Spanish after the fashion of prowar Catholics; instead, they defended the authenticity of Spanish Catholicism. In particular, the *Ave Maria* and the St. Louis *Review* both demonstrated sympathy for Spain and avoided criticizing the Spanish as diabolical and un-Catholic. On July 23, for example, the *Ave Maria* referred to the respect that Spain's Admiral Pascual Cervera had gained among Americans by observing that "the Spaniards . . . may well feel proud of representatives who could make such an impression on their foes as Admiral Cervera and his officers have made. Gentlemen know one another by instinct and brave men recognize their kind." It continued, "the American people are just beginning to learn the true character of the enemy they are fighting," adding ominously, "and that of the insurgents in Cuba whose cause they espoused." In contrast to the *Northwestern Chronicle*'s negative judgment, the *Ave Maria* saw the Spanish as a noble foe. Similarly, in the *Review*'s opinion, the United States had no right to claim any sort of moral superiority over its European opponent. In response to critics of Spanish Catholicism, the *Review* argued that "so long as 'yellow journalism' flourishes among us and the theatre is a hotbed of corruption in the city, town, and village, we have no reason to turn up our noses at the Dons."[48]

In fact, the *Review* implied that the Spanish were more righteous than the Americans. In the closest instance of a Catholic newspaper siding with the enemy, its May 12 edition reprinted excerpts from an editorial appearing in the Catholic *Western Watchman* (St. Louis), which portrayed the Spanish as innocent victims of American aggression: "Spain is praying. She is on her knees before the shrines of the Blessed Mother, and her prayers and her vows are going up daily that God may protect her from her mighty foe 'that comes out from the West.' We have taken our vows before the shrine of Bellona and our prayer is a hoarse cry of 'revenge for the Maine.' The Lord of hosts will decide." The *Globe*'s William Henry Thorne likewise left no doubts concerning where he thought blame for the war lay. In one of his harshest critiques of the United States, Thorne declared: "I look upon this war as an impudent crime brought about by American greed and ignorance; and if John Ireland and [other supporters of the war] . . . would only study the American as he is in actual history . . . they might be better prelates and more sensible men."[49] In this view, Spain had a better plea than the United States before the divine tribunal.

The *Ave Maria* and the *Review* also defended Spain by critiquing interpretations of the war that attributed Spain's decline to its Catholicism. Although the *Review*'s immediate target was a German Protestant newspaper (the *Evangelischer Kirklicher Anzeiger*) making this charge, its analysis also served as a rebuttal to similar assertions from Americans. The *Review* celebrated Spain's medieval golden age, when the nation "was permeated most thoroughly by the spirit of the Catholic Church." Military defeats and a rising "anti-Catholic spirit" had gradually opened the door for "Liberalism," sapping the nation's strength, but neither of these unfortunate events could be blamed on the church. In narrating Spain's long religious decline, the *Review* portrayed the nation as a victim rather than as a villain. Moreover, the *Review* refused to find an easy connection between American Protestantism, providential blessing, and financial prosperity. Instead, it argued, "if the United States be more powerful than Spain, that is a matter which is explained, not by religious differences, but by the simple fact that they possess infinitely greater resources."[50]

The *Ave Maria* also demonstrated this sort of unconventional thinking in its analysis of Spanish character and culture. When a writer in the *Atlantic Monthly* ascribed Spain's weakness to its "pride, conservatism, and clericalism," the *Ave Maria* shot back that Spain had "exhausted herself by a century of ceaseless conquest in the New World" (actions that, in nineteenth-century fashion, the *Ave Maria* regarded as praiseworthy). To acknowledge this was simply "to give her justice." Similarly, in response to Protestant criticisms that "Spain is degenerate because she is Catholic," the *Ave Maria* reprinted an editorial from the *Springfield Republican* (Massachusetts) acknowledging that Catholic Spain was struggling but arguing that Catholic Mexico was flourishing. Accordingly, the *Ave Maria* provocatively argued, "material prosperity or adversity depends on other causes than religion, and in no case can it be interpreted as the visible sign of God's pleasure or displeasure." Then, in a pointed biblical reference, the editors turned the tables on those who blamed Spain for its current impoverished condition: "The only promise of temporal prosperity recorded in the Bible was made, not by Christ, but by Satan on the pinnacle of the temple. Pointing to the kingdoms of the earth, he said: 'All these I will give thee if, falling down, thou wilt adore me.'"[51] Unlike the prowar writers, Catholics opposing the conflict routinely went out of their way to defend Spain, often at the expense of the United States. The attitudes of the *Review* and *Ave Maria* toward the United States and Spain, in turn, motivated opposition to the war.

In sum, these antiwar writings illuminate an alternative to the mainstream American rhetoric and assumptions of the prowar Catholics and well-known Anglo-Protestant clergy. Unlike mainstream Protestants, Ireland, the *Northwestern Chronicle*, and other prowar voices, antiwar Catholics resisted a providentialist reading of the war in which American victory and expansion were the natural results of divine favor. Although only some Catholics took this tack, their perspective demonstrates the possibility of a counterpoint to thorough Americanization in the late nineteenth century. In other words, the fact that a majority of Catholics supported the war was a historical contingency with a viable alternative. If they could not fully escape the influences and ideas of American culture, antiwar Catholics challenged accepted American patterns of thinking, clinging to a greater sense of the transnational nature of the church.

Ultimately, the debate in the American Catholic church was only partly about the war itself. Relatively few of the editorials on either side of the question gave sustained treatment to military ethics, just war theory, or the actual conditions in Cuba. Instead, American armed conflict provided the impetus for a larger discussion of the church's relationship to the American nation-state as a whole. To some extent the results were predictable. Noted theological "Americanists" such as John Ireland lined up on the prowar side, while opponents of Americanism like Arthur Preuss protested the conflict. Yet some surprising alliances developed as well. Bernard McQuaid had once referred to the "impulsiveness and rashness of the Archbishop of St. Paul," denigrating his policies as "extreme." Still, McQuaid's conservative sentiments did not prevent him from aligning with Ireland in declaring the war a righteous one.[52] Likewise, even someone as progressive as Ireland harbored private doubts about the war's validity. By bringing questions of patriotism, international loyalties, and the nature of American culture to the forefront of the national consciousness, the Spanish-American War simultaneously revealed and remade the American church's complicated relationship with nationalism.

Comparison with the AME Church

Although John Hay considered the conflict a "splendid little war," it was hardly splendid for a sizeable portion of the American Catholic communion. The resentment expressed by antiwar Catholics was similar to that of another marginalized group, African Americans. The most thorough study of the Black press's attitude toward the war concludes that "black patriotism during the Spanish-American War was restrained, critical, and often bitter."[53] George Marks's compilation of editorials in African American newspapers during the war yields few examples of American Providentialism or Manifest Destiny.[54]

In the Black Methodist Church, Bishop Henry McNeal Turner found that he had no more positive things to say about the United States during the 1898 conflict than he had during the Civil War. As early as 1896, Turner warned against American involvement in Cuba, predicting, "The United States is fixing to get what it justly needs, a good flogging." When the war came in 1898, Turner discouraged Blacks from enlisting in the army and, like Daniel Hudson, railed against the hypocrisy of a nation that practiced lynch law daring to claim the mantle of humanitarianism. Turner thought the future of Blacks in the United States completely hopeless, arguing that African Americans have "no country here and *never will* have." Instead of condemning Spain, he praised the racial equality he had experienced there. He put his attitude toward the nation most memorably in 1896: "Vote for the gold standard, if you think it will help to kill this rotten old sham of a nation; vote for the silver platform, or 16 to 1, if you think that will assist in its destruction." While Turner hardly spoke for everyone, his was a prominent voice within the AME church.[55]

AME spokesmen offered equally critical views regarding American imperialism. In April 1899, the *Christian Recorder* editor H.T. Johnson published a satirical poem in response to the popularity of Rudyard Kipling's "The White Man's Burden." Where Kipling had lauded Anglo-American efforts to "civilize" darker peoples, Johnson acidly condemned American actions at home and abroad. In a representative stanza that referenced the treatment of Native Americans, Johnson wrote: "Pile on the Black Man's Burden / His wail with laughter drown / You've sealed the Red Man's problem / And will take up the Brown." Uniquely positioned to see the prevalent racism of America's leaders, Johnson echoed Turner in his condemnation of American attempts at self-righteous colonization.[56]

Division or Unity?

Without question, the Spanish-American War helped to unify a nation still divided from a Civil War that had ended barely thirty years before. The last time Americans had taken up arms, they had been killing one another. Many contemporaries celebrated the war with Spain as a unifying moment for the North and South.[57] Moreover, the easy military successes of the United States during the war inaugurated an era of expansion and world power. Expeditions in Panama (1903) and Mexico (1914) as well as a bloody war in the Philippines soon followed on the heels of victory over Spain. This interventionist mood would culminate in the nation's participation in the Great War several years later.

This sunny picture of growing national power overlooks the acrimonious debates that preceded the conflict and that in many cases continued during it. If the struggle was a time of healing for some Americans, it was a time of bitterness and alienation for others. The debate within the American Catholic church illustrates this tension well. Although the war brought many of the church's factions together, it alienated people like the editors of the *Ave Maria*, *Globe*, and *Review*. Indeed, some felt the world they had grown up in was rapidly vanishing altogether. From a hospital in Yonkers, New York, in April 1898, an elderly correspondent wrote discouragingly to the *Ave Maria's* Daniel Hudson of "the diabolic fever now rampant," predicting that "imminent foreign complications will inaugurate a new era for us, and will be the beginning of the end of our prosperity as a state." Although disclaiming the label of pessimist, he concluded, "I often now thank God that I am growing old."[58] Clearly, the war separated and divided some Americans while it united others. Only by paying more attention to opponents of the conflict will we enjoy a fuller grasp of the Spanish-American War as a divisive as well as uniting moment for American communities in general.

CHAPTER 5

"A Louder Call for War"

The Protestant Mainline and the
Twentieth-Century Crusade

On the evening of January 9, 1912, guests of New York's Aldine Association—an organization composed mainly of publishers—gathered on the fifteenth floor of the club's building on Fifth Avenue. They came that evening to celebrate two guests of honor: ex-president Theodore Roosevelt and his current employer, Lyman Abbott. Henry Van Dyke Jr., formerly pastor of Manhattan's Brick Presbyterian Church, and now professor of English at Princeton University, served as toastmaster of the tony affair. A fine dinner followed by musical entertainment began the program, with Abbott making a few brief remarks in praise of his fellow honoree. Roosevelt, as usual, stole the show, delivering a forty-five-minute speech intimating a presidential run. The ex-president's remarks and his anger later that night at having been betrayed (he had barred all journalists from the event and sworn the guests to silence) dominated headlines the following morning.[1]

As the *New York Times* the next day focused on Roosevelt's speech, it overlooked just how central Abbott and the *Outlook* had been earlier in the evening's proceedings. Wags at the Aldine Association had written for the occasion several "political parodies of popular airs," satirizing the guests of honor.[2] The most insightful one adapted Irving Berlin's "Alexander's Ragtime Band" (1911), renaming it "The *Outlook*'s Ragtime Band." The new lyrics alluded to the periodical's stance on mollycoddles, Progressivism, and international arbitration; however, the real insight lay in a line from the chorus: "They can play a

FIGURE 6. Theodore Roosevelt. Library of Congress, Prints & Photographs Division, LC-DIG-ppmsca-35660.

call for peace or a louder call for war."[3] With these prescient words, the Aldine Association's parody hit home for a magazine that had consistently backed American military action against Spain and the Philippines. Yet in January 1912, no one could have predicted the extreme lengths to which the *Outlook*, Abbott, and his mainline Protestant colleagues would go to support American involvement in the Great War.

FIGURE 7. Lyman Abbott, c. 1915. Library of Congress, Prints & Photographs Division, LC-DIG-bellcm-00111.

Among American clergy, no one in the period from 1914 to 1917 led the charge for military preparedness more enthusiastically than the *Outlook* editor. Likewise, when the nation finally entered the war in April 1917, Abbott occupied the vanguard, interpreting the war as "a twentieth century crusade." Although he took the rhetoric one or two steps farther than some of his colleagues, Abbott articulated positions common among the nation's white Protestant leadership, especially those hailing from historically Calvinist denominations in the Northeast. As in America's other military struggles, ideological commitments and social position best explain these leaders' vociferous rhetoric in support of military action. Theologically, they saw the United States as a Christ-like nation locked in an irrepressible conflict with demonic Germany over the fate of worldwide democracy. Defending democracy around the world, in turn, became a Social Gospel imperative. Socially, privileged white Protestant leaders interpreted the war as a collision between all that was best in Anglo-American civilization and a rising German barbarism. We cannot fully understand the United States during the war years without recovering this disturbing but influential mentality.

New Perspectives

Those who have studied how American cultural leaders manufactured support for the Great War have often focused on government propaganda.[4] That work largely misses the central role religion played in ginning up support for the conflict. Unfortunately, ignoring the clergy's agency in promoting the government's aims contributes to a distorted view of American wartime society. E. Brooks Holifield demonstrates that although rural ministers in the Gilded Age and Progressive Era generally lacked social clout, urban clergy commanded considerable cultural authority. "Some became local, regional, even national celebrities," he writes. "Tourists came to hear them preach, newspapers covered their sermons, and young pastors emulated their innovations."[5] Although Holifield records a general decline in ministers' public authority from 1861 to 1929, some contemporary observers stressed the continuing influence of the clerical profession.[6] Disregarding clerical roles in promoting the war can assume an anachronistically secular society.

Despite this neglect, the groundwork exists for a more accurate assessment of religion's role in World War I. In 1933, the University of Pennsylvania sociologist Ray H. Abrams published his seminal study *Preachers Present Arms*. Abrams, a pacifist, looked back on the conflict with disgust, noting with satisfaction in his preface that the "confessions," "secrets," and methods of the "professional propagandists" had come to light a decade and a half later. He argued that the churches were both victims and agents of social control. That is, clergymen helped to stifle dissent about the war even as the federal government pressured them to do their part to ensure American victory.[7] Fifty-two years after Abrams published *Preachers Present Arms*, the historian John F. Piper, Jr. reopened the question of American religion during World War I. Piper highlighted the positive and responsible role played by such organizations as the Federal Council of Churches and the National Catholic War Council. As they staked out a middle ground between irresponsible militants and idealist pacifists, Piper argued, mainstream Protestant and Catholic leaders fulfilled their patriotic duty while maintaining the moral gravitas befitting their calling.[8]

Since the 2000s, interest has grown in the clergy and the Great War. William H. Thomas, Jr.'s thorough study of the Justice Department's investigations of sedition during the war echoed Abrams by portraying the clergy solely as victims of nationalistic hysteria.[9] In *The War for Righteousness* (2003), historian Richard M. Gamble conducted the most penetrating analysis to date of elite religious liberals and the war. Revising both Abrams and Piper, Gamble argued that Social Gospel Protestants embraced the war wholeheartedly because they saw it as a chance to implement the Kingdom of God—a vision for which they had been longing for the past decades. According to Gamble, however, their rhetoric lacked both moderation and responsibility; instead, it represented the apotheosis of Victorian optimism, ridiculed by the next generation of chastened neoorthodox church leaders.[10] Andrew Preston argues that American religious communities created an "idealistic synthesis" of pacifist and belligerent extremists. This majority supported the war reluctantly, becoming "America's first-ever liberal internationalists."[11]

The following narrative aligns most closely with Gamble's interpretation. Religious progressives embraced the war because they saw it as both a duty and an opportunity—not primarily, as Abrams would have it, because they felt the strong hand of the federal government bearing down.[12] Moreover, the characters in this chapter—leading spokesmen like Abbott, Newell Dwight Hillis, and Harry Emerson Fosdick—in no way exuded the moderation Piper and Preston attribute to the clergy.

Attending closely to white Protestant leaders illuminates a widespread understanding of the Great War as a religious struggle. Particularly among this group, the idea of an American crusade often prevailed. Moreover, recognizing Abbott's World War I statements as mostly continuous with his commentary on previous conflicts allows us to see more clearly how a certain kind of religious investment in the United States became central to national self-understanding in late Victorian America. What Ernest Tuveson identified as a "redeemer nation" mentality for early America took on new dimensions as Americans adopted an increasing world role in the Progressive Era.[13]

Before April 1917

On June 28, 1914, Slavic nationalist Gavrilo Princip assassinated Austro-Hungarian Archduke Franz Ferdinand. This event escalated tensions between Austria-Hungary and Serbia, with each side calling upon its allies for military assistance. By August, the continent found itself engulfed in what contemporaries simply called the "Great War." Despite President Woodrow Wilson's admonition to be "neutral in fact as well as in name . . . impartial in thought as well as in action," Americans disagreed passionately over which side to support and whether the nation should even be involved in the distant conflict.[14]

American Protestant leaders were also divided on what policy the nation should pursue. Unsurprisingly, Abbott led the preparedness charge, agreeing with his friend Theodore Roosevelt that the United States must pursue "righteousness above peace."[15] This would mean supporting the Allies against the allegedly barbaric Germans, who had invaded neutral Belgium. Although Abbott preferred peace to war, he believed national obligations sometimes necessitated armed conflict. Thus, the *Outlook* cheered the resignation of Wilson's Presbyterian pacifist Secretary of State William Jennings Bryan in June 1915 for these reasons: "Mr. Bryan stands not for freedom first, but for peace; not for the triumph of law first, but for peace; not for righteousness first, but for peace." The magazine thought its own militant stand reminiscent of that of the Patriots of 1776 and the Republicans of 1860 while Bryan's position called to mind the Tories and cowardly compromisers with the Confederacy. Abbott was not alone in these views. Episcopalian leaders in Massachusetts and Arkansas as well as Congregationalists and Presbyterians in New York called down divine blessing on the Allies and wrath on Germany.[16]

When war broke out, the *Outlook* covered the conflict thoroughly, sending several correspondents to Europe for firsthand reporting.[17] Like many New Yorkers of his social station and ethnicity, Abbott took the side of the Allies.[18] For one who came of English stock and believed in a common Anglo-American culture, the decision came naturally.[19] As early as January 1915 the *Outlook* strongly implied the Allies were engaged in a Christian struggle to defeat Germany.[20] Abbott's anti-German convictions only strengthened over the next months as Germany began to wage unrestricted submarine warfare. The sinking of the British merchant ship *Lusitania* in May 1915 (resulting in the deaths of over one hundred American passengers) the magazine condemned as "murder"; it recommended severing all relations with Germany, a step just short of war.[21] In an interview a year later Abbott laid the blame for the conflict at the feet of Germany.[22] When Wilson finally broke relations with Germany in February 1917, the *Outlook* wired Abbott's enthusiasm to the president.[23]

Yet many mainline Protestants disagreed with such a militaristic stance. The nation's most famous Presbyterian, President Wilson, strove to keep the nation neutral. The son and grandson of Presbyterian ministers, Wilson took his faith seriously, even becoming a ruling elder in his denomination in 1897. Wilson refused to keep his religion a private affair, attempting to apply broadly Christian principles to public life.[24] After the Great War broke out, Wilson tried to keep the United States out of the conflict even if he sympathized with the Allies. In this posture he was joined by the Federal Council of Churches (FCC), an organization comprised of the nation's largest mainline denominations. The FCC specifically approved William Jennings Bryan's efforts for peace and neutrality. Conservatives, too, could praise neutrality. The best known of them, Billy Sunday, for the first two years of the war dismissed the conflict as a European problem for which Americans bore no responsibility.[25]

When war finally did come to the United States, however, divisions among white mainline Protestants mostly vanished. As usual, warfare meant both that the clergy enlisted in the national cause and that they went over and above the call of duty. The atmosphere of armed conflict, of a draft, of the loss of life, and of the national propaganda put forth by the Wilson administration made it hard for nuanced or dissenting points of view to gain traction with the general public. During the war's duration, with rhetoric even more vociferous than in previous conflicts, the clergy portrayed the contest as a holy war. This extravagant language sprang directly from ideological views of the world as well as from social factors like ethnic background and geographical location. Ultimately, many white Protestant leaders depicted the conflict in Manichaean terms foreign to what we now know about relative national moral responsibility during World War I. Still, patient examination of this worldview reveals how influential white Protestant leaders understood the meaning of the Great War and America's world role.

American Providentialism

Because his country generally promoted democracy, Abbott interpreted the United States as a messianic nation chosen by God to accomplish His purposes in the war. Drawing again on some of the same ideas he had expressed in the Civil War and Spanish-American War, he made the case that America served as nothing less than God's ally in the cause of liberty. Referring to the war as a "Christian crusade," Abbott explained the thesis of his latest book, *The Twentieth Century Crusade*, in a letter to Roosevelt: "This book affirmatively, I might almost say aggressively, contends that our participation in this world war primarily for the sake of the people whom most of us do not know, furnishes a striking evidence of the power of Christianity, and the extent with which its spirit has pervaded the nation."[26] In a chapter on "Christ's Peace," Abbott distinguished between a nation asking God to be on its side in war and a nation consciously fighting on God's side. The first position Abbott dismissed as "faith in ourselves" combined with a desire for "a silent partner who will enable us to carry out our plan." Against this idea, he posited the notion that "we want to be the ally of God," rejoicing that "he wants us to fight his battles with him."[27]

How did Abbott know the United States really fought on God's side? The answer lay in the fact that God had ordained the war and had commanded the United States to slay the powers of evil. Abbott drew this idea from Jesus' saying, "all they that take the sword shall perish by the sword" (Matt. 26:52). The *Outlook* editor observed that aggressors would be punished "not by pestilence, nor by thunder-bolt, nor by the act of God—but by the sword in the hands of man." Some might have taken this verse to mean the United States should rarely take up arms, but Abbott drew the opposite conclusion: "That sword has been given to us by our Master and we must not sheathe it until the Predatory Potsdam Gang has perished from the face of the earth."[28]

This view echoed an idea the *Outlook* had championed a year before. In an October 1917 article celebrating the four hundredth anniversary of Martin Luther's ninety-five theses, the *Outlook* reflected on the sorry state of German society in the twentieth century. Jingoistic German ministers had "drugged" the "docile" German people into accepting the state's perfidious actions. In order to liberate them, the *Outlook* thought, the United States must "take the sword thrust upon us and beat the madness of their masters out!"[29] In this interpretation, America had not chosen to wage a war of aggression; instead, God had "thrust" a sword of war into the nation's hands, using it to accomplish his purposes. When Americans destroyed their enemies, they simply executed God's will. Long-time readers of the *Outlook* might have remembered what Abbott had said in 1898: "It is . . . a Christian duty to accept the sword Excalibur, when divine providence puts it into our hands."[30]

As the war progressed, Abbott applied biblical passages about Christ to the United States. First, he identified the Allied army with Christ's incarnational mission of peace and deliverance. In an article written for Christmas 1917, the *Outlook* reflected on the Virgin Mary's Magnificat found in Luke 1:46–56, noting the song's militant tone and characterizing it as "a song of victorious democracy." The *Outlook* refused to believe the Magnificat's message spoke only of the role of Jesus, asking, "To-day who are they that are fulfilling the words of the song of Mary?" The editors thought they saw in the prosecution of the war the strong arm of the Lord smiting His foes and bringing peace to the earth, leading them to conclude that "the armies of the Allies" had inherited Mary's messianic prophecy. Christmas Day, the *Outlook* stated, could be "reverently observed by the very sounding of artillery."[31]

Abbott and his fellow editors used the same article to apply other prophecies about Christ's birth to America and its allies. Both "peace on earth" and "good will among men"—the Christmas message proclaimed by the angels in Luke 2:14—described the mission of the Allied armies, the *Outlook* declared. Switching the metaphor slightly but keeping the biblical theme, the article also argued that the Allies were "fit successors" to the sacred heroes of Hebrews 11, who died for their faith. Like the biblical saints, the Allies too "subdued kingdoms, wrought righteousness . . . waxed mighty in war, [and] turned to flight armies of aliens," making them "to-day the bearers of the message of Christmas."[32] The article concluded by returning explicitly to the messianic theme. In Abbott's judgment, the Allies were helping to effect an era of world peace surpassing even what Christ had wrought: "In their victories there is coming to pass that which was said of old: 'The people that walk in darkness have seen a great light; they that dwell in the land of the shadow of death, upon them hath the light shined.'"[33] This prophecy, Isaiah 9:2, originally applied to Jesus's birth. As the *Outlook* conflated the military success of earthly armies with Christ's spiritual mission, it deployed theological language and associations to buttress the Allied cause.

In addition to identifying the Allies with Christ's incarnation, Abbott connected the work of American and Allied soldiers with Christ's atonement. Not long after the United States declared war on Germany, he took to the pages of the *Outlook* to encourage his fellow Americans in their sufferings. He noted that wartime required those on the home front to make material sacrifices, congratulating children as well as adults for their willingness to forgo accustomed peacetime luxuries. Ultimately, American sacrifices reminded Abbott of Christ's suffering on the cross. In a remarkable statement, the *Outlook* editor wrote, "We are learning by experience what it is to bear the sins of the world." Moreover, Abbott thought that selfless Americans were learning the "deeper meaning" behind the Apostle Paul's declaration in Colossians 1:24: "I rejoice in my sufferings and fill up that which is lacking of the afflictions of Christ."[34] In Abbott's typology, Americans composed an innocent, Christ-like nation, suffering for the sins of its enemies.

The war also reminded Abbott of Christ's sacrificial death because of American soldiers' willingness to die in the place of their fellowmen. Just as Horace Bushnell during the Civil War had associated Union soldiers' deaths with Christ's atonement, Abbott saw Allied soldiers laying down their lives for others in the Great War. The *Outlook* explicated this idea most thoroughly in Easter reflections written in 1918. The periodical recounted how Christianity had grown cold throughout history before rejoicing that "to-day" the Christian spirit could be found in abundance at the Western front. With the approaching Good Friday in mind, the *Outlook* celebrated the "hundreds of thousands of Americans who, with their faces set toward their Passion, are marching steadfastly toward the field of battle to lay down their lives for their unknown brethren, while we who stay at home follow them with our unuttered prayer, 'Let us also go, that we may die with them.'"[35]

Strikingly, Abbott argued that all American soldiers who perished in the great crusade would go to heaven when they died. (*The Stars and Stripes*, the official periodical of the American Expeditionary Force, also advocated this view.)[36] Throwing aside all historic Christian teaching, Abbott acknowledged, "What the Beyond may have for [American soldiers] we do not know and cannot guess." "But," he affirmed, "we may be very sure that whatever may have been their faults or their transgressions here below, the righteous Father will not refuse these heroic cross-bearers the crown of righteousness."[37] Here was the doctrine the conservative Baptist *Western Recorder* (Louisville, KY) ridiculed as "salvation by khaki."[38] Although Abbott took pains to stress that heaven was "not for sale" and maintained that the soldiers' sacrificial attitudes were a good demonstration of the state of their souls, readers could hardly escape the conclusion that death in such a glorious cause would cover over "whatever may have been their faults or transgressions here below."[39] Conservative Baptists, unwilling to depart from the letter of Scripture in their understanding of salvation, naturally recoiled at such statements. By contrast, Abbott's theological liberalism, with its penchant for overturning historic understandings of Christian doctrines, allowed him to soft-pedal traditional Christian teachings on salvation.

The idea of soldierly atonement fit well with a key principle enunciated in the opening pages of Abbott's *Twentieth Century Crusade*. Here, in some of the war's most purple prose, Abbott used the imagery of atonement to describe American suffering, setting the stage for what followed in the rest of the book. He began the introduction by discussing the "three crosses" on the hill of Golgotha, the setting of Christ's crucifixion. The first cross, he noted, contained a criminal "who to the end was defiant of God and man," possessing an "unrepentant conscience." The second cross held the repentant thief, to whom

Jesus promised forgiveness and the hope of paradise (Luke 23:43), while Christ himself suffered on the third cross. Extending this image, Abbott maintained, "There are to-day in Europe three crosses and three groups of sufferers." Germany, a nation that had "broken alike the laws of God and man," represented the rebellious first criminal. The repentant thief, in Abbott's modern-day reading, was analogous to the Allies. They bore responsibility for some of the evils of the nineteenth century but had since abandoned their sins and repented of them. Abbott included the United States in this category as well, although he spent more time justifying America's imperialist exploits and celebrating its social reforms than in condemning American faults. The third cross, then, was occupied by those who were not "sinless" but who, nevertheless, "l[aid] down their lives for crimes in which they had no share and which never had their approval." This class included hospital workers, but those "sailing the sea and defying torpedo boats," "serving in the trenches," and "flying in the airplanes" composed most of its ranks. These, Abbott wrote, "are laying down their lives for their fellow-men."[40]

Direct references to biblical passages solidified Abbott's interpretation of the war as atonement. He did this most often with Hebrews 9:22—"And almost all things are by the Law purged with blood; and without shedding of blood there is no remission"—a verse describing the necessity of blood sacrifice under both the Old Covenant (Judaism) and the New Covenant (Christianity). In a December 1917 article, Abbott acknowledged that his generation of liberals "may have lost something in exact definitions of doctrine"; still, he held that the church as a whole had gained the "faith, hope, and love" common to all religions. The war itself demonstrated that the modern church had discovered "a wider and diviner meaning in the saying, 'Without the shedding of blood there is no remission of sin.'"[41]

In Abbott's interpretation, the supernatural implications of Christ's death should not be taken literally; instead, Allied doughboys too could attain messianic status through their sacrifices. Moreover, the sufferings of American soldiers would create a regenerated German nation in the postwar period. Demonstrating this idea in *The Twentieth Century Crusade*, Abbott quoted Hebrews 9:22, arguing that only the deaths of innocent Americans could overthrow Germanic "falsehood," "despotism," and "injustice."[42] Like Horace Bushnell rejoicing fifty years earlier over the regenerative power of the Civil War's baptism of blood, so Abbott also saw sacrificial death ultimately bringing life in the Great War. By suffering "for the sins they have never committed," Abbott implied, the soldiers of the United States would help to create a reborn world.[43] In these paragraphs, all metaphors and analogies broke down. Sacred and secular categories became so entangled as to be indistinguishable. God and country, the soldier and Christ, the cross and the trenches merged into one indissoluble whole.[44]

Equating American soldiers with Jesus, their deaths with Calvary, and their blood with the blood of Christ exploited images, feelings, and emotions deeply resonant for Abbott's Christian audience. Indeed, it is hard to understand fully what these identifications would have meant for devout believers accustomed to thinking of Christ's death as both utterly holy and distinctly historical. Dragging such viscerally sacred associations into the European trenches elevated an earthly military conflict to a holy war in a manner unsurpassed by apologists for Christian crusades of a different era.[45] For Abbott and his cobelligerents, these images did not merely serve as rhetorical flourishes for an argument based on realpolitik; such spiritual associations supplied the fundamental meaning of the war. Abbott's rhetoric also had the effect of minimizing distinctions between God and the United States. When American soldiers were frequently compared to Christ, it became hard to retain traditional conceptions of the Almighty as the impartial judge of all nations.[46]

Many of Abbott's compatriots echoed his rhetoric, including prominent religious spokesmen who pictured Christ garbed in American khaki. Harold Bell Wright, a novelist, Social Gospel advocate, and erstwhile Disciples of Christ minister, argued that "a thirty-centimeter gun may voice the edict of God as truly as the notes of a cooing dove . . . The sword of America is the sword of Jesus."[47] In 1918 the Unitarian editor Albert C. Dieffenbach provided an even more graphic description of Jesus at the front lines: "There is not an opportunity to deal death to the enemy that [Jesus] would shirk from or delay in seizing! He would take bayonet and grenade and bomb and rifle and do the work of deadliness against that which is the most deadly enemy of his Father's kingdom in a thousand years . . . That is the inexorable truth about Jesus Christ and this war; and we rejoice to say it."[48] Likewise, in April 1918 the Reverend John Elliott Wishart of Xenia, Ohio, used the pages of *Bibliotheca Sacra* to make a case for "The Christian Attitude Toward War." Although Wishart admitted that "War is essentially an evil," he believed that all wars could not be classified as un-Christian.[49] Indeed, in this conflict, Wishart found nothing less than "the struggle of light against darkness . . . of the kingdom of God against the kingdom of this world, of Christ against Belial."[50]

The Baptist minister Harry Emerson Fosdick (1878–1969), who would go on to become the liberal standard-bearer in the 1920s and 1930s, also lent his pen to the cause of the war, identifying the allied struggle with Christ and the Kingdom of God. Although Fosdick later became a pacifist, his *Challenge of the Present Crisis* (1918), written at the height of the war, sounded the militant note. Fosdick's conclusion to the book tugged at his readers' heartstrings, calling all slackers and shirkers to their rightful duty. He recounted the story of a French mother who had written to one of her sons who was living abroad. The mother's other two sons had both been killed in the war, but nevertheless she pleaded with this remaining son to come to the aid of his beleaguered country, essentially threatening to disown him if he continued his cowardly course. Fosdick applied this story to Americans, accusing reluctant young men of possessing a "callous soul," unable to "hear a voice, whose call a man must answer, or else lose his soul." Fosdick concluded by identifying the Allies with Christ: "Your country needs *you*. The Kingdom of God on earth needs *you*. The Cause of Christ is hard bestead and righteousness is having a heavy battle in the earth—they need *you*."[51]

Fosdick repeated some of these ideas in a 1919 article for the *Atlantic Monthly*. After visiting France, he reported on the spiritual state of the American troops as he had encountered them in the trenches. Although the popular minister acknowledged that soldiers struggled to maintain their religiosity at the front, he was not unduly troubled, for he found in the doughboys a manly, self-sacrificing religion far outranking the old, doctrinally centered variety excessively focused on heaven.[52] One soldier, in particular, epitomized the attitude: "'I used to wonder at the Cross,' an American soldier in France said to me; 'not now! I think that Jesus was a lucky man to have a chance to die for a great cause.'"[53] This soldier (and Fosdick) evidently saw both Christ's death and the Great War simply as two examples of a "great cause." The historian Jonathan H. Ebel summarizes such sentiments most directly: "From pulpits, podia, and the pages of periodicals, [the mainline Protestant clergy] argued for the Christianity of the nation and of the war effort."[54]

Demonization of Germany

The necessary corollary of American providentialism was the demonization of the German foe. Even more than in the Civil War or Spanish-American War, white mainline clergymen denounced Germany in religious terms. "History will hold the German Emperor responsible for the war in Europe," the *Outlook* editorialized as early as August 15, 1914. Only the willfully blind could not see that Germany and Austria had partnered in the act of "brigandage" against Serbia.[55] As the war progressed, Abbott's hostility increased as Germany, in his recital, consistently disregarded the rules of civilized warfare. Over the next few years the sinking of the *Lusitania* (May 1915), the violation of the Sussex Pledge regarding submarine warfare (October 1916), and the publication of the Zimmerman Telegram (February 1917) added fuel to the fire of Abbott's

Figure 8. Harry Emerson Fosdick in Pulpit of Park Avenue Baptist Church, c. 1925. Public Domain. Courtesy of Wikimedia Commons. https://commons.wikimedia.org/wiki/File:Harry _Emerson_Fosdick_in_the_pulpit_of_Park_Avenue_Baptist.jpg

anti-Germanism. These events, combined with Germany's invasion of Belgium at the beginning of the war, formed the basis for the *Outlook*'s belligerent stance. As the conflict progressed, this antagonistic attitude led to a myriad of accusations against the Kaiser and his nation.[56] Some of these charges, like alleged German insanity, did not traffic in religious language while other allegations elevated the conflict to the religious realm, as when Abbott associated Germany with Satan, Pontius Pilate, and pagan religions. There was not a simple cause-and-effect relationship here; instead both kinds of indictments reinforced each other in building up American righteousness and German viciousness.

Often, Abbott's paper offered a venue for others to share their views. Seven months after the war began, the *Outlook* printed an extraordinary article by the popular psychologist Joseph Jastrow titled "Mania Teutonica."[57] Jastrow began by acknowledging that during the first years of the conflict, he had considered the Germans simply to be acting as should be expected in a time of war. However, as the struggle continued, Germany's position had "ceased to be intelligible to me in that light." Instead, he had "come to consider the state of the German mind as a state of madness assuming a military form; the madness is far more significant than the military expression." Classifying this state of "war madness" as *"Mania Teutonica,"* Jastrow devoted the rest of the article to documenting the ways in which German society as a whole manifested its insanity, leaving no doubt how he believed the United States ought to respond: "The patient must be overpowered to be cured."[58]

Similar statements appeared over the next few months. As the tide of the war turned in 1918, the *Outlook* editors addressed the topic of the peace negotiations that would follow Germany's surrender. Only unconditional surrender was permissible, the magazine believed, perhaps in part because the Allies were negotiating with a mentally unbalanced people. The *Outlook* quoted one observer as saying that all Germans were megalomaniacs, while by the end of the war the paper refused to distinguish—as it initially did—between the Kaiser and the German people. At this juncture, the *Outlook* argued, "the entire German people are obsessed with the insane delusion that the German nation is divinely ordained to the rule the world."[59]

For Abbott, a mad Germany required not pity but hate. He advocated this view in his most infamous wartime article, "To Love Is to Hate," published in May 1918. The *Outlook* editor scoffed at the Archbishop of York's suggestion to follow the example of Christ and forgive the Germans, who did not know what they were doing. On the contrary, Abbott argued, he might forgive the German masses, but he refused to forgive the Kaiser and "the Predatory Potsdam Gang" because "they do know what they do." Because Christians are filled

with the love of God, Abbott argued, they must necessarily hate God's enemies. True, Christ commanded his followers to love their foes, "but he nowhere
commands us to love God's enemies or those who treat his children with ma-
lignant cruelty." Because Germany had not injured him personally, he could
hate its rulers with a righteous hatred: "I hate it because it is a robber, a murderer, a destroyer of homes, a pillager of churches, a violator of women. I do
well to hate it." Devout Christians ought to pray for the defeat of the Central
Powers, Abbott maintained, so that Germans would "hate themselves as the
civilized world now hates them." Jesus, he reminded his readers, offered no
words of hope to the unrepentant criminal on the cross.[60] A few months later
he stated that atrocity-committing Germans had so purposefully chosen evil
as to commit the unpardonable sin (Luke 12:10), putting them "beyond forgiveness" from God or man.[61]

The *Outlook*'s positions on Germany's madness and the necessity of hate
did not remain in the realm of ideas. In June 1918, Abbott began advocating
reprisals (what he preferred to call "retorsion") against enemy combatants.
Germans' habitual infliction of atrocities proved their military understood only
brute force, the *Outlook* reasoned. If that was the case, then the Allies ought
to oblige them. To be sure, there were limits: American soldiers must not commit criminal acts or outrage women, for example. Still, instead of imprison-
ing submarine crews—a despicable lot that had "almost uniformly played the
part of pirates"—the Allies could "make sure that no German submarine officer or seaman found and seized should ever be heard of again."[62] The exact
meaning of this prescription remained, perhaps intentionally, a little ambiguous. Still, it would not have been unreasonable, in the context, for a reader to
conclude that the Reverend Doctor Lyman Abbott advocated shooting captured German sailors in cold blood.

The *Outlook* also employed the language of extermination. In August 1917,
Abbott's journal recounted Germany's diabolical record in the war—its broken
promises, its submarine warfare, and its outrageous proposal enticing Mexico
to attack the United States. Illustrating well the mentality of "total war," Abbott argued that only one solution remained: "A war with such a nation
means just one thing—the extermination of the government and the system
and the national state of mind that have made such faithlessness possible."
Conditional surrender or negotiated peace terms were out of the question:
"Until that Power is destroyed—not merely subdued, but utterly done away
with—there can be no peace."[63] Others took this position one step further. A
writer named Pamela Victor Pike offered the following sentiments a year later
in a letter to the editor: "After this war there should be no Germany, no Germans.
Allow every man and woman the right to become voluntarily any nationality

preferred; legalize the right, and make it easy for any one to become French, Italian, British, American, *Hottentot*—anything! Then forever recognize them and their descendants by and according to that choice. I see no necessary embarrassment—to the loyalist."[64]

At the furthest extreme, proposals circulated to rid the world of the German people. One of the most prominent advocates of such extermination was Abbott's friend Newell Dwight Hillis (1858–1929). Hillis, an underappreciated figure in American religious history, began his clerical career in Illinois. After pastoral stints in Peoria and Evanston, he became the controversial David Swing's successor at Chicago's progressive Central Church from 1895 to 1899. When Abbott resigned as Plymouth's pastor in 1899, Hillis moved to Brooklyn to take over the esteemed pulpit.[65] (Ironically, Plymouth's "Germania Club" gave a dinner in honor of Abbott and Hillis in November of that year.)[66] Hillis's celebrity increased during the war, with a Navy Department official describing him as "with the exception of ex-President Taft and ex-President Roosevelt . . . the most prominent figure on the American lecture platform."[67] Although financial problems dogged his personal life, Hillis provided strong leadership at Plymouth until his resignation in 1924.

Like Henry Ward Beecher and Abbott, Hillis believed his ministerial vocation at Plymouth should include political and social activity. This became especially evident during World War I when his work on behalf of the first Liberty Loan and the Red Cross drew praise from Roosevelt, whom he knew personally.[68] During this time, however, Hillis primarily earned his fame as a peddler of German atrocity tales. After touring Europe in July 1917, the Plymouth minister returned to the United States with a fierce hatred for the Kaiser's land. Claiming to have verified ten thousand German atrocities, Hillis asked, "Shall this foul creature that is in the German saddle, with hoofs of fire, trample down all the sweet growths in the garden of God[?]"[69] In 1918 he wrote two books documenting such sins: *German Atrocities* and *The Blot on the Kaiser's 'Scutcheon.* The Treasury Department planned to use this sort of material in its fundraising efforts for the Third Liberty Loan.[70] Hillis rejoiced in that campaign, describing the war as "a religious crusade."[71]

Not one to mince words, Hillis provided *The Blot on the Kaiser's 'Scutcheon* with chapter titles such as "The Arch-Criminal," "The Judas among Nations," "The Black Soul of the Hun," and, most chillingly, "Must German Men Be Exterminated?"[72] Hillis defended his argument for German extermination by maintaining that respectable citizens such as philanthropists, scholars, and statesmen were now considering this question. Just as previous cultures had conspired to abolish rattlesnakes, yellow fever, wolves, and the Black Plague, Hillis explained, modern civilization could no longer tolerate Germans.[73] Ob-

FIGURE 9. Newell Dwight Hillis, c. 1915. Library of Congress, Prints & Photographs Division, LC-DIG-ggbain-18048.

servers as old as the Roman historian Tacitus had observed the barbaric German character while contemporary events made it unmistakably clear that "the leopard has not changed its spots."[74] Therefore, Hillis wrote, he was examining a plan—ostensibly being considered by surgeons—to forcibly sterilize "ten million German soldiers" and to segregate "their women" so that "this awful cancer" could be "cut clean out of the body of society."[75] Where the *Northwestern Chronicle* advocated the end of the Spanish empire in 1898, Hillis in 1918 did them one better: he advocated the extinction of German people themselves. As evidenced by such proposals, the *Outlook*'s language of extermination was in tune with wider cultural currents. In the language of insanity, extermination, and hatred, the vitriolic rhetoric expressed in the pages of the *Outlook* toward Germany in World War I surpassed even that expressed toward the South in the Civil War or the Spanish in the war of 1898.

What possibly could have accounted for this language of madness, extermination, and hatred? Partly it had to do with prosaic reasons: prowar clergy believed Germany had unlawfully invaded Belgium, violated numerous agreements, and failed to protect the rights of neutrals. But it also certainly had to do with the way ministers deployed theological language and associations in demonizing Germany. Several examples will show how mainline Christian leaders regularly identified Germany with evil biblical characters and questioned Germans' Christianity. Investing the earthly conflict with otherworldly significance allowed, if not required, unrestrained language. One might respect a worthy foe, but who could compromise with Satan, Pontius Pilate, or Judas?

The *Outlook* consistently used religious imagery to associate Germany with evil biblical characters such as Satan. In January 1918, the journal printed a letter from "A Pastor of a City Congregation." This writer began by noting, "the German as I have known him in the church is not a spiritual-minded person." The pastor went on to recount anecdotes of his troubles with his German and German-American congregants. Yet, this fiery parson reserved his most explosive rhetoric for the German nation itself: "Patriotism for a country such as ours I somehow cannot disassociate from my religion. My business is to fight the devil, and I have never met him so clearly in the open as in this war."[76]

Abbott himself echoed these charges in *The Twentieth Century Crusade*. In a use of hellfire imagery unusual for Abbott, the *Outlook* editor argued that peace could not be attained in the world until the Kaiser and his ilk "converted to a God of truth and goodness, or are utterly destroyed with unquenchable fire." Abbott made the comparison even more explicit a few lines later. Discussing the prophecy recorded in Genesis 3:15, which Christians commonly considered a promise that Christ would crush the head of serpent Satan, Abbott wrote, "Now the head of the serpent is erect, its forked tongue is running out, its eyes red with wrath, its very breath is poisonous. We have a difficult task to get our heel on the head but when we do we must grind it to powder."[77] Instead of being a worthy enemy, Germany reminded Abbott of the devil himself.

The *Outlook* also conflated Germany with many other notorious biblical figures. A brief survey of the journal's efforts in this direction underscores the frequency (and elasticity) of the trope. As peace arrangements began in the fall of 1918, the *Outlook* argued that Germany must not be allowed to become a member of the proposed League of Nations. To permit this, the paper argued, would be to construct "a league of Apostles with Caiaphas to promote Christianity."[78] Abbott and his colleagues also applauded when S. De Lancey Townsend, the rector of the Protestant Episcopal Church of All Angels, New York City, connected another of Jesus' persecutors, Pontius Pilate, with the Germans. In a Palm Sunday 1918 message, Townsend told his parishioners that military power alone impressed Pilate. The Roman procurator could not understand Jesus because "Pilate was a product of a military *Kultur*" that only respected brute force. Lest his possibly drowsy congregation miss the point, Townsend stated bluntly, "Pilate was a Prussian." "To the Prussian," Townsend insisted, "truth and goodness rest for their authority upon the power to 'crucify.'" To this message, the *Outlook* appended that "it is also what we would say" to those ready to compromise with Germany.[79]

By incessantly portraying the war as a crusade, perhaps the mainline clergy strove to counteract the apathy of less militaristic congregations. They had some reason to do so. A national postwar survey of Congregationalist churches found that not all made the war central to their mission. In response to the question, "What did your pastor consider the main message of the pulpit during the war?" one church responded, "Prayer." Likewise, an Alabama pastor ministering to soldiers considered "the main emphasis of the message" not to be social salvation, manly courage at the front, or the defeat of a Satanic foe, but simply, "Jesus Christ."[80] These answers would have failed to satisfy militaristic clergy who considered war to be the all-absorbing problem.

The fighting parsons might also have been targeting pacifist clerical colleagues. Traditional peace churches, like the Mennonites and Quakers, predictably found their communions deeply divided about the permissibility of serving in the armed forces.[81] Pacifists were found in the mainline denominations as well. In 1915, Congregationalist Charles E. Jefferson delivered six lectures at Grinnell College on "Christianity and International Peace." Probably with preparedness advocates like Abbott and Roosevelt in mind, Jefferson warned that "Christianity and militarism are implacable and deadly foes." In New York, the Unitarian John Haynes Holmes published a statement of "radical pacifism" in 1916; his preface denounced the so-called Christian pacifists of all lands who had marched "with enthusiasm" to the front lines when the war broke out.[82] Even as respected a member of the Social Gospel clergy as Walter Rauschenbusch, whose father had been born in Westphalia, as late as 1917 doubted the righteousness of the war. Where prowar advocates saw American military action embodying love for one's neighbor, Rauschenbusch wrote that "in actual practice we do not love when we kill." That Jesus could approve of violence he ridiculed as "theoretical twaddle." Whether it was out of theological conviction, ethnic background, or a combination of both, not all white Protestants joined the wartime crusade.[83]

Thus, the prevailing heated rhetoric emanating from the militant clergy probably resulted at least in part from desires to drown out the voices of the uncommitted, the opposed, and the nonresistant. For them, Abbott had another biblical text in mind, one employed as far back as the Seven Years' War and the American Revolution to quell antiwar dissent—Deborah's cursing of Meroz in Judges 5:23: "Curse ye Meroz, said the angel of the Lord, curse ye bitterly the inhabitants thereof; because they came not to the help of the Lord, to the help of the Lord against the mighty."[84] In February 1917, the *Outlook* reported that Roosevelt had applied this text to those who stood neutral between martyred Belgium and its murderer, Germany. Abbott, too, thought the passage applied to neutrals in the present day.[85]

Religiously inspired militarists also demonized Germans by associating them with paganism. On May 2, 1917, Abbott editorialized on "The Duty of Christ's Church Today." One of the duties, Abbott thought, included taking a stand for Christian civilization against Germany's paganism. Because Abbott knew that Protestantism had a long history in Germany, he sought to prove that contemporary Germans had abandoned anything that could be described as Christianity. To demonstrate this, Abbott reprinted a German poem (translated into English) that he believed "enjoyed a large circulation in Germany." This poem asserted that the Germans enjoyed the protection of Odin, an ancient Germanic god. In response, Abbott stated that the present contest was one "between Christianity and paganism," urging his readers to "transform" the "pagan world" into the Kingdom of God.[86] In June 1918, the *Outlook* repeated the charge: "[Prussianism] has endeavored to drive love from the pulpit, and for loyal love for a heavenly Father, God of love, it has sought to substitute abject fear of Odin, god of force."[87]

Again, such views resonated in the larger American Protestant world. A letter to the Methodist *Christian Advocate* (New York), for instance, rehearsed the familiar trope of Germany as devilish. This letter writer, George D. Beattys from Westfield, New Jersey, took issue with an earlier editorial lamenting the sad spectacle of Christians fighting each other. Whereas the first writer had identified war with "the Furies of the Pit . . . doing their diabolical work of desolation in all the world," Beattys applied that characterization to the "arrogant, tyrannous, Prussian military autocracy." The "Prussian war lords," moreover, he described as "Godless" practitioners of "unrighteousness."[88]

One of the most prominent liberal Protestant theologians joined Beattys in these sentiments. Shailer Mathews (1863–1941), dean of the divinity school at the University of Chicago, qualified as one of the most theologically learned supporters of the war. In May 1918, Mathews delivered a series of lectures at the University of North Carolina, subsequently published as *Patriotism and Religion*. In this work, Mathews argued that the German Kaiser and his cohorts prayed to someone different than the Christian God when they asked for divine aid.[89] Because Germans connected their God to an earthly "sovereign's will" and the divine right of kings, the end result inevitably led to "massacre, deportation, [and] terrorization." Echoing the themes of German paganism, Mathews asserted that "the continuity of history between the German God and the ancient tribal god is unbroken." In reference to an obscure biblical passage (2 Kings 19:1–37), Mathews again associated Germany with paganism: "German patriotism is as truly identified with official German religion as was the pride of Sennacherib with the praise of Marduk."[90]

It was not only theological liberals who made such charges, however. No matter the topic, Billy Sunday could always be counted upon for a colorful quotation, and his denunciations of Germany during the Great War were no different. After having stood on the sidelines during the early years of the war, Sunday eventually became a vocal supporter of the Allies. "I tell you it is [Kaiser] Bill against Woodrow, Germany against America, Hell against Heaven," he declared after the United States had entered the conflict. In a prayer before the House of Representatives, Sunday characterized the Germans as "that great pack of wolfish Huns whose fangs drip with blood and gore." Most famously, he explained that "if you turn hell upside down, you will find 'Made in Germany' stamped on the bottom."[91] Such religiously charged references dehumanized the German enemy, perhaps helping to make a de-Germanized world thinkable.

The Social Gospel

In *The War for Righteousness*, Richard Gamble argues that theologically progressive clergymen interpreted World War I as an extension of the Social Gospel, the liberal Protestant impulse to remake American society along Christian lines. He has interpreted widespread Protestant support for the war as part of a broader American evangelical impulse to ameliorate social ills.[92] Regardless of whether one considers such impulses to be strictly based on the social gospel or more generally on the evangelical ethos, it is clear that the application of Christian principles to world affairs also motivated American Christians to support the Great War.

Following this line of thought, Abbott argued in the pages of the *Outlook* that Christ's teachings on church discipline (found in Matthew 18:15–17) equally applied to nations when international conflicts arose. To those who objected that Christ intended his prescriptions only for individuals, Abbott prepared a ready answer: "the same principles apply to the settlement of disputes between organizations as between individuals."[93] Similarly, in *The Twentieth Century Crusade*, Abbott maintained that adherence to "the Old Gospel" required national action on behalf of suffering Europe. Quoting Jesus' description of his mission of deliverance (Luke 4:16–21), Abbott averred that Christians should emulate their Master in this duty as well.[94] Therefore, since Germany had allegedly enslaved Belgium and France, Christianity demanded the United States act to liberate these latter-day captives. Referencing German poison gas, Abbott queried, "How can we allow that process to go on and pretend to fulfill our divine mission to give sight to the blind?"[95] Nations as well as individuals must imitate Christ.

Abbott even held out hope that Europe's social salvation would come by means of victorious Allied forces. On its front page, the June 6, 1917 issue of the *Outlook* carried an editorial urging its readers to buy Liberty Bonds. The *Outlook* called the war "the greatest philanthropic enterprise in the history of the world," promising that it would bring "salvation" to "nations and races." Buying the bonds would help to ensure the success of this effort.[96] Liberty Loan Sunday in the fall of 1918 provided another occasion for Abbott to reinforce the urgency of the call. As a guest preacher in an unrecorded location, Abbott took for his text Luke 22:36: "Then said he unto them, But now, he that hath a purse, let him take it, and likewise his scrip: and he that hath no sword, let him sell his garment, and buy one." His diary remarks suggest the character of his message: "the time may come when it is wise to sell" one's own clothes "if necessary to secure arms for the battle."[97]

In August 1917, Abbott made one of his most emotional appeals of the war. In an editorial titled, "The Call of the Nation," the eighty-one-year-old editor described the present conflict as "the greatest task which has ever been given to men," expressing a wish to "shoulder a rifle or fly an airplane" in the service of his country. In his praise of the soldiers who epitomized the "spirit of heroism and self-sacrifice," Abbott passionately summarized the Social Gospel nature of the war. Because the struggle would ultimately end "in a world freedom and a world peace," he invoked the lines of the Battle Hymn of the Republic, a hymn equally pertinent to the Great War as it had been to the Civil War: "As [Christ] died to make men holy, let us die to make men free."[98] In this reading of the conflict, American war-making could actually help to usher in a new era of world democracy—something God surely endorsed. To fight the war, therefore, meant obedience to Christ as the nation practiced "applied Christianity."

This warlike Social Gospel even had the power to save Germany. Abbott admitted the war would cause "many German children" to become "orphans" and German wives, "widows." Yet the conflict would ultimately benefit the enemy: "It is also true that we are fighting to emancipate Germany no less than to emancipate Belgium, France and Italy." Adapting President Wilson's rationale for the war, he declared, "We are going to make the whole world safe for the Brotherhood of Man—Germany no less than the countries which German autocracy has attacked."[99] To illustrate this view, Abbott recounted the biblical story in which Christ exorcised a demon from a boy (Luke 9:37–43). After Jesus expelled the demon, but before the child was completely re-stored, "the boy became as one dead; in so much that the more part said, He is dead." Abbott wrote that the cleansing that would come to Germany as a result of the war might also involve pain, but would ultimately prove salvific: "This war must not end until the demon of lawless self-conceit and self-will is driven out of the German nation, though the nation be left as one dead by the very act which saves its people from the madness which possesses them."[100] Ultimately, the war would bring social and political righteousness to Germany.

The same Social Gospel convictions also motivated other mainline leaders to support the conflict as well. Shailer Mathews too used religious language in his support for the war effort. Mathews argued in *Patriotism and Religion* that the nature of one's religion and the nature of one's patriotism could not be separated: "When one considers the historical kinship of patriotism and reli-gion, it is seen to be something more than an inheritance. It is psychological. Each is a complementary aspect of the same mood of the social mind. Loy-alty to one set of political institutions involves loyalty to a conception of reli-gion, both positively and negatively." Now, he went on, the world witnessed a conflict between "two types of patriotism and two types of religion." On one side stood "a religion which is the servant of the state" while the other side embodied "a social order that is already finding its way into a religion that promises light and freedom for the human soul." What was ultimately at stake, Mathews insisted, was "a new future for democracy and a religion worthy of democracy." Allied victory would ensure the abolition of Germanic reaction-ary religion, bringing in its place a true religion, which worships "God who is a Father . . . rather than a God of battles and conquest."[101] Thus, the war be-came a Social Gospel enterprise because it promised to bring both true free-dom and true religion to Europe.

George Beattys, the writer to the *Christian Advocate*, agreed with Mathews's exposition of social Christianity. In his view, history had never produced such an extraordinary example of "men and women dedicated to the brotherhood of man." "Countless thousands," he exclaimed, "are sacrificing their lives for a really Christian ideal—that of human liberty and justice and the principles that Christ exemplifies."[102]

Fosdick took up similar themes in his *Atlantic Monthly* article. He rejoiced that American soldiers had not gone to France "to save their souls." Rather, "they forgot themselves, and went to France to save the world. They are learning that innermost salvation that never comes except through social sacrifice; they have found their lives by losing them in a cause."[103] For Fosdick, the war would bring redemption not only to Europe but to the lives of American soldiers as well. Perhaps V.G.A. Tressler, the president of the General Synod of the Lutheran Church in the U.S.A., put the sentiment most explicitly: "In this Liberty Loan we are in no small measure achieving the aspirations of this government and the commands of the Gospel."[104]

Social Position

In contrast to the well-publicized opinions of influential writers, the marginalized social position of America's Missouri Synod Lutherans, Black Methodists, and Roman Catholics produced divided commentary in their communities about the righteousness of World War I (discussed in chapter 6). Social location played an important role in determining white mainline Protestants' position as well.

In private Lyman Abbott revealed a few of the regional and ethnic prejudices bearing on his views. In a 1915 letter to Britain's Lord Aberdeen, Abbott sought to explain why the United States had not rushed to the aid of the Allies. While those on the East Coast recognized the stakes of the war, he implied, those in the "middle and far west" cared little about a conflict that seemed "a long way off." Ethnically, German Americans were torn between "loyalty to liberty and love for the Fatherland" while Irish Americans still held "anti-English" sentiments.[105] Apprising himself of German-American opinion, Abbott underlined pro-German phrases in an August 1914 edition of *The Lutheran*.[106] Although he did not directly condemn these groups, he made it clear that the nation's "heterogeneous population" made it difficult to achieve concerted national opinion.[107]

As in the Spanish-American War, gender also played a role for some in their enthusiastic support of the Great War. Recycling the "muscular Christianity" themes of the 1890s, Henry Hallam Tweedy at Yale Divinity School explained that the experience of war would turn soft, complacent men into masculine warriors. A committee of the FCC agreed with this characterization, praising the toughening effects war was having on the soldiers. Women, too, could echo this point of view. The Episcopalian Social Gospel activist Vida D. Scudder disagreed with other socialists when she maintained that the experiences of American doughboys were likely to stimulate the traditional martial virtues. Unlike in 1898, however, Anglo-Saxonism was not as much of a factor in prompting war in 1917.[108] It did not make as much sense for clergy to trumpet "Anglo-Saxonism" when the nation's opponents were Germans.

More broadly, perhaps mainline clergymen also observed the shrinking role of the ministerial vocation and wished to shore up the cultural authority of both Christianity in general and of the ministry in particular. Darrel Bigham and Ann Douglas have advanced this thesis in their studies of the clergy in the Gilded Age and Progressive Era.[109] Although Bigham overstates "status anxiety" motivations, his analysis does cast light on mainline stances during the Great War. If Americans accepted a religious understanding of the conflict, perhaps they would continue to entrust the church with cultural authority and listen to its pronouncements even on secular affairs. Indeed, during the conflict nervous Protestant leaders repeatedly addressed the issue of soldiers' religion, wondering what kind of expectations veterans would bring with them on their return. While ideology best accounts for the vociferous support the war received, more earthly reasons like ethnic prejudices, regional locations, concerns about manliness, and status anxiety must not be overlooked.[110]

Continuity with Earlier Wars

Mirroring the patterns they displayed in the Civil War and the Spanish-American War, elite mainline Protestants often supported the Great War because of their social station and ideological understanding of the conflict. Although American culture and society had changed considerably from 1860 to 1920, the general attitude toward war had not. Although historians must always be alert to change over time, sometimes the more interesting stories can be found in continuities between periods that are commonly thought of as distinct.

Abbott's conduct after the war reinforced the persistence of older ideas. After the storm had passed, some of the progressive clergy repented of their jingoism. Marginalized during the war, in retrospect the perspectives of pacifists like Charles Jefferson and John Haynes Holmes seemed prescient to some.

Nonresistance again became fashionable in some quarters while a chastened "theology of crisis," with a greater awareness of sin and humanity's limitations, arose during the following decades. In World War II, America's clergy promoted what one historian has called "a cautious patriotism."[111] Abbott belonged to a different generation. In the four years he had to live after the 1918 armistice, he showed no signs of rethinking his wartime positions. In March 1922, the president of the French Republic made Abbott "chevalier" of the Legion of Honor in recognition of the editor's outstanding service to the Allied cause. In his acceptance speech, Abbott praised the ideals the two countries shared, recounting the righteous war they had waged in defense of a common vision.[112] Ever gifted in the use of words, a few months before his death, Abbott wrote simply, "The World War was worth all that it cost."[113]

For a more complete understanding of this world, scholars must examine those religious groups opposed to majority wartime positions. One particularly interesting outsider group, the Missouri Synod Lutherans, offered a significantly different take on the Great War. Their leaders disdained mainline Protestant theological commitments, recoiled from blending sacred and secular categories to justify the conflict, and valued their German heritage. Chapter Six will illustrate the war's different reception among Midwestern Lutheran communities. Their perspective sheds light on American intellectual, cultural, and social life during these years while it also brings mainline Protestants' own assumptions into stark relief.

CHAPTER 6

"There Will Be a Day of Reckoning for Our Country"

Missouri Synod Lutherans Face World War I

When a portion of white mainline Protestant leaders supported the Great War with such ferocity, they spoke for many American Christians, but not for all of them. One important group, in particular, the German Evangelical Lutheran Synod of Missouri, Ohio, and Other States (abbreviations: LCMS or Missouri Synod), offered a stark contrast. Often of German heritage (with a goodly number of Scandinavians as well), centered in the Midwest, focused on developing their own communities, averse to any mingling of church and state, and committed to a "two-kingdoms" theology that distinguished sharply between the City of Man and the City of God—not many groups stood as far from the mainline theological and social world in 1914–18 as Missouri Synod Lutherans. This chapter analyzes LCMS views of World War I to highlight the critical role that ideology and social location played in influencing American Christians' positions on the conflict. Where such factors had led many to full-throated support of the war, theology and social position combined to cause much anxiety about the conflict within the LCMS community.

The Missouri Synod was organized in the United States in 1847 to preserve strict adherence to Reformation doctrines (the Augsburg Confession of 1530) over against German rationalism, on the one hand, and Americanization, on the other.[1] Conservatism was its hallmark. Indeed, the Missouri Synod clung tightly to its tradition while building an impressive subculture (including about

2,100 parochial schools) by the early twentieth century.[2] Since in this period the synod was primarily composed of second- and third-generation immigrants, many of the denomination's congregations and schools still used the German language as did two of the synod's official periodicals.[3] At the beginning of the war, such phenomena kept LCMS members relatively isolated from the dominant American culture. As we will see, the crisis of the war forced some changes in the LCMS, allowing the denomination to become more fully "American" by the end of the conflict.[4] In the main, though, continuity rather than change prevailed.

Two of the denomination's official publications, the biweekly English language newspaper *Lutheran Witness* and the biweekly German-language newspaper *Der Lutheraner*, commented frequently on the Great War from August 1914 to November 1918. In 1918 subscription rates approximated 43,000 for *Der Lutheraner* and 19,000 for the *Lutheran Witness*.[5] Controlled by the faculty at the LCMS's Concordia Seminary in St. Louis, the two publications were well-positioned to represent the synod's views.[6]

The editors of these two LCMS publications shared a common background and outlook. Ludwig Fuerbringer (1864–1947) of *Der Lutheraner* served as a professor at Concordia. Fuerbringer's colleague on the faculty, Theodore Graebner (1876–1950), edited the *Lutheran Witness* along with denominational leader Martin Sommer (1869–1949), who would join Concordia in 1920. All three men were also Concordia graduates with pastoral experience.[7] They well represented an important subculture in the Midwest since the LCMS claimed 728,000 adherents by 1900.[8] Speaking for thousands of serious Christians but far removed from mainstream American culture, the Missouri Synod provides an ideal comparison with the Protestant mainline.

Overall, LCMS Lutherans rarely agreed with popular positions during the war. Whereas leaders like Lyman Abbott championed the Allied cause from an early date, before April 1917 LCMS periodicals favored Germany or advocated strict neutrality. Where some mainline clerics marshaled biblical images and Christian rhetoric to label the war a righteous one, the Missouri Synod offered a much more restrained patriotism. And where many Protestant spokesmen seemed to lose all distinction between earthly and heavenly kingdoms, in the main these Lutherans refused to baptize the conflict. From the beginning of the struggle in August 1914 until around the spring of 1918, the LCMS steadfastly clung to its apolitical stance, supporting the war dutifully only after American intervention in April 1917. Until the beginning of 1918, the synod's newspapers routinely denounced the mingling of church and state, insisting that secular affairs must remain separate from churchly functions. From January 1918 until the armistice in November, external pressures forced

LCMS leaders to adjust, but not exactly renounce, their previous positions. Even in this atmosphere, Missouri Synod pronouncements rarely resembled the views offered by white Protestant mainline leaders.

Setting LCMS commentary next to the mainline's wartime writings provides historical insight by continuing to show how crucial ideology and social position (in this case, ethnicity and geographical location) were for determining Christians' views on American wars. In this case, mainline theology allowed an easy blending of the sacred and secular. In the mainline world, latent Calvinist background (with its emphasis on transforming the world) melded with immanentist theology (with its stress on God's presence in human affairs) to reduce distinctions between religion and politics. By contrast, Lutherans' distinctive theology of "two-kingdoms" (explained below) taught that church and state must not be mixed. Likewise, LCMS Lutherans were often recent German immigrants, sometimes spoke no English, and were inclined to favor *der Vaterland*. Geographically, their largest city was St. Louis, their more rural communities spread out in the hinterlands of the upper Midwest. In short, among these two groups of American Protestants, different theological and social backgrounds helped produced strikingly different perspectives on the Great War.

New Contributions

Histories of American Lutheranism have generally suffered from parochialism. Accounts of denominational politics and institutional changes proliferate without much attention to American culture more broadly.[9] These traits especially characterize treatments of Missouri Synod Lutherans and the Great War. Even the best work, an early chapter in Wayne Wilke's larger study of twentieth-century LCMS attitudes toward church and state, remains relatively internalist.[10] Most studies give approximately the same picture: the LCMS favored Germany prior to the American declaration of war in April 1917. After that time the denomination loyally supported the Allied cause, albeit without much enthusiasm. Wartime hysteria in the form of moderate persecution forced the Missouri Synod to proclaim its patriotism more loudly as 1918 wore on. In the end, the war's main effect was the reduction of the German language in churches and schools.[11] This chapter does not contest the foregoing account. Instead, it extends Wilke's work in examining the assumptions underpinning LCMS commentary on the conflict. It seeks to show what made the Missouri Synod stand out from mainline Protestants with Calvinist roots. It also demonstrates why their views matter for understanding American religion and the Great War more completely.

This focus is especially important because the broader accounts of the American churches in World War I have not adequately explored the Lutheran case. The first such study, Ray Abrams's classic *Preachers Present Arms* (1933), dutifully noted Lutheran perspectives on various events but failed to explore in any depth why Lutherans reacted to wartime developments as they did.[12] John F. Piper Jr.'s revision of Abrams, *The American Churches in World War I* (1985), focuses on the mainline Protestant bodies with only scattered references to the LCMS.[13] Richard M. Gamble's exposé of liberal Protestant excesses during the war likewise leaves Lutherans out of the story.[14] Recent surveys of religion and the Great War, such as Andrew Preston's *Sword of the Spirit, Shield of Faith* (2012) and Philip Jenkins's *The Great and Holy War* (2014) likewise pass over American Lutheran experiences.[15] This chapter enriches our understanding of broader American history by demonstrating the payoff for including the Missouri Synod in the story of American churches in the conflict.

Finally, adding the LCMS into the story enriches our accounts of the World War I home front, which currently omit engagement with the Missouri Synod. Despite facing persecution in the Midwest due to its ethnic heritage, the denomination does not appear in the index of David Kennedy's standard resource on the domestic scene, *Over Here* (1982).[16] More localized treatments of Missouri and the Great War also give Lutherans short shrift.[17] Petra DeWitt's recent volume *Degrees of Allegiance* (2012) improves matters slightly, but more work must still be done to integrate the Missouri Synod into the story of German American experiences during the conflict.[18] We must not conceive of the LCMS as simply one more German American group pining for the Fatherland during the war; the synod's distinctive theology, combined with its members' ethnic sympathies, led to its refusal to baptize the conflict. Their story is different and needs to be better understood for a more complete account of American experiences on the home front.

Lutheran Theology and the War

Most Progressive Era American Protestants envisioned relatively porous boundaries between sacred and secular affairs. Although few in this period denied the benefits of the separation of church and state, many moral reformers considered it their duty to make American laws reflect Protestant values. Attempts to legislate Prohibition, advocacy of "blue laws," sponsorship of Bible reading in public schools, and efforts to create a "Christian Amendment" to the Constitution recognizing God's sovereignty over the nation all represented an activist impulse to make the City of Man become like the City of God.[19]

Missouri Synod Lutherans largely opposed such policies because of their understanding of the divine order. In their view, God ruled over two kingdoms: a temporal one and a spiritual one. The temporal kingdom included facets of life like government, economics, and everything else to do with this world; the spiritual kingdom manifested itself in believers coming together in church for Word and Sacrament under the power of the Holy Spirit. Christians should keep the two realms separate, LCMS leaders taught, since each kingdom operated according to its own nature. Good Lutherans could be active citizens, but the church must avoid advocating specific policies. The state, in turn, should never interfere with the church's activities.[20] The church was the church, and the state was the state.

Because of such convictions, during the war LCMS ministers as well as official LCMS organs like *Der Lutheraner* and the *Lutheran Witness* hesitated even to discuss secular matters. When they did find it necessary to touch upon the conflict, they frequently prefaced their remarks with disclaimers. "You will bear me witness," the Missouri Synod minister Louis Buchheimer (1872–1953) told his St. Louis congregation during the war, "that I have never unduly introduced any reference to political matters or agitated public questions into this place," before explaining that buying war bonds was a "supreme duty."[21] Likewise, prior to discussing Lutheran soldiers, the Red Cross, and war bonds, *Der Lutheraner* editor Ludwig Fuerbringer insisted that "The LUTHERANER has never discussed political issues, and does not purpose to do so in the future."[22] The extent of Fuerbringer's fidelity to traditional Lutheran doctrine can be gauged from the periodical's motto: "God's word and Luther's teaching shall never pass away."[23] As the war went on, Missouri Synod Lutherans sometimes departed from these practices, commenting on various kinds of secular affairs. Most of the time, however, they followed their stated principle of keeping religious and worldly affairs separate.

Indeed, only the crisis of American entry forced these Lutherans to use their denominational magazines to urge patriotism. Before April 1917, the LCMS papers consistently maintained that politics and religion ought to be kept far apart, attacking those who violated the separation of church and state. The *Lutheran Witness*'s comments on a November 1915 speech of President Woodrow Wilson illustrate the point well. When Wilson inveighed against Americans whose real loyalties allegedly lay elsewhere, the paper's coeditor Graebner interpreted the remark as an anti-German slur. Graebner thought the comment more accurately applied to the rabidly pro-Allied newspaper editors. He chose, however, not to pursue that line of thought further: "the LUTHERAN

WITNESS, as a religious paper, is not concerned with that portion of President Wilson's speech." Instead, Graebner found fault with Wilson's call for religious harmony in the nation. Although such a plea sounded harmless enough, Graebner came to the defense of anti-Mormon and anti-Catholic movements since he considered both Mormons and Catholics politically dangerous. Neither, he alleged, believed in the separation of church and state. Hence, Americans should not tolerate these menaces but oppose them.[24] As a good Lutheran editor, Graebner did not think it his role to elaborate on Wilson's ethnic prejudices; however, he did make it a point to stand up for a strict church-state separation.[25]

Graebner's assumptions became even more explicit in a follow-up editorial. Here he trained his sights on Wilson's ecumenism. "We are a God-fearing nation," the president had said. "We agree to differ about the methods of worship, but we are united in believing in a Divine Providence and in worshiping the God of Nations." Nonsense, Graebner retorted, there were "sixty odd million Americans who are not even nominally connected with any Church." The president therefore harmfully divided Americans on the basis of "religion against irreligion." Graebner declared that the government "is simply non-religious," insisting that atheists must be protected in their freedom not to worship at all. No one could miss the warning: "Let our political leaders beware of mingling religion and government."[26] This remarkable editorial illustrates just how committed the synod was to "two-kingdoms" theology and the separation of church and state. Unlike mainliners, LCMS Lutherans harbored deep theological suspicions of any conflation of sacred and secular realms.

Following this conviction, LCMS commentary on the war (at least in the early days) often emphasized its spiritual aspects. When the conflict began, the *Lutheran Witness* did not take sides, editorializing instead that all parties had "much abused the blessings of God." The paper's wartime prayer had little to do with battlefield victory; instead co-editor Martin Sommer prayed for spiritual renewal across Europe: "If the terror of facing murderous cannon, if the pains of the wounded, if the agonies of the dying, if the sorrows of those who are weeping at home, will cause souls to be aroused to seek the face of the Heavenly Father, to make confession of sin, and to visit the altar where His pardon is bestowed, then the war will 'pay.'"[27] A few weeks later, the editors turned a discussion of the heroism and sacrifice of European soldiers into a lesson on warfare of the spiritual sort.[28] As late as May 1918, over a year after American entry, *Der Lutheraner* still refused to baptize the Allied cause. In giving some suggestions for war prayers to be used in church services, the paper avoided commonplace triumphalist rhetoric about the righteous war. Instead, *Der Lutheraner*'s petitions demonstrated humility and repentance: "We have well deserved such affliction with our many and great sins; but they give us sorrow in our hearts and make us repentant. And because you are gracious and merciful, patient and merciful, and slow to punish—so we ask that you would neither treat us according to our sins nor repay us according to our iniquity."[29] War's privations served the larger purpose of spiritual renewal.

Lutherans' preference for stark divisions between church and state affected their wartime commentary in other ways as well. For example, "two-kingdoms" theology determined what kind of wars were lawful. In May 1916 the *Lutheran Witness* derided President Wilson's notion that the United States should follow the interests of "humanity" in determining whether or not to become involved in the war. The New Testament gave governments distinct authority to rule their own subjects, Graebner stated. "Unutterable confusion" would result if nations began dictating to each other what was lawful and what was not. In short, the United States had no right to interfere in another nation's affairs (much less make war), even for humanitarian considerations.[30]

Graebner based his argument on Romans 13, a key text for the synod throughout the war. The relevant parts of the Apostle Paul's letter read as follows:

Let every soul be subject unto the higher powers. For there is no power but of God: the powers that be are ordained of God. Whosoever therefore resisteth the power, resisteth the ordinance of God: and they that resist shall receive to themselves damnation. For rulers are not a terror to good works, but to the evil. Wilt thou then not be afraid of the power? do that which is good, and thou shalt have praise of the same: For he is the minister of God to thee for good. But if thou do that which is evil, be afraid; for he beareth not the sword in vain: for he is the minister of God, a revenger to execute wrath upon him that doeth evil. Wherefore ye must needs be subject, not only for wrath, but also for conscience sake. For this cause pay ye tribute also: for they are God's ministers, attending continually upon this very thing. Render therefore to all their dues: tribute to whom tribute is due; custom to whom custom; fear to whom fear; honor to whom honor.[31]

LCMS leaders believed this passage taught that government was a godly institution ordained by the Lord Himself. As subjects, people must obey the government even if they disagreed with its laws. By implication, the United States had no right to go to war simply because Germany's military tactics were disagreeable.

To be sure, Graebner admitted that Christians lived according to a different standard—one of self-sacrifice and love of one's neighbor. *"But it is not the function of government to enforce this principle,"* Graebner insisted. That was the mistake of the "Calvinistic system of theology. It is another case of mixing politics and religion."[32] What would we do if Japan attacked us because it disapproved of our treatment of Mexico? Graebner asked.[33] A war "for humanity" was sheer nonsense anyway. How could one "choke, starve, slash, hack, cut asunder, and blow into the air" in the name of humanity?[34] Like Shailer Matthews, LCMS leaders employed theology to justify their views of the war; however, the "two kingdoms" theory led them to very different conclusions.

Since governments should not wage war for abstract principles like "humanity," few Lutherans endorsed the extravagant, self-righteous language of crusading. "No synod," several historians have stated, "endorsed the popular view of a 'holy war'" even after American entry.[35] Two months after the United States entered the conflict, Graebner explicitly disavowed the concept of the war as a Christian enterprise. Responding to a Presbyterian pastor's assertion that "this war is a struggle for the Christian order of things," Graebner rebuked "such wretched perversions of the doctrine of Scripture regarding the Church, her nature, her functions and purpose." He also blasted a treasury department official who had stated that America would become "Messianic" if it saw the war through to a successful conclusion. Reminding his readers that the purely secular issue of Germany's use of submarines prompted the American declaration of war, Graebner lamented the "political heresy and perversion of religious teaching" characteristic of the treasury official's statements.[36] Where Harry Emerson Fosdick's theology allowed him to picture the American soldiers in the place of the crucified Christ, Lutheran understandings strongly militated against any such equation.

Indeed, Missouri Synod Lutherans tended to reject the application of biblical typology to modern states altogether, which shaped how they viewed America's role in the war. A writer for *Der Lutheraner* made this clear in a January 1918 editorial about the propriety of praying Psalm 60 in the present day. "C.M.Z." worried that Americans might directly apply King David's plea for help in the midst of God's chastisement to the current situation. In refuting this idea, the writer made rare and incisive statements about the problems entailed in making the United States God's New Israel:

> But where is there now a political body that means a people live together in a land under a single authority, which has the promise of God, and can raise a banner in the manner that Israel once did? Where is now such a people that can pray this psalm in the privations of war and know that victory is certain? Nowhere. Because no such people is the church of God, even though the church of God is found in their midst. Can this psalm, then, not be used now when there is war? O yes, but in correct and modest ways.[37]

Such convictions seemed to derive, at least in part, from Lutheran conceptions of the clear boundaries between sacred and secular spheres. Where mainline leaders often associated Old Testament Israel with the United States, Missouri Synod spokesmen refused to do so.

A final way the LCMS's emphasis on "two-kingdoms" theology and the separation of church and state affected its wartime commentary occurred in a controversy over promoting Liberty Loans from the pulpit. In the spring of 1917 the federal government established June 3 as "Liberty Loan Sunday" to promote the sale of war bonds. The treasury department even sent ministers a list of suggested patriotic sermon outlines. Where figures like Newell Dwight Hillis embraced such initiatives due to their understanding of Christianity and democracy, the *Lutheran Witness* protested emphatically. Although Graebner acknowledged the government's right to promote the purchase of war bonds, his conception of the nature of the church impelled him to reject the request: "But what has this bond issue to do with the Christian pulpit? Is the Church of God a house of merchandise? Does it come within the function of the American government to suggest texts and sermon outlines . . . to Christian preachers?"[38]

As the Wilson administration continued to apply pressure on this issue in the coming months, the *Witness* stood firm. In September the paper reprinted a resolution from some Southern Presbyterians declaring that "political or war sermons have no rightful place in the pulpit."[39] As late as February 1918, Graebner insisted that Missouri Synod ministers must stick to spiritual themes for Sunday morning sermons, although they might find other times to honor federal requests.[40] "Our preachers do not write sermons on The Epic of the Panama Canal or on The Ventilation of Public Buildings," Graebner explained. "The Lutheran pulpit recognizes only one purpose: to declare the will of God revealed in the inspired Scriptures."[41] Theological convictions prompted him to oppose any intrusion of political matters into the spiritual realm.

In addition to emphasizing church-state separation, Lutheran theology also prompted its adherents to oppose mainline Protestants like Lyman Abbott on other wartime issues. Like many periodicals, the *Lutheran Witness* paid attention to the *Outlook*, engaging with Abbott several times from 1914 to 1918. Since the synod rejected Abbott's theological liberalism, the *Witness's* general opinion was not very favorable. In November 1914 Martin Sommer styled the *Outlook* editor one of America's "greatest rationalists," laughing at his theological "surmises and ridiculous guesses."[42] Two years later Graebner struck a more serious tone: "Every week [the *Outlook*] has its dole of poison."[43]

The *Witness's* attitude toward the *Outlook* editor hardly improved after the United States entered the war. In particular, the journal attacked Abbott after his infamous sermon "To Love Is to Hate" suggested American Christians need not pray for the Kaiser because Jesus supposedly did not pray for the leaders who condemned him. Sommer ridiculed Abbott's notion that Jesus did not pray for Pontius Pilate or the Jewish high priest Caiaphas: "Why does [Abbott] not continue and assert also that Jesus may have loved those poor ignorant soldiers, but that He certainly did not love Caiaphas or Pilate?" he asked. "Jesus did not only love the soldiers who crucified Him, He sincerely loved also Caiaphas and Pilate," Sommer insisted. "He loved Pilate enough to die for him." This statement led to an obvious implication: "We American Christians are to pray also for the German people, for the German soldiers, for the German generals, and for the German Kaiser."[44]

The *Witness* also condemned "salvation by khaki," another doctrine that Abbott advocated. In this view, soldiers who died fighting in a righteous cause went straight to heaven, despite their previous sins. Just as theological convictions prompted African American Methodists to rebuke Henry Ward Beecher for allegedly teaching this doctrine in the Civil War, so Missouri Synod Lutherans denounced the idea fifty years later. In an October 1918 editorial, Sommer discussed this issue, first appealing to Martin Luther to legitimate the soldier's profession. Lutherans, he explained, rejected the supposedly medieval error of doubting that soldiers could be good Christians. Still, Sommer demonstrated even more carefully that "a soldier, be he commander-in-chief, officer, or private, does not go to heaven simply because he is a soldier, or because he happens to die upon the field of battle." There remained only one way to heaven: "faith in Jesus Christ, the Lamb of God, which taketh away the sin of the world."[45] This belief echoed a statement made by another LCMS leader in the paper's pages a few months before: "In death [the Christian soldier] enters into life eternal, *not because he died as a soldier*, but because he died as a Christian soldier, died as a Christian in the patriotic discharge of his duty to his country. The death on the battlefield, *if it be a death in Christ*, cannot separate from Christ."[46] The strain of wartime could not compel LCMS leaders to modify their doctrine of heaven. Only Christ's work on the cross, not a selfless death, could atone for sin.

The distinctive theology of the LCMS prevented the synod from embracing the "holy war" or "crusading" rhetoric promoted by outspoken white mainline Protestants. Missouri Synod Lutherans lived in a world where true righteousness could only be obtained by faith in Christ; where governments could legitimately carry out their duties without justifying them on the basis of Christian teaching; and where Christians combined church and state at their peril. These assumptions simply could not permit the "holy war" language that prevailed for many American Protestants during the conflict.

Social Position

In their view of the church's role in the war, in their general conception of the distinction between sacred and secular realms, and in their opposition to Abbott and his friends on controversial issues, Missouri Synod Lutherans demonstrated that theology mattered for determining their convictions about the struggle. Still, other factors such as geographical location and ethnicity influenced LCMS leaders as well. Never deterministic, such factors nevertheless impacted the denomination's outlook on the nation and the war.

In the early twentieth century, the Missouri Synod dwelt on the margins of American life. The point must not be overstated: LCMS leaders exercised cultural authority within their own communities. In the nation at large their status as white male Protestants also put them well ahead of African Americans, women, and non-Christians, to name only a few groups. Still, compared to figures like Hillis or Fosdick, they occupied an outsider status. Even in peacetime no LCMS leaders exercised the kind of national political or religious influence enjoyed by the white Protestant mainline. When war came, they found this marginal position reinforced by German ethnicity and allegedly divided loyalties. As a result, LCMS spokesmen held a more favorable attitude toward Germany because their ethnicity and marginal location allowed them to see Germany's merits and America's demerits more clearly than did the pro-war Anglo-Protestant clergy. Whereas mainline leaders were closely associated with cultural power, the LCMS approached the United States with more critical distance.

Before the United States entered the war, the *Lutheran Witness* regularly complained that American newspapers treated Germany unfairly. "Pharisaic hypocrisy comes to a climax in the solemn curses called down upon the Germanic armies by the American press because of the 'barbaric,' 'inhuman,' 'Hunnic,' 'savage' mode of their warfare," Graebner grumbled in July 1915, "while the actions of the Allies are never made the object of the most gentle censure, no matter what the methods employed."[47] In an editorial the following year, Graebner attacked the religious press in particular for giving in to fanaticism. When another periodical editorialized that the Allies "not only have a righteous cause, but are rendering a service to humanity," Graebner scoffed, "Consider this, when a German is blown up by a mine, or rammed with a bayonet, a service has been rendered to humanity! We have received the *London Times* regularly for the past year, but have never read in it statements that would surpass this in ferocity."[48]

Sometimes the pro-German sympathies took other forms. LCMS Lutherans contributed over $4,000 for war relief in Germany during the fall of 1914.[49]

Occasionally individual ministers even expressed outright disloyalty. O.D. Baltzly of Omaha, Nebraska, referred to the conflict in May 1917 as an "unrighteous war" more properly termed "Mr. Wilson's war." He refused to cooperate with federal initiatives and advised his congregants to do the same. Baltzly argued that the real despotism lay closer to home.[50] Similarly, one Kansas minister wrote to another in 1918, "I hate this land. I am now here twenty-five years, but I hate this land."[51] Another clergyman feared, after returning from a Lutheran pastors' conference, that "if the government had had clever detectives out on the lawn, a half dozen of our ministers would now be at Leavenworth."[52] Such cases remained relatively isolated, but they do illustrate the extent to which German sympathies pervaded the Missouri Synod.

The more moderate *Lutheran Witness* did not go that far. Instead, the paper's preference for Germany in the early years manifested itself only in occasional pro-German editorials. Although the editors generally tried to remain neutral, sometimes their ethnic sympathies gave them away. In August 1915, Martin Sommer quoted long extracts from an *Atlantic Monthly* profile of German general Paul Von Hindenburg. In his own commentary, Sommer drew special attention to Hindenburg's religious beliefs. The general's preference for orthodox doctrine led the editor to label Hindenburg "a Lutheran of the old school"—a tag meant sincerely as a compliment. The *Atlantic Monthly*'s article caused Sommer to feel justified "in classifying this latest hero of the battlefield among Christian soldiers."[53] No such profile of any Allied leader appeared.

Before American entry the editors also defended German honor. Graebner charged the British government censors with regularly lying about the success of the Allies in the war, leading to laughable misinformation in the press. By contrast, although German newspapers admittedly lied, censored, and exaggerated, "it can be truthfully said that the German people as well as the outside world has never been deceived in the German government bulletins as to the course that events were taking." Getting away from his typical religious focus, he implied Russian militarism and British prevarication, rather than German aggression, were responsible for starting the war.[54] In another case, Graebner defended Germany on the question of intellectual freedom at its universities. A *New York Evening Telegram* allegation provoked a visceral response from the Lutheran editor: "The statement that the German Government has muzzled the universities and churches, throttling freedom and thought and utterance, is a stupid falsehood, invented for the purpose of strengthening the impression that the German Government is a ruthless tyranny, crushing out the free development of national life at every point." In fact, he went on, professors at American, not German, universities had recently been fired because of their unpopular views. Only typical American hypocrisy would suggest otherwise.[55]

Missouri Synod Lutherans' position as social outsiders also afforded them a standpoint from which to denounce America's sins. Americans selling arms to the Allies (while the United States was ostensibly neutral) topped their list. In 1916 the *Lutheran Witness* severely criticized the Bethlehem Steel Corporation (Pennsylvania) for manufacturing millions of shells for Britain and its co-belligerents. Graebner was horrified at the profits the owner and his wife made from their abominable trade, labeling them "MURDERERS in the sight of God." He castigated America's Christians for their silence on "the atrocious trade in arms," insisting that the laws of God rather than "nationalistic bias" prompted his fury.[56] Indeed, God would not long withhold his wrath against a nation that profited in this way. In condemning the United States, Graebner sounded the note of an Old Testament prophet:

> The exportation of arms to European battlefields, which have now been reddened a year longer by reason of such exportation than would have been the case otherwise, is a clear case of coining gold eagles out of the blood of fellow-men. These manufacturers and exporters of arms have brought blood-guilt upon the nation. Without question, there will be a day of reckoning for our country. Eternal Justice cannot be outraged without the most dire results. An enormous moral debt has piled up against our nation. It will be liquidated to the last penny by an Authority which *discounts no bills*. Is it possible that these bills have already begun to mature? If the next weeks will not tell, the years will.[57]

Although Charles Jefferson, John Haynes Holmes, or William Jennings Bryan might have agreed with Graebner's antimilitarism, most mainline Protestants avoided using such denunciatory language about their fellow Americans. Far removed from the halls of power, Graebner brought critical distance to bear on dominant assumptions about American righteousness.

When war finally came to the United States the following year, LCMS spokesmen continued the theme of divine punishment. "God has lifted and is even now striking our nation with the direst temporal curse," Martin Sommer wrote in May 1917. The presence of "this awful judgment," he continued, should prompt the nation to repent of its sins.[58] Six months later, as crusading language prevailed elsewhere, the *Lutheran Witness* maintained its humbler outlook. It reprinted an editorial from the *Detroit Messenger* interpreting the war as God's chastisement. "Sin, disobedience to God's Word and will, is always the cause for which God punishes a land with war," it proclaimed, listing a score of sins of which Americans were guilty.[59]

Others in the Missouri Synod said much the same. As late as 1918, a writer to *Der Lutheraner* urged national repentance. The nation as a whole, even its Christians, had merited divine punishment. "Should then God not become angry, nor punish, when the mass of the people despise his word of mercy, riding roughshod over it; when the Christians, who have received so much grace, do not bring forth the fruits that God is looking for?" the author asked.[60]

The St. Louis minister Louis Buchheimer also advanced this view in a wartime sermon. Although the Wilson administration had requested ministers to address the war from the pulpit, government officials would probably have shuddered at Buchheimer's choice of James 4:1 as his text: "From whence come wars and fighting among you? come they not hence, even of your lusts that war in your members?" Although Buchheimer approved the American cause, his sermon also pointed to American faults. Even more unconventionally, he noted that Germans and Americans shared a common human nature. Yes, Germans were a depraved lot, he admitted, but "we must draw the same conclusion concerning ourselves." Buchheimer, too, used the language of divine chastisement while declaring that "the Lord justly has a controversy with us."[61] When Lutherans humbled themselves in national repentance, they echoed the statements of Elisha Weaver and other black Methodist leaders during the Civil War. Rather than interpret the conflict in terms of absolute right and wrong, "counterpoint" leaders recognized the sins in their own communities. LCMS Lutherans' outsider status during the World War I years allowed them to see the manifold sins of the nation more clearly than most.

Accordingly, LCMS papers pounded away at America's faults during the conflict. If arms-dealing was a cardinal sin, others trailed close behind. The editors of the *Lutheran Witness* highlighted quite a few national flaws, regularly targeting American hypocrisy as especially wicked. When the American press scolded Austria-Hungary for its annexation of Serbia, Graebner wondered why the journalists did not also chide the very similar way the United States had acquired Texas seventy years before. Moreover, if the newspapers were so interested in Germany's broken treaties and alleged atrocities, why did they keep silent on the United States' four hundred broken treaties with Native Americans and torture of innocent Filipinos?[62] The following year Sommer repeated the same charge, labeling the "most grievous" American sin as "blindness to our own faults, Pharisaism." He hoped that repentance could "avert the disasters which are approaching."[63]

Although its fiercely anti-Catholic editors would not have appreciated the analogy, the *Lutheran Witness*'s critique of the nation sometimes sounded like Catholic complaints during the Spanish-American War. Like Arthur Preuss's *Review*, also published in St. Louis, some in the LCMS doubted the United

States was an authentically Christian nation. In November 1915, a writer to the *Witness* named W.M. Czamanske answered the question "Is the United States a Christian Nation?" in the negative. Only 40 percent of Americans were church members, he maintained, with 10 percent of those adhering to congregations that were Christian in name only.[64] Instead of a city on a hill, the United States reminded Czamanske more of pagan Athens at the time of the Apostle Paul; a tourist in America would find "altars and temples erected to gods and demigods, male and female, far surpassing that wilderness of gods of which the Athenians were so proud."[65] Likewise, late in 1918 "R. Jesse" of St. Louis admitted in the *Witness*, "Boasters call us a Christian nation." However, he wanted to know, "where are the evidences of our national Christianity?" Surely not, he concluded, in the epidemics of irreligion, sectarianism, profanity, juvenile delinquency, divorce, greed, and other sins engulfing the nation. Like others in the synod, "R. Jesse" called for national repentance rather than national celebration.[66]

In some ways, LCMS interpretations of war as a divine punishment for sin hearkened back to older views like Beecher's Fast Day sermon in 1860. Like Beecher on that occasion, Lutheran critics perceived real flaws in the nation and were unafraid to call it to account. Unlike Beecher, however, Missouri Synod Lutherans rarely if ever got around to equating the American cause with the Kingdom of God. LCMS Lutherans' distinctive theological convictions, more remote habitation, and ethnic heritage militated against a close identification between the fortunes of the United States and those of the church. Therefore, for the most part they refused to entangle church and state in their commentary on the conflict.

AME and Catholic Commentary

LCMS perspectives on the Great War sounded similar to those of the other "counterpoint" groups. Writing in 1922, AME historian Charles Smith found little to praise about the Great War. "While the white race was solely and absolutely responsible for the World War," he maintained, "the darker races made victory possible for the Allies." Yet, he went on, those brave black troops seemed to have "died in vain" because of America's ongoing racial injustice. The character of the United States still appeared deeply flawed: "It cannot be said that America is 'safe for democracy' so long as mob law prevails. It cannot be said that righteousness has exalted any people who delight in making bonfires of human bodies."[67] Most African Americans supported the war, but quite a few registered skepticism about the nation for which they were asked to risk their lives.[68] This attitude echoed the AME's outlook during the Civil War, where the *Christian Recorder* supported the Union but where many of its writers questioned the righteousness of the American nation.

Catholic opinion about the war was likewise divided. The American archbishops sounded like Abbott when they referred in 1917 to "the holy sentiments of truest patriotic fervor and zeal" and "the great and holy cause of liberty." Indeed, the burden of Michael Williams's *American Catholics in the War* (1921) was to showcase the loyalty of the nation's Catholics, a finding that has been borne out by recent studies as well.[69] As in the Spanish-American War, however, other Catholics dissented from the hierarchy's enthusiasm. Neither Arthur Preuss's periodical (now called the *Fortnightly Review*) nor Daniel Hudson's *Ave Maria* offered much direct commentary on the war, which was telling in and of itself. Still, their occasional notes urged national humility and love of the enemy. Soon after the United States entered the conflict, Preuss reprinted a pastoral letter from the Archbishop of Cincinnati attributing the divine judgment of war to a long list of American sins.[70] Both the *Fortnightly Review* and the *Ave Maria* warned against casting stones at Germany for its alleged atrocities when Allied nations were guilty of similar crimes.[71] Likewise, both papers decried the spread of hatred toward Germany. As late as August 1918, Preuss nostalgically recalled "how often we have been stirred by German song, and responded to German hospitality, been mersed [*sic*] in German poetry, music, and literature!" The second-generation German immigrant labeled Germanophobia a "virulent poison."[72] Throughout American wars, black Methodists as well as Catholics remained divided about popular kinds of Christian nationalism. In this case, despite historic differences with Lutherans, their views more closely resembled those of the LCMS than those of most mainline Protestant leaders.

Changes in the Synod

Missouri Synod Lutherans saw the conflict much differently than many white mainline leaders did. Still, as 1918 wore on, their patriotism grew louder, and they occasionally applied spiritual language to earthly affairs. By the war's end, they had taken a few steps to sound more like mainstream Protestants concerning the relationship between Christianity and patriotism. Such modifications also forced the synod to reassess its relationship with national culture. Although the change was not as dramatic as with the AME in the Civil War or Catholics in 1898, Lutherans too found their position vis-à-vis the dominant culture in flux due to the war.

The shift occurred in part because of the persecution German Americans encountered during the nineteen months America was at war. Even before the United States entered the conflict, ex-president Theodore Roosevelt repeatedly warned of "hyphenated Americans" ("those evil enemies of America"), who failed to give full loyalty to the United States.[73] During the war, zealots took such sentiments further than Roosevelt intended. The most extreme case took place in April 1918 in Collinsville, Illinois, when a mob lynched a German-born miner named Robert Prager on suspicion of sedition.[74] There is no indication that Prager was a Lutheran, but German American Lutherans in the Midwest also routinely faced persecution of varying levels. The *Lutheran Witness* reported in the fall of 1918 that a Lutheran school in Missouri had been burned to the ground and a church in Ohio bombed because German was taught in the parochial schools.[75] More common was a notice posted on an LCMS church in Missouri: "NOTICE.—This notice is to notify you as pastor of this church not to teach German in the church, or preach German in the church. Comply with notice at once, before a committee waits on you."[76]

The experiences of the persecuted German Americans had something in common with those of Native Americans during the Great War. Like German Americans, a high percentage of Indians voluntarily enlisted. Many of these volunteers were graduates of Indian boarding schools, like the well-known one in Carlisle, Pennsylvania. In some cases, authorities urged even those students who were too young to go ahead and enlist. Following such advice, one Navajo eighth-grader volunteered (and was accepted), and a Yuma boy joined up at age fifteen—only to be killed less than a year later. Thus, in a cruel irony, the American government had taken these Indian children from their homes, stripped them of their identities, and then sent them to be killed to defend that government. Perhaps perceiving this, some natives refused even to register for the draft. Following patterns that went back a century or more, in these cases armed American troops were called in to put down the resistance. Like the persecutions experienced by German American Lutherans, arrests and detentions of eligible Goshute men occurred on the Deep Creek Reservation in Utah and Nevada; likewise, the organizer of the Creek Draft Rebellion in 1919 found herself on the run from federal authorities. Although the experiences of Missouri Synod Lutherans and Native Americans were far from identical, both groups experienced the strong hand of American violence during this period of domestic unrest.[77]

Above all else the Missouri Synod's use of German in its extensive school systems and congregational services typically made its members targets of abuse and discrimination. During the war, governments at every level passed legislation aimed at eliminating the use of the Kaiser's tongue.[78] The

FIGURE 10.   Student-Athletes at the Carlisle, Pennsylvania, Indian School, 1912. Public Domain. Courtesy of Wikimedia Commons. https://commons.wikimedia.org/wiki/File:1912-carlisle -indian-school-track-team.jpg.

Smith-Towner Act (1918) required states to pass laws making English the pri-mary medium of instruction in all schools (including parochial ones) if they wished to receive federal funding.[79] State councils, such as the infamous one in Nebraska, hunted down potential dissidents.[80]

The *Lutheran Witness* felt this pressure keenly in 1918, devoting quite a bit of space to the language issue over the year. Although Graebner and Sommer criticized the hysteria that equated speaking German with disloyalty, they were no fools. They were unwilling to sacrifice the life of their synod on the altar of language. Accordingly, Graebner argued in April against the "general and frantic abolition of German" but maintained that "local conditions in every case must be the deciding factor."[81] He also stressed the benefits of using English.[82] By September, although Graebner still insisted that local conditions must govern language policies for individual congregations, he also announced that he now favored eliminating German from most parochial schools.[83]

The language issue proved to be only one case among many where the synod reacted to instances of persecution by accommodating the prevailing mood. Most of the time LCMS members did not compromise their principles but rather promoted their latent patriotism more loudly. To begin with, they took pains to distinguish themselves from the pacifist Mennonites, another sect of heavily German extraction with a sizeable Midwestern presence. In July 1918 *Der Lutheraner* attacked the Mennonite *Gospel Herald* (Scottdale, PA) for its non-resistant stance. In contrast to the *Herald*'s position, "E.P." in the *Lutheraner* sought to prove from the teachings of John the Baptist and Christ the lawful-ness of bearing the sword.[84] Sommer, writing in the *Lutheran Witness*, con-demned all pacifists as "unreasonable people" who were being treated quite generously by the government.[85] Although Lutherans' "two-kingdoms" the-ology had always permitted Christians to bear arms, the wartime atmosphere made it especially valuable to emphasize that teaching.

Additionally, as the war went on, the *Witness* ratcheted up its critique of German excesses. In August 1918 the periodical printed an address from Fred-erick Brand, third vice-president of the LCMS, denouncing the doctrine of "Pan-Germanism." Ostensibly popular with Germany's military and intellec-tual elite, this teaching held that the German people were superior to all others by virtue of their cultural evolution and divine election. Therefore, like Nietz-schean "super-men," ordinary morality did not apply to them. Brand main-tained that Pan-Germanism was "an abomination and an execration to our soul, to the soul of the Lutheran Church in America."[86] Such ideas could never have gained currency, Martin Sommer added, if Lutheranism had not been marginalized in Germany. Sadly, however, rationalism had taken over, result-ing in what Sommer (echoing the psychologist Joseph Jastrow) called "a pecu-liar madness."[87]

Lutherans disassociated themselves as far as possible from the Kaiser as well. Historical investigation from *The Lutheran* (published in Philadelphia by the Evangelical Lutheran Church in North America) sought to prove the royal family had long ago ceased to be Lutheran in any meaningful way.[88] To the *Witness*, Wilhelm II had demonstrated his personal apostasy by approving the work of Friedrich Delitzsch, a scholar whose historical-critical methods cast doubt on traditional interpretations of the Bible. If the Kaiser liked Delitzch's views, he was no Lutheran.[89] Although LCMS leaders never went as far as some in condemning Germany, in 1918 they sought to distance themselves from the more unsavory aspects of German *Kultur*.

The synod also went out of its way to promote its patriotism publicly. The Walther League (an organization of "young people" named after LCMS founder C.F.W. Walther) provided detailed instructions to *Witness* readers about the placement of American flags and service flags in church buildings. The League urged cooperation with the Red Cross and the hospitable treat-ment of soldiers stationed at local camps.[90] The *Witness* itself applauded an

LCMS school in Chicago displaying a service flag while admitting the liberty of individual congregations to follow or disregard that example as they saw fit. Likewise, the periodical encouraged ministers to use part of the Sunday morning service to pass along messages from the government as long as this did not entail changing "our church-year to include all manner of special Sundays." "Those who avoid giving public testimony to the Americanism that is in them," the paper advised, "are making a serious mistake."[91]

Perhaps the paper wished to promote something like the practices of the Reverend Henry Frincke, who delivered "short and instructive talk[s]" on patriotic themes "after the sermon on Sundays." Frincke, an LCMS pastor in Monroe, Michigan, wrote to the *Witness* in January 1918 boasting of the local recognition his congregation had received for its patriotic activities. Patriotism, after all, had its payoffs. C.E. Scheidker of Hannibal, Missouri put the new attitude best: "We Lutherans here still maintain our position with regard to separation of Church and State . . . but are all the time placing ourselves before the public in a proper manner, so that no one can question our Americanism."[92]

Finally, in 1918 Graebner compiled a collection of documents demonstrating Lutheran loyalty, publishing them under the title *A Testimony and Proof Bearing on the Relation of the American Lutheran Church to the German Emperor* (alternative title: *"The Lutheran Church vs. Hohenzollernism."*). In addition to rebutting accusations of Lutheran connections with the Kaiser and sedition in parochial schools, *A Testimony and Proof* trumpeted the "thousands" of Lutherans in the American military and the money pledged on its behalf.[93] By this point, the LCMS had apparently gained some traction with its patriotic pleas. At the beginning of 1918 the government entrusted Sommer to oversee the sale of war stamps to Lutherans in Missouri, while the Treasury Department congratulated Graebner in February on Lutheran "intense patriotic interest."[94]

Such examples demonstrated that Missouri Synod Lutherans could be loyal without a great deal of compromise in their position regarding two kingdoms and the separation of church and state. On occasion, however, members of the synod briefly indulged in the blending of sacred and secular. The following examples document how the LCMS found itself caught up in the religiopolitical zeitgeist in 1918 while still remaining relatively distant from the rhetoric of the mainline Protestant leadership.

First, over time the emphasis on strict church-state separation faded in the *Lutheran Witness*. When the United States entered the war in the spring of 1917, the paper applied biblical prophecy directly to the nation. After claiming that American sins had brought on the punishment of armed conflict, Sommer used the words of Isaiah 1:4–6 to urge the nation as a whole to repent.[95]

Although LCMS teaching usually frowned on applying biblical texts directly to modern states, here Sommer disregarded that principle. Likewise, when President Wilson announced a national day of prayer in May 1918, the *Witness* advised its readers to participate. Although it must have troubled his Lutheran soul to hear the president enjoin religious duties upon the nation, Sommer encouraged Lutherans to repent and fast on the appointed day.[96] Likewise, the paper seemed to modify its position on the Liberty Loan. Where it had earlier protested against ministers using their pulpits to promote secular matters, the *Witness* itself carried a call to support the Third and Fourth Liberty Loans in April and October 1918.[97] Although this was not quite the same thing as advertising war bonds from the pulpit, it came fairly close since the *Witness* considered itself a strictly religious periodical.

Second, on occasion the *Witness* suggested the Christian character of the war. In August 1918 the paper advertised a compilation of hymns, published by the LCMS-sponsored American Lutheran Publicity Bureau (ALPB), titled "War-Time Hymns for Church and Home." The advertisement noted this collection's hymns were "mainly of a patriotic or warlike character," recommending that "congregations arranging patriotic meetings, flag-raisings, etc. should investigate."[98] Sometimes phrases that reflected the holy war mentality also appeared in the pages of the *Lutheran Witness*. Soldiers were said to be dying "on the altar of patriotism"; a writer reported a Lutheran minister's emphasis on this "righteous war"; and a resolution of the LCMS's Northern Illinois District referenced "the high and holy principles for which our Constitution stands."[99] The LCMS could not entirely resist the "holy war" impulse.

Another LCMS publication, the *American Lutheran*, seemed to be even more at home with such language. This monthly paper was the product of the ALPB, the institution responsible for the wartime hymns. Founded in 1914 and located in Manhattan, the ALPB hoped to demonstrate Lutheran patriotism to the rest of the nation. To this end, it founded the *American Lutheran* in 1918.

The *American Lutheran* mostly promoted garden-variety displays of patriotism through the first half of the year. In June, however, the magazine struck a different note. Under the title, "Following the Flag a Holy Act," the publication reprinted excerpts from an address given by a Concordia Seminary professor at the dedication of a building for Lutheran soldiers stationed in Kansas. (The *Lutheran Witness* carried a nearly identical excerpt.) This professor, W.H.T. Dau, declared enlistment "a holy act," one answering "the summons of God."[100] Likewise, the publication reported favorably of a parochial school in St. Louis that had installed portraits of George Washington, Abraham Lincoln, and Woodrow Wilson in one of its classrooms. When the portraits were unveiled, the local Lutheran minister emphasized the "Christian example" of these three presidents.[101] Although Missouri Synod Lutherans did not normally applaud the "Christian example" of non-Lutherans of questionable religious commitment, wartime forced them to make an exception.

Like the *Lutheran Witness*, the *American Lutheran* also promoted displays of patriotism, even if that meant the intrusion of warfare into the church. In November 1918, subscribers read of "a patriotic service" held the evening of September 29 at St. Andrew's Lutheran Church in Pittsburgh, Pennsylvania. After singing "the great English War Hymn, No. 172, 'O God, our Help in Ages Past,'" the congregation heard a sermon on the text, "Render therefore unto Caesar the things which are Caesar's; and unto God the things that are God's." Officials then unfurled an American flag while the church launched into "The Star-Spangled Banner."[102] All this (and a good bit more) would not have caused much of a stir at many old-stock Protestant congregations; for Lutherans, however, such events symbolized the distance the LCMS had traveled from April 1917 to September 1918. Although synod leaders rarely renounced their earlier views, their public presentation changed over time to accommodate a patriotism more in tune with that of the dominant culture.

Other Lutheran groups equaled or outdid their Missouri Synod brethren in their use of such language. One journal, the *Lutheran Quarterly* (Gettysburg, PA), published by the newly formed United Lutheran Church in America, featured Christian patriotism just after the war had concluded. Reflecting on the prospects for lasting postwar peace, the Reverend Arthur J. Hall sounded the messianic note usually associated with Protestant elites. Quoting British Prime Minister David Lloyd George, Hall framed the peace question starkly: "Are we to lapse back into the old national rivalries, animosities and competitive armaments, or are we to initiate the reign on earth of the Prince of Peace?" In Hall's view, another British leader also had it right when he offered the choice as "Berlin or Nazareth; the Kaiser or the Christ." Hall even went on to advocate the possibility of the abolition of wars, the sort of utopian dream that LCMS Lutherans scoffed at.[103] Strict adherence to "two-kingdoms theology," resistance to blending the sacred and secular, a more pro-German stance, and skepticism about the human ability to bring in permanent peace made the publication of such opinion in the *Lutheran Witness* almost unthinkable.

LCMS reactions to the war changed over time, with increased patriotism of various kinds picking up in 1918. By the end of the war, the LCMS had undergone some changes and accepted some slight compromises with its beliefs. The most permanent one proved to be the eventual abolition of German from many Lutheran schools and churches.[104] The synod's reversal on language, the establishment of the ALPB, and the Treasury Department's commendation of

Graebner testified to the changes taking place in the LCMS—developments only warfare could have caused.

Still, when viewed from a longer angle, more continuities than changes prevailed. After the armistice in November, a sign appeared that LCMS flirtation with extreme wartime rhetoric had been brief. In December Graebner denounced those who would enlist the church to help in the postwar reconstruction work. In his view, the church had "this one and only commission: to preach the Gospel for the salvation of immortal souls." When the church was "employed *as a moral and spiritual agency* for the purpose of enforcing government measures," he went on, "she is out of her proper territory." All Lutherans should stand against "this perversion of the Church's functions."[105] Here was "two-kingdoms" theology par excellence. Although the war had helped modify LCMS positions on some matters, it had not fundamentally changed the outlook of the synod. As two historians have judged, "Essentially, the Synod in 1920 was the Synod of 1865."[106] The relatively separatist position of the LCMS in the twenty-first century witnesses to the denomination's consistent lack of interest in becoming part of mainstream American religious culture.

Comparison with the Mainline

A distinctive theology and a marginal social location caused Missouri Synod Lutherans to advocate quite different views on World War I than some of their mainline counterparts. Where spokesmen for the latter group like Matthews or Fosdick often embraced a world-transforming theological ethos that disdained distinctions between the City of Man and the City of God, the LCMS tried to maintain a "two-kingdoms" theology that forbade the mixing of religion and politics. Likewise, as a self-described descendant of Puritans, a figure like Lyman Abbott sensed a duty to preserve the best of Anglo-American civilization from the encroachments of bloodthirsty Huns. As an influential New Yorker, he regularly associated with the nation's power brokers. And as the former minister of a prosperous city church, he enjoyed the social prestige that attached itself to that occupation in early twentieth-century America. Such prestige would decline in the coming decades, but ministerial experience still carried some cultural cachet at this historical moment.[107] This prosperous social position, in turn, led him to a proprietary interest in the fate of the United States. LCMS Lutherans, by contrast, built separatist enclaves, maintaining relatively strong ties to their homeland. Although rarely disloyal, they showed more interest in maintaining orthodox churches in the Midwest than in directing the fate of the United States.

Reformed, liberal Protestant, and evangelical strains—all of which to one degree or another emphasized the transformation of the City of Man into the City of God—predominated too much in American Protestant life for "two-kingdoms" theology to make much of an impact outside of Lutheranism. The reformist, activist impulse common to the more mainstream American Protestant churches was too deeply entrenched in common American ways of thinking. Still, for wartime commentary, the LCMS demonstrated an alternative, a counterpoint that merits further study. Though their approach was a road not taken by most Americans, observers must wrestle with it if they are to understand the assumptions that did guide a significant portion of American society in the World War I years.

Conclusion
The Mere Echo of the Warring Masses

The Eclipse of Christian Nationalism

In more than one sense, the end of the Great War provided the punctuation to a distinctive period in American history. Going back to mid-century, American cultural leaders had stressed religion, hard work, the nuclear family, and above all, earnestness. While such values by no means disappeared in the postwar world, others seemed to take their place. The rise of psychology, therapy, the New Woman, jazz, the flapper lifestyle, and other cultural developments marked the 1920s as distinct. Although continuities remained, change dominated.[1]

The memory of the Great War changed as well in the postwar period; in the 1920s American intellectuals recoiled from the struggle's world-transforming ethos. The Lost Generation, indelibly shaped by the horrors of the war and the self-destruction of the West, abandoned Victorian ideals once and for all. The old civilization, Ezra Pound famously said, was nothing more than "an old bitch gone in the teeth."[2] Although expatriate poets like Pound and T.S. Eliot articulated the feeling especially well, such sentiments reached beyond their class. As historian William McLoughlin has noted, in the postwar period the masses also tired of crusades and "world-saving."[3]

Younger liberal Protestant leaders grew more circumspect about the conflict's legacy in the following decade as well. Harry Emerson Fosdick, writing in 1928 for the *Christian Century*, publicly repented: "I do not propose to bless war again, or support it, or expect from it any valuable thing. It is an unmitigated curse, and with each change in modern life it becomes more unqualifiedly disastrous." Where mainline leaders in previous decades had consistently characterized American wars as Christian enterprises, Fosdick's religious faith prompted his newly found pacifism: "War's motives, methods, and results are essentially anti-Christian; no device of argument or trick phrase can make war and Christian principles harmonious—I ought to know for I have tried hard enough to achieve that impossible task."[4] Fosdick was not alone. The *Christian Century*'s own editor, Charles Clayton Morrison, has been described as a "staunch, perhaps even extreme, advocate for peace" in the 1920s.[5]

Change came in other ways as well. Some in the post–World War I era reacted against liberal Protestantism in part because of mainline Protestants' common holy war rhetoric. Neo-orthodox theology, typified in the writings of Swiss theologian Karl Barth and adapted by the American theologian Reinhold Niebuhr, expressed greater pessimism about the purity of people's personal motivations as well as humans' ability to live unstained by the world they necessarily inhabited. In 1928 Niebuhr used the *Christian Century* to attack the legacy of American Protestant support for the Great War. Like Fosdick (whose article had appeared only eight months before), Niebuhr by his own admission had been "more than ordinarily patriotic" during the conflict. Looking back, however, he disdained the disgusting spectacle of "the church playing up to the nation, an ancient religion maintaining its waning life by skillfully compounding itself with the new religion of nationalism." Niebuhr pessimistically argued that "if Christianity is to be killed in this new world of nationalism and commercialism, it would be better for it to die splendidly than to survive by adding the odor of an old sanctity to the worship of mammon and Caesar."[6] Although Niebuhr's strongest moral reflections came in the 1930s in the midst of the Great Depression, even at this earlier date one can see his reaction against the sort of Protestant liberalism that so easily and heartily endorsed American war-making.[7] Like the Lost Generation as well as mainline Protestant leaders, Niebuhr had no stomach for another American crusade.

These sentiments persisted beyond the calm of peacetime. Representative Protestant responses to World War II suggested that a more nuanced view of the church's role in American warfare could be sustained even in difficult circumstances. When Japanese bombers attacked Pearl Harbor in December 1941 (a provocation far greater than anything experienced twenty-five years earlier), the *Christian Century* reminded its readers that Christians were divided over the appropriate response, denouncing ministers who used the pulpit to support warfare wholeheartedly.[8] "Caution" characterized the moment. One historian has labeled ordinary Americans' struggle against Nazism "a cautious crusade." Likewise, Gerald Sittser's study of American churches and the Second World War describes the general approach as "a cautious patriotism."[9] Remembering the often-unrestrained ways the mainline had blessed the Great War, liberal Protestants approached World War II much differently. In this struggle, soul searching, careful statements of the church's position, and some persistent pacifism prevailed.[10]

To be sure, American Christian leaders often recognized the stakes of World War II. In 1942 a group of Methodist bishops announced that the contest pitted a tyrannical worldview that "exalts the State as supreme" against a democratic one defending "the intrinsic worth of every man."[11] According to Sittser, such leaders interpreted the war as a decisive event in world history, one that would change the course of Western civilization permanently. In their view, he says, the conflict "was a judgment and turning point."[12]

But it was a "judgment and turning point" in another sense as well. Never again in American history, including World War II, would America's mainline leadership endorse a war as unqualifiedly as it had during the Civil War, Spanish-American War, and World War I. In the same article where the Methodist bishops drew a stark contrast between the Allied and Axis Powers, they also defended the rights of conscientious objectors and declared that "the Church . . . should not be used for military recruiting." Like the Missouri Synod in the Great War, the bishops stressed the church's complicity in American social sins and urged Methodists to pray for their enemies.[13] In the same spirit, six months before Pearl Harbor, Fosdick doubled down on his earlier antiwar sentiments: "The Church in wartime easily becomes the mere echo of the warring masses, with every distinctive quality of Christ's teaching well-nigh forgotten; it is tempted to lose its international, interracial, ecumenical nature, and to become only one more agency for hallowing and waging war; it is lured to accept a theology of escape, by which the ethical teachings of Christ are interpreted as inapplicable and unlivable; and in the end it too commonly divests itself of any function that differentiates it from a world gone mad with mutual hatred and suicidal strife."[14] Unlike earlier generations of white mainliners, Fosdick took special care to ensure the church not duplicate "the voice of any government or the echo of any popular opinion or passion."[15]

The Anomalous Generation

Why the change in public posture during World War II and after? As we have seen, part of the adjustment certainly had to do with the desire not to replicate the excesses of 1917–18. Still, other factors mattered too. Some of this newfound caution and moderation had to do with the changing composition of the nation as a whole as well as the slow decline of white mainline Protestants' public influence. The mid-century Protestant-Catholic-Jew establishment of Will Herberg's typology quickly gave way to increasing pluralism of all kinds in the 1960s and after.[16] The reasons for this development, extensively described in secondary literature, lie beyond the scope of this book.[17] The upshot was that after mid-century the United States witnessed the public proliferation of racial, ethnic, sexual, and ideological diversity.

Such diversity, in turn, proved uncongenial to the deference the white Protestant male clergy were accustomed to receiving in earlier times. To be sure, the second half of the twentieth century only slowly witnessed the death of an American public and intellectual life characterized by mainline Protestant mores and leadership.[18] Nevertheless, especially after 1970, white Protestant clergymen no longer enjoyed the influence they had had at the turn of the century; indeed, by this time no such unified group even existed. The "restructuring of American religion" along ideological rather than denominational lines eventually divided white Protestants into competing sides in the national "culture wars."[19] This development, combined with conservative Protestants' eclipse of the mainline in terms of national visibility and political influence during the Seventies and Eighties, assured that the relatively generic white Protestant hegemony of the older day had passed for good.

Still, an even more important part of the "judgement and turning point" of World War II had to do with mainline Protestantism's increasing distrust of celebratory Christian nationalism. When progressive Protestants at mid-century took more critical positions on American race relations, empire (broadly understood), capitalism, and nationalism, as David Hollinger has shown, they naturally grew more suspicious of American self-righteousness vis-à-vis other nations.[20] Conflicts in Vietnam and Iraq, to take only the most prominent examples from the past fifty years, failed to garner the kind of mainline Protestant endorsement given to the three wars in this study.[21] William Sloane Coffin Jr., nephew of the prominent early twentieth-century theologian Henry Sloane Coffin, represented the changing attitude as well as anyone when he used his privileged position as Yale University's chaplain to denounce American involvement in Vietnam.[22] In opposing war, sometimes liberal Protestant leaders specifically cited American moral failures. In 2007, leaders of the United Church of Christ condemned American "abuse and torture" of political prisoners in their call for an immediate end to the conflict in Iraq.[23] Strong commitments to peace coupled with doubts about intrinsic American righteousness fueled mainline Protestant antiwar protests.

Just as foreign wars continued in the twentieth century, so did conflicts with Native Americans. Empowered by the successes of the civil rights movement, in 1969 a group of Native Americans occupied Alcatraz Island and tried to negotiate with the federal government for ownership. When that failed, in 1973 the American Indian Movement took control of sites around Wounded Knee, South Dakota, where the massacre of the Lakota had occurred in 1890. Federal troops exchanged gunfire with the protestors and attempted to starve them out. In 2016–17, natives from hundreds of different tribes camped near the Standing Rock Reservation to protest the Dakota Access Pipeline begun under President Donald Trump.[24]

In these cases, however, the white Protestant elite was much more sympathetic to the plight of American Indians than previous generations had been. An Episcopal church in Pine Ridge, South Dakota, assisted in the 1973 Wounded Knee negotiations, for instance, while in 2004 the National Cathedral in Washington, DC, held a special service to bless the opening of the Smithsonian's National Museum of the American Indian. Natives themselves took an active part in the ceremony as a Potawatomi man celebrated the Eucharist and a Cherokee woman preached the sermon. The demonstrations at Standing Rock also gained the strong support of the mainline, ecumenical National Council of Churches (NCC), the successor group to the old Federal Council of Churches. The NCC sent members to stand alongside the Sioux protestors and issued statements expressing opposition to any oil pipelines that would transverse natives' sacred ground. Although conflicts between Native American groups and the American state have continued over the past half-century, the attitudes of white mainline leaders concerning Indians' rights have changed dramatically.[25]

When viewed from the broader perspective of American religious history as a whole, the story of the Protestant mainline baptizing America's wars from 1860 to 1920 looks quite anomalous. Indeed, the caution and ambivalence about American war that reigned after 1920 had deep roots in similarly skeptical Protestant attitudes before 1860. Fewer than two decades before the Civil War, important Protestant leaders and organizations decried the Mexican-American War as unjust.[26] Christian nationalist ideas could not persuasively be applied to the Mexican-American War, even though some tried. According to historian John C. Pinheiro, many Protestant leaders' anti-Catholic convictions and missionary motivations operated in tension with their feeling that the war could not be defended on moral grounds. Northern Baptists, for example, accurately perceived the blatant desire for more slave territory motivating Southern support for the conflict.[27] In 1847 Old School Presbyterians passed a resolution condemning the struggle while Northern New School Presbyterians "typically decried the war as evil."[28] Some individuals opposed the conflict throughout its duration.[29]

When viewed from this angle, then, the Civil War, Spanish-American War, and World War I must be understood as a unit. These conflicts and the United States they occurred in represented a distinct period in American life. Neither previous conflicts nor future ones would meet with the same level of support from the nation's most influential Protestant leaders. As Sydney Ahlstrom recognized in 1972: "Never have patriotism, imperialism, and the religion of American Protestants stood in such fervent coalescence as during the McKinley-Roosevelt era."[30] Future scholars should consider how our view of American history changes when we think of these wars as having a good deal in common.

As Ahlstrom implied, the period between 1860 and 1920 is also unique because it witnessed the rise of imperial America. American empire did not begin or end in this period, but it did expand rapidly. In the late nineteenth century, the American military put down the last of the major armed uprisings from Native Americans. When in 1893 Frederick Jackson Turner declared the frontier closed, he was not all wrong; the domestic imperialism that began in the earliest days of the nation now seemed complete.[31] The acquisition of Hawaii, Guam, Puerto Rico, and the Philippines a few years later stretched the (formal) empire further. Religious leaders like Lyman Abbott, Josiah Strong, and John Ireland all leveraged their considerable influence to justify and support these endeavors. For them, deep-seated convictions about America's divine destiny undeniably justified and spurred this imperialism. Yet religious beliefs could also be used to critique, protest, and prophetically denounce colonial expansion; some white Protestants like Edward Abbott and William Jennings Bryan as well as a host of Catholic and Black Methodist figures each opposed imperialism based on their understanding of their faith. The majority support that white mainline Protestants gave to the American empire, though, helped make the Gilded Age and Progressive Era stand out as distinctive.

Thus, standard periodizations that distinguish sharply between the Civil War Era, the Gilded Age, and the Progressive Era must be rethought in light of this research. Though no one would deny that the nation looked quite a bit different in 1920 than it did in 1860, important commonalities remained as well. Victorianism, with all its earnestness, certainties, and paradoxes, persisted as a powerful, persuasive way of understanding the world. This remained especially true for those, like Abbott, who had come of age during the Civil War. While we already know a good deal about the changes occurring in these years, we know less about what lingered and remained. When scholars look for continuities between 1860 and 1920 as well as for change over time, they will find much more united American cultural life in this period than is commonly realized.

The story of mainline Protestantism and war before 1860 and after 1920 provokes an inevitable question: What made that generation different? Why did American warfare in this period garner such vociferous support from prosperous white Protestants? Relatively prosaic reasons begin to answer the question. The South did treat its slaves abominably and had fired on Fort Sumter. Spain had been terrorizing rebellious Cubans. Germans were allegedly committing atrocities and had certainly authored the Zimmerman Note. It did not take extensive ideological schema to oppose such practices and interpret the conflict in terms of moral right and wrong.

Social location mattered as well. Anxieties about race suicide, loss of manliness, national decadence, and other earthly concerns helped prompt white elite Protestant enthusiasm for adventuresome war and imperialism. Moreover, by virtue of race, class, and gender configurations in the late nineteenth and early twentieth century, white male Protestants held positions of enormous privilege, although some of that privilege was fading by the end of the period. High levels of investment in a White Anglo-Saxon Protestant nation, combined with fears of losing ministerial social prestige, played a significant role in motivating support for America's wars. It did not hurt that sometimes American victories reinforced white ministers' social privilege.

Still, behind these reasons lurked a distinctive ideology even more important for understanding the mainline leadership's consistent justifications of the conflicts as holy wars. One experience unique to this period and these conflicts was simply a common confidence among the Protestant mainline in the inherent righteousness of the American nation-state. Patriotic ministers never had to accept the blind patriotism of Steven Decatur's motto, "My country right or wrong," because they rarely allowed the United States could be wrong. In their view, the nation conceived in liberty and dedicated to the proposition that all men are created equal need only espouse those ideals consistently to be assured of its righteousness. As long as the United States lived up to its founding principles, it necessarily did good in spreading freedom and democracy abroad. For Abbott, this was the meaning of America: a nation that did God's will insofar as it upheld democracy (defined as the weak serving the strong). Whatever the empirical merits of that description, Abbott consistently interpreted the nation in those messianic terms.

The task of justifying American wars became all the easier when the nation's opponents could be characterized as (variously), rebellious, tyrannical slaveholders; Catholic colonial oppressors; and barbaric Huns. This was the sort of ideological scheme that fit so well with democratic Christian republicanism.

Not only could struggles be described as democracy versus despotism, but democratic Christian republicanism elevated the stakes even further: democratic nations were invariably Christian nations, while despotic nations inevitably opposed Christian moral teaching. Such devilish enemies, in turn, deserved destruction. From these premises, then, proceeded the language of crusades and holy wars that so consistently characterized mainline commentary on America's military conflicts.

Theological and social factors are seen even more readily when we juxtapose mainline perspectives with those of "counterpoint" groups like African American Methodists, Catholics, and Missouri Synod Lutherans. Here, too, social location combined with ideology to determine these groups' outlooks on America's military conflicts. In many cases, the ordeal of warfare afforded crucial occasions to reflect on and even remake these groups' relationships with the nation-state. Members of these groups protested the righteousness of each conflict and rejected the idea of America as a Christian nation. The individual counterpoint stories possess importance in and of themselves for determining questions of group identity, Americanization, and cultural assimilation. However, since they operated under such different assumptions, their stories also cast light on the presuppositions of privileged white Protestants.

Never Again?

The significance of the end of the Progressive Era around 1920, then, stretched far beyond the passing of a simple historical marker. Its death signified the end of a distinct chapter in American religious, intellectual, and cultural life, symbolically spelling the decline (among mainline Protestant spokesmen) of a worldview eager to closely associate democratic arrangements, the righteousness of the United States, and the Christian faith. Although few would want to return to this world or embrace the crusading convictions of the characters in this study, it is imperative that we appreciate the prevalence of the worldview and reckon with its legacy.

Indeed, arguably the impulses animating the leaders of the white Protestant mainline in the late nineteenth and early twentieth century never went away at all. In the mid-twentieth century, another group willing to forge links between Christianity, democracy, and American righteousness arose. It declared that the United States had been, and must again be, a Christian nation. This group's leaders, however, did not usually hail from patrician backgrounds or lead from the symbolic centers of American religious life; they ordinarily came to national prominence from the South or the West. They found theological liberalism repulsive, favoring instead a supernaturalist interpretation of the Bible replete with evangelical understandings of sin, redemption, heaven, and hell.[32] Forged in the Cold War, the Religious Right and its political hero, Ronald Reagan, sometimes echoed the same confidence in God and country as the white Protestant mainline had three-quarters of a century earlier. For better or worse, we live with this influence still.

The convictions of the counterpoint groups offer more hope to some readers. They illustrate that American Christians could also put their faith to use for peaceful purposes, remain humble in the face of national success, and maintain an ability to separate church and state. Their example, too, lingers and inspires. We need their voices now more than ever.

Notes

Introduction

1. "Dr. Hillis Assails Lansdowne's Plea," *New York Times*, Dec. 3, 1917.

2. Lyman Abbott, *The Twentieth Century Crusade* (New York: Macmillan, 1918).

3. Examples of the genre include William Warren Sweet, *The Story of Religion in America*, revised and enlarged edition (New York: Harper & Brothers, 1950); Sidney E. Mead, *The Lively Experiment: The Shaping of Christianity in America* (New York: Harper & Row, 1963); and Sydney Ahlstrom, *A Religious History of the American People* (New Haven, CT: Yale University Press, 1972).

4. Harry S. Stout, "Review Essay: Religion, War, and the Meaning of America," *Religion and American Culture: A Journal of Interpretation* 19 (Summer 2009): 286, https://doi.org/10.1525/rac.2009.19.2.275.

5. Stout, "Review Essay," 286. Brackets in the original.

6. See, for example, on the American Revolution: Thomas S. Kidd, *God of Liberty: A Religious History of the American Revolution* (New York: Basic Books, 2010), and James P. Byrd, *Sacred Scripture, Sacred War: The Bible and the American Revolution* (New York: Oxford University Press, 2013); on the War of 1812: William Gribbin, *The Churches Militant: The War of 1812 and American Religion* (New Haven, CT: Yale University Press, 1973); on the Mexican-American War: John C. Pinheiro, *Missionaries of Republicanism: A Religious History of the Mexican-American War* (New York: Oxford University Press, 2014); on the Civil War (selected): Mark A. Noll, *The Civil War as a Theological Crisis* (Chapel Hill: University of North Carolina Press, 2006); Harry S. Stout, *Upon the Altar of the Nation: A Moral History of the Civil War* (New York: Viking, 2006); George C. Rable, *God's Almost Chosen Peoples: A Religious History of the American Civil War* (Chapel Hill: University of North Carolina Press, 2010); and Timothy L. Wesley, *The Politics of Faith During the Civil War* (Baton Rouge: Louisiana State University Press, 2013); on the Spanish-American War: McCullough, *Cross of War*; on World War I: John F. Piper, Jr., *The American Churches in World War I* (Athens: Ohio University Press, 1985); and Richard M. Gamble, *The War for Righteousness: Progressive Christianity, the Great War, and the Rise of the Messianic Nation* (Wilmington, DE: ISI Books, 2003); on World War II: Gerald L. Sittser, *A Cautious Patriotism: The American Churches & the Second World War* (Chapel Hill: University of North Carolina Press, 1997); and on Vietnam: George Bogaski, *American Protestants and the Debate over the Vietnam War: Evil Was Loose in the World* (Lanham, MD: Lexington Books, 2014).

7. Rebecca Edwards, *New Spirits: Americans in the "Gilded Age," 1865–1905*, 2nd ed. (New York: Oxford University Press, 2011), 3–5; T.J. Jackson Lears, *No Place of Grace:*

Antimodernism and the Transformation of American Culture, 1880–1920 (New York: Pantheon, 1981); Louis Menand, *The Metaphysical Club* (New York: Farrar, Straus and Giroux), 2001; Allen Guelzo, "Did Religion Make the American Civil War Worse?" *The Atlantic*, Aug. 23, 2015, http://www.theatlantic.com/politics/archive/2015/08/did-religion-make-the-american-civil-war-worse/401633/.

8. For example, Ernest Tuveson, *Redeemer Nation: The Idea of America's Millennial Role* (Chicago: University of Chicago Press, 1968); Nicholas Guyatt, *Providence and the Invention of the United States, 1607–1876* (New York: Cambridge University Press, 2007); Eran Shalev, *American Zion: The Old Testament as a Political Text from the Revolution to the Civil War* (New Haven, CT: Yale University Press, 2013); and Sam Haselby, *The Origins of American Religious Nationalism* (New York: Oxford University Press, 2015).

9. Jon Butler, *God in Gotham: The Miracle of Religion in Modern Manhattan* (Cambridge, MA: Harvard University Press, 2020).

10. Stout, "Review Essay," 275–79.

11. Jennifer Graber, *The Gods of Indian Country: Religion and the Struggle for the American West* (New York: Oxford University Press, 2018), 11–13, quote from 12; Rachel Wheeler, "Hendrick Aupaumut: Christian-Mahican Prophet," in *Native Americans, Christianity, and the Reshaping of the American Religious Landscape*, ed. Joel W. Martin and Mark A. Nichols (Chapel Hill: University of North Carolina Press, 2010), 225–49; David Treuer, *The Heartbeat of Wounded Knee: Native America from 1890 to the Present* (New York: Penguin, 2019), 26, 59; Henry Warner Bowden, *American Indians and Christian Missions: Studies in Cultural Conflict* (Chicago: University of Chicago Press, 1981), xv–xvi, quote from xv.

1. "The God of Justice Is the God of Battles"

A few paragraphs of this chapter first appeared in "'This Sacred Warfare': Northern Congregationalists Interpret the Civil War," *Bulletin of the Congregational Library* 8, no. 2 (Fall 2011): 2–10. Used by permission of the Congregational Library & Archives and the *Bulletin of the Congregational Library*.

1. Lyman Abbott, "The Crisis—Its Cause and Cure," *Wabash Express* (Terre Haute, IN), Dec. 19, 1860, 1.

2. Eric Foner, *Free Soil, Free Labor, Free Men: The Ideology of the Republican Party before the Civil War*, 2nd ed. (New York: Oxford University Press, 1995), 9–10.

3. Fatality figure from James Oakes, *Freedom National: The Destruction of Slavery in the United States, 1861–1865* (New York: Norton, 2013), xiv.

4. Lewis O. Saum, *The Popular Mood of Pre-Civil War America* (Westport, CT: Greenwood Press, 1980), 33–36.

5. George C. Rable, *God's Almost Chosen Peoples: A Religious History of the American Civil War* (Chapel Hill: University of North Carolina Press, 2010).

6. Chester F. Dunham, *The Attitude of the Northern Clergy toward the South, 1860–1865* (Philadelphia: Porcupine Press, 1974), 110, 118, 134, cf. 143–50; Paul Eugene Grosjean, "The Concept of American Nationhood: Theological Interpretation as Reflected by the Northern Mainline Protestant Preachers in the Late Civil War Period" (PhD diss., Drew University, 1977), 182; Daniel W. Stowell, *Rebuilding Zion: The Religious*

Reconstruction of the South, 1863–1877 (New York: Oxford University Press, 1998), 49; George M. Fredrickson, "The Coming of the Lord: The Northern Protestant Clergy and the Civil War Crisis," in *Religion and the American Civil War*, ed. Randall M. Miller, Harry S. Stout, and Charles Reagan Wilson (New York: Oxford University Press, 1998), 118; Peter J. Parish, "The Just War," in *The North and the Nation in the Era of the Civil War*, ed. Adam I.P. Smith and Susan-Mary Grant (New York: Fordham University Press, 2003), 171–72; Harry S. Stout, *Upon the Altar of the Nation: A Moral History of the Civil War* (New York: Penguin, 2006), xvii; Rable, *God's Almost Chosen Peoples*, 83.

7. Timothy L. Wesley, *The Politics of Faith during the Civil War* (Baton Rouge: Louisiana State University Press, 2013), 1.

8. Wesley, *Politics of Faith*, 94–100, 103–11.

9. Stout, *Upon the Altar of a Nation*, 70.

10. John F. Wilson, *Public Religion in American Culture* (Philadelphia: Temple University Press, 1979), 12; Mark Y. Hanley, *Beyond a Christian Commonwealth: The Protestant Quarrel with the American Republic, 1830–1860* (Chapel Hill: University of North Carolina Press, 1994).

11. Ira V. Brown, *Lyman Abbott, Christian Evolutionist: A Study in Religious Liberalism* (Cambridge: Harvard University Press, 1953), 1–24.

12. Quoted in Lyman Abbott, *Reminiscences* (Boston: Houghton Mifflin, 1915), 99.

13. In using this phrase, I draw on some of the concepts in Nicholas Guyatt, *Providence and the Invention of the United States, 1607–1876* (New York: Cambridge University Press, 2007). Such beliefs about national righteousness were not unique to Americans, but they still help explain why some Americans were eager to support national conflicts. For a comparative perspective, see the essays in William R. Hutchison and Hartmut Lehmann, eds., *Many Are Chosen: Divine Election and Western Nationalism* (Minneapolis: Fortress Press, 1994).

14. Parish, "The Just War," 172.

15. Lyman Abbott, "The Ministry for the South," *The Home Missionary* 38 (Nov. 1865): 158.

16. Lyman Abbott, "Southern Evangelization," *New Englander* 23 (Oct. 1864): 709.

17. "Citizen, Go to Church," *Weekly Wabash Express*, Oct. 28, 1863.

18. Lyman Abbott, "The Issue and Duty of the Hour," Sep. 17, 1862, typescript, pp. 4, 20, 21, in box 28, folder 7, Abbott Memorial Collection, George J. Mitchell Department of Special Collections & Archives, Bowdoin College Library.

19. Abbott, "The Crisis—Its Cause and Cure," 1. At first, Abbott held strictly to the position of the Republican Party—that slavery should not be allowed to expand in the territories, but that it should also not be immediately abolished. Henry Ward Beecher's writings supporting emancipation possibly influenced Abbott's change of mind. See Brown, *Lyman Abbott, Christian Evolutionist*, 30, and Abbott, *Reminiscences*, 98. For Abbott's changing views on civil rights for African Americans after the Civil War, see Colin B. Chapell, "The Third Strand: Race, Gender, and Self-Government in the Mind of Lyman Abbott," *Fides et Historia* 42 (Summer/Fall 2010): 27–54; Ronald C. White, *Liberty and Justice for All: Racial Reform and the Social Gospel (1877–1925)* (1990; repr. Louisville, KY: Westminster John Knox Press, 2002), 25–26; and Ralph E. Luker, *The Social Gospel in Black and White: American Racial Reform, 1885–1912* (Chapel Hill: University of North Carolina Press, 1991).

20. Abbott, "The Issue and Duty," 2, 4, 5, 17, 24.

21. Abbott, "The Issue and Duty," 17–24.

22. On the prevalence of millennial and apocalyptic rhetoric during the war, see James H. Moorhead, *American Apocalypse: Yankee Protestants and the Civil War, 1860–1869* (New Haven, CT: Yale University Press, 1978); Moorhead, "Between Progress and Apocalypse: A Reassessment of Millennialism in American Religious Thought, 1800–1860," *Journal of American History* 71, no. 3 (Dec. 1984): 524–42, https://doi.org/10.2307/1887470; and Terrie Dopp Aamodt, *Righteous Armies, Holy Cause: Apocalyptic Imagery and the Civil War* (Macon, GA: Mercer University Press, 2002).

23. Abbott, "The Crisis—Its Cause and Cure," 1.

24. Abbott, "Southern Evangelization," 704–5.

25. Abbott, "The Ministry for the South," 160.

26. Abbott, "The Ministry for the South," 160.

27. Abbott, "Southern Evangelization," 705.

28. Abbott, "The Ministry for the South," 162.

29. Debby Applegate, *The Most Famous Man in America: The Biography of Henry Ward Beecher* (New York: Doubleday, 2006), 237.

30. William G. McLoughlin, *The Meaning of Henry Ward Beecher: An Essay on the Shifting Values of Mid-Victorian America, 1840–1870* (New York: Knopf, 1970), xi.

31. McLoughlin, *The Meaning of Henry Ward Beecher*, 252.

32. Applegate, *The Most Famous Man in America*; Clifford E. Clark, Jr., *Henry Ward Beecher: Spokesman for a Middle-Class America* (Urbana: University of Illinois Press, 1978), 2.

33. Ann Douglas, *The Feminization of American Culture* (New York: Knopf, 1977), 17–22.

34. This position, increasingly common in antebellum America, saw the Pilgrims and Puritans as the progenitors of liberty and democracy. It was given full expression in John Gorham Palfrey, *History of New England*, 5 vols. (Boston: Houghton Mifflin, 1858–89). The last volume was completed by Palfrey's son Francis.

35. Henry Ward Beecher, "Our Blameworthiness," in *Freedom and War: Discourses on Topics Suggested by the Times by Henry Ward Beecher* (Freeport, NY: Books for Libraries Press, [1863] 1971), 69–71.

36. The Pilgrims, who were Separatists, arrived in Plymouth in 1620; Puritans, who did not officially separate from Anglicanism, came to Massachusetts Bay in 1630. In addition, 1619 is usually the date given for the introduction of slavery into Virginia.

37. Beecher, "Our Blameworthiness," 66, 68.

38. Beecher paid for the equipment of an additional regiment out of pocket. Lyman Abbott, *Henry Ward Beecher* (Boston: Houghton Mifflin, 1903), 238.

39. Beecher, "The National Flag," in *Freedom and War*, 111, 112, 113. The text is Isaiah 9:2.

40. Henry Ward Beecher, "Address at the Raising of the Union Flag over Fort Sumter," in *Patriotic Addresses in America and England, from 1850 to 1885, on Slavery, the Civil War, and the Development of Civil Liberty in the United States*, ed. John R. Howard (New York: Fords, Howard, and Hulbert, 1887), 676, 681–82.

41. Beecher, "Our National Flag," 122–23.

42. Beecher, "The Southern Babylon," in *Freedom and War*, 435.

43. Beecher, "Our National Flag," 115.

44. Beecher, "The Beginning of Freedom," in *Freedom and War*, 231.

45. Beecher, "Address at the Raising of the Flag," 689.

46. Mark A. Noll, *America's God: From Jonathan Edwards to Abraham Lincoln* (New York: Oxford University Press, 2002), 264, 319–20.

47. For a more positive assessment concerning Bushnell's views on American nationality, see Conrad Cherry, "The Structure of Organic Thinking: Horace Bushnell's Approach to Language, Nature, and Nation," *Journal of the American Academy of Religion* 40 (Mar. 1972), 13–20, https://www.jstor.org/stable/1461913. Mark Y. Hanley showed that prior to the war Bushnell did make distinctions between sacred and secular categories. See Hanley, *Beyond a Christian Commonwealth*, 9, 45.

48. Stout, *Upon the Altar of the Nation*, 66–67.

49. Horace Bushnell, *Reverses Needed: A Discourse Delivered on the Sunday after the Disaster at Bull Run, in the North Church, Hartford* (Hartford, CT: L.E. Hunt, 1861), 9–12.

50. Bushnell, *Reverses Needed*, 22, 23, 25, 27. See also Grosjean, "The Concept of American Nationhood," 105–6.

51. Horace Bushnell, "Our Obligations to the Dead," in *God's New Israel: Religious Interpretations of American Destiny*, ed. Conrad Cherry, rev. ed. (Chapel Hill: University of North Carolina Press, 1998), 210.

52. Bushnell, "Our Obligations to the Dead," 206–7.

53. For a detailed analysis of this topic, see Christopher C. Moore, "'Blood, Blood, Rivers of Blood': Horace Bushnell and the Atonement of America," *Fides et Historia* 50, no. 1 (Winter/Spring 2018): 1–14.

54. Paul C. Nagel, *This Sacred Trust: American Nationality, 1798–1898* (New York: Oxford University Press, 1971), 129–94.

55. Bushnell, "Our Obligations to the Dead," 205.

56. Horace Bushnell, *Work and Play: Or, Literary Varieties* (New York: Charles Scribner, 1864), 355.

57. William Clebsch, "Baptism of Blood: A Study of Christian Contributions to the Interpretation of the Civil War in American History" (Th.D. diss., Union Theological Seminary, 1957), 90–91; Bushnell, "Our Obligations to the Dead," 214. The phrase "baptized for the dead" comes from 1 Corinthians 15:29.

58. Barbara M. Cross, *Horace Bushnell: Minister to a Changing America* (Chicago: University of Chicago Press, 1958), 137.

59. Horace Bushnell, *The Vicarious Sacrifice: Grounded in Principles of Universal Obligation* (New York: Scribner, 1866), 41.

60. Bushnell, *The Vicarious Sacrifice*, 46–47.

61. All quotations from Dunham, *The Attitude of the Northern Clergy Toward the South*, 111, 112, 114; Richard M. Gamble, *A Fiery Gospel: The Battle Hymn of the Republic and the Road to Righteous War* (Ithaca, NY: Cornell University Press, 2019), ix, 6–7.

62. I use "democratic" here to distinguish this form of Christian republicanism from other varieties more suspicious of democracy.

63. Noll, *America's God*, 564, 213; Noll, *The Civil War as a Theological Crisis* (Chapel Hill: University of North Carolina Press, 2006), 18.

64. The characteristic not mentioned is, in fact, the idea of America's covenantal relationship with God. I place more emphasis on this view than Noll does, which is why I designated a separate section to discuss it.

65. Noll, *Civil War as a Theological Crisis*, 19.

66. Noll, *Civil War as a Theological Crisis*, 19.

67. Like many at the time and since, Abbott did not make clear distinctions between "republicanism" and "democracy," even though the two terms are not technically synonymous.

68. *Minutes of the General Association of Congregational Churches and Ministers of Indiana at its Meeting in Terre Haute, May 16, 1861* (Indianapolis: Congregational Churches [?], 1861), 4, quoted in Brown, *Lyman Abbott, Christian Evolutionist*, 29.

69. Beecher, "The Southern Babylon," 439.

70. "Untitled," *Weekly Wabash Express*, May 20, 1863, 1. See also the sarcastic editorial, "Religion a Bad Thing for Slaves," *Weekly Wabash Express*, Dec. 2, 1863.

71. Lyman Abbott to Abby Frances Hamlin, Apr. 17, 1856, quoted in *Reminiscences*, 100–2.

72. Abbott, "Southern Evangelization," 703.

73. Abbott, "Southern Evangelization," 701, 704, 707–8.

74. Abbott, *Reminiscences*, 99.

75. Abbott, "Southern Evangelization," 700.

76. Beecher, "The Ground and Forms of Government," in *Freedom and War*, 341, 359.

77. Beecher, "Christianity in Government," in *Freedom and War*, 279.

78. He also made clear his opposition to racial intermarriage and social equality for African Americans. Beecher, "Christianity in Government," 292.

79. Beecher, "Christianity in Government," 289–92.

80. Beecher, "The Southern Babylon," 432, 433.

81. Henry Ward Beecher, "Abraham Lincoln," in *Lectures and Orations by Henry Ward Beecher*, ed. Newell Dwight Hillis (New York: Fleming H. Revell, 1913), 280–81.

82. Beecher, "The Battle Set in Array," in *Freedom and War*, 98.

83. Beecher "The Beginning of Freedom," 231–32.

84. Beecher, "The Beginning of Freedom," 230.

85. Beecher, "Our Good Progress and Prospects," in *Freedom and War*, 380.

86. Beecher, "National Injustice and Penalty," in *Freedom and War*, 324.

87. Beecher, "National Injustice and Penalty," 325.

88. Beecher, "Address at the Raising of the Union Flag," 685–87.

89. Bushnell, *Reverses Needed*, 16–17.

90. Bushnell, *Reverses Needed*, 18–19.

91. Quoted in Dunham, *Attitude of the Northern Clergy*, 84, 88, 96.

92. Wesley, *Politics of Faith*, 94–100, 103–11.

93. See Dietrich Bonhoeffer, *No Rusty Swords: Letters, Lectures and Notes, 1928–1936 from the Collected Works of Dietrich Bonhoeffer*, vol. 1, ed. Edwin H. Robertson, trans. Edwin H. Robertson and John Bowden (London: Collins, 1965).

94. Reginald Horsman, *Race and Manifest Destiny: The Origins of American Racial Anglo-Saxonism* (Cambridge: Harvard University Press, 1981), 209.

95. Chandra Manning, *What This Cruel War Was Over: Soldiers, Slavery, and the Civil War* (New York: Vintage, 2007), 193, 221.

96. For the term "greater reconstruction," see Elliott West, "Reconstructing Race," *Western Historical Quarterly* 34, no. 1 (2003): 6, https://doi.org/10.2307/25047206. West locates the beginning of the "greater reconstruction" in 1846. I follow Richard White's

use of the term in *The Republic for Which It Stands: The United States during Reconstruction and the Gilded Age, 1865–1896* (New York: Oxford University Press, 2017), 103–35; Heather Cox Richardson, *West from Appomattox: The Reconstruction of America After the Civil War* (New Haven, CT: Yale University Press, 2007), 1–7; Jennifer Graber, *The Gods of Indian Country: Religion and the Struggle for the American West* (New York: Oxford University Press, 2018), 78–81; Harry S. Stout, "Review Essay: Religion, War, and the Meaning of America," *Religion and American Culture* 19, no. 2 (Summer 2009): 275–76, https://doi.org/10.1525/rac.2009.19.2.275.

97. Abbott, "The Crisis," 1.

98. David Blight, *Race and Reunion: The Civil War in American Memory* (Cambridge: Harvard University Press, 2001).

99. Edward L. Ayers, *What Caused the Civil War? Reflections on the South and Southern History* (New York: Norton, 2005), 103–30.

100. Blight, *Race and Reunion*, 2–3.

2. "Heavy Is the Guilt That Hangs upon the Neck of This Nation"

1. Patricia L. Pastore, "Allen Chapel Congregation, Church have helped shape Wabash Valley History," *Tribune-Star*, http://specials.tribstar.com/terrehautestop40/stories/allen.html.

2. Gilbert Anthony Williams, *The Christian Recorder, A.M.E. Church, 1854–1902* (Jefferson, NC: McFarland, 1996), 12.

3. Williams, *The Christian Recorder*, 17–18. From July 1861 through December 1861, Anthony L. Stanford technically served as editor, with Weaver providing close assistance. There were also seven "corresponding editors," but Eric Gardner states that they were not intended to be a "working editorial board." Given Weaver's desire for authority and continuous influence, it is improbable that the *Recorder* printed anything with which he strongly disagreed. I have thus treated the *Recorder*'s editorial page during the war as mostly the product of one person. On Weaver, Stanford, and battles for control of the *Recorder*, see Eric Gardner, *Black Print Unbound: The Christian Recorder, African American Literature, and Periodical Culture* (New York: Oxford University Press, 2015), 44–49, quotation from 45.

4. Eric Gardner, "Remembered (Black) Readers: Subscribers to the *Christian Recorder*, 1864–1865," *American Literary History* 23 (2011): 242, 245–46, 231, 240; Frank Luther Mott, *A History of American Magazines, 1850–1865* (Cambridge, MA: Harvard University Press, 1938), 315. For the context of the *Recorder* within nineteenth-century black literature, see Gardner, *Unexpected Places: Relocating Nineteenth-Century African American Literature* (Jackson: University Press of Mississippi, 2009).

5. Williams, *The Christian Recorder*, 15.

6. Elizabeth McHenry, *Forgotten Readers: Recovering the Lost History of African American Literary Societies* (Durham, NC: Duke University Press, 2002), 130; Jean Lee Cole and Aaron Sheehan-Dean, eds., *Freedom's Witness: The Civil War Writings of Henry McNeal Turner* (Morgantown: University of West Virginia Press, 2013), 5.

7. Clarence E. Walker, *A Rock in a Weary Land: The African Methodist Episcopal Church during the Civil War and Reconstruction* (Baton Rouge: Louisiana State University Press, 1982), 15.

8. *The American Annual Cyclopedia and Register of Important Events, of the Year 1866: Embracing Political, Civil, Military, and Social Affairs; Public Documents; Biography, Statistics, Commerce, Finance, Literature, Science, Agriculture, and Mechanical Industry*(New York: D. Appleton, 1869), 6:492.

9. Many of these letters have been reprinted (though sometimes abridged) in Edwin S. Redkey, ed., *A Grand Army of Black Men: Letters from African-American Soldiers in the Union Army, 1861–1865* (New York: Cambridge University Press, 1992). Coincidentally, Weaver also came from Terre Haute.

10. Lizzie [Hart], "For the Christian Recorder," *Christian Recorder*, Apr. 8, 1865, 2. On Hart, see Eric Gardner, "'Yours, for the Cause': The *Christian Recorder* Writings of Lizzie Hart," *Legacy: A Journal of American Women Writers* 27 (2010): 367–75, https://doi.org/10.5250/legacy.27.2.0367.

11. Edmund S. Morgan, *American Slavery, American Freedom: The Ordeal of Colonial Virginia* (New York: Norton, 1975).

12. Perhaps the best-known example is John Hope Franklin [and Evelyn Higginbotham], *From Slavery to Freedom: A History of African Americans*, 9th ed. (New York: McGraw-Hill, 2011). See also Chandra Manning, *What This Cruel War Was Over: Soldiers, Slavery, and the Civil War* (New York: Vintage, 2007), 181–212.

13. Timothy L. Wesley, *The Politics of Faith During the Civil War* (Baton Rouge: Louisiana State University Press, 2013), 168–193; David W. Stowell, *Rebuilding Zion: The Religious Reconstruction of the South, 1863–1877* (New York: Oxford University Press, 1998), 65–79.

14. Hazel Dicken-Garcia and Linus Abraham, "African Americans and the Civil War as Reflected in the *Christian Recorder*, 1861–1862," in *Words at War: The Civil War and American Journalism*, ed. David B. Sachsman, S. Kittrell Rushing, and Roy Morris, Jr. (West Lafayette, IN: Purdue University Press, 2008), 249–60.

15. Gardner, *Black Print Unbound*, 135–65.

16. Sandy Dwayne Martin, "Black Churches and the Civil War: Theological and Ecclesiastical Significance of Black Methodist Involvement, 1861–1865," *Methodist History* 32 (Apr. 1994): 186, 174.

17. Walker, *Rock in a Weary Land*, 30–45.

18. Daniel Alexander Payne, *History of the African Methodist Episcopal Church* (New York: Johnson Reprint Corporation, 1968). Chapters 31 and 32 cover the relevant years, but Payne did not say much about the war itself.

19. Charles Spencer Smith, *A History of the African Methodist Episcopal Church: Being a Volume Supplemental to a* History of the African Methodist Episcopal Church, *By Daniel Alexander Payne, D.D. LL.D., Late One of Its Bishops, Chronicling the Principal Events in the Advance of the African Methodist Episcopal Church From 1856 to 1922* (New York: Johnson Reprint Corporation, 1968).

20. Williams, *The* Christian Recorder, 16; Julius Bailey, *Race Patriotism: Protest and Print Culture in the AME Church* (Knoxville: University of Tennessee Press, 2012).

21. Nelson T. Strobert, *Daniel Alexander Payne: The Venerable Preceptor of the African Methodist Episcopal Church* (Lanham, MD: University Press of America, 2012); Stephen W. Angell and Anthony B. Pinn, eds., *Social Protest Thought in the African Methodist Episcopal Church, 1862–1939* (Knoxville: University Press of Tennessee, 2000); and A. Nevell Owens, *Formation of the African Methodist Episcopal Church in the Nineteenth Century: Rhetoric of Identification* (New York: Palgrave Macmillan, 2014).

22. "Better Than Peace," *Christian Recorder*, Apr. 27, 1861, 61.

23. "The Star-Spangled Banner, and the Duty of Colored Americans to That Flag," *Christian Recorder*, Apr. 27, 1861, 62.

24. "Errors of the South," *Christian Recorder*, Jun. 1, 1861, 81. The biblical reference is to Psalm 55:9, 15. The text varies slightly from the King James Version. It is not clear what translation Weaver was using.

25. "War Reading," *Christian Recorder*, Jun. 22, 1861, 94.

26. Samuel Watts, "Ohio Correspondence," Aug. 6, 1864, 125. John 15:1–6 reads "I am the true vine, and my Father is the husbandman. Every branch in me that beareth not fruit he taketh away: and every branch that beareth fruit, he purgeth it, that it may bring forth more fruit. Now ye are clean through the word which I have spoken unto you. Abide in me, and I in you. As the branch cannot bear fruit of itself, except it abide in the vine; no more can ye, except ye abide in me. I am the vine, ye are the branches: He that abideth in me, and I in him, the same bringeth forth much fruit: for without me ye can do nothing. If a man abide not in me, he is cast forth as a branch, and is withered; and men gather them, and cast them into the fire, and they are burned." Romans 11:17–24 reads "And if some of the branches be broken off, and thou, being a wild olive tree, wert grafted in among them, and with them partakest of the root and fatness of the olive tree; Boast not against the branches. But if thou boast, thou bearest not the root, but the root thee. Thou wilt say then, The branches were broken off, that I might be grafted in. Well; because of unbelief they were broken off, and thou standest by faith. Be not highminded, but fear: For if God spared not the natural branches, take heed lest he also spare not thee. Behold therefore the goodness and severity of God: on them which fell, severity; but toward thee, goodness, if thou continue in his goodness: otherwise thou also shalt be cut off. And they also, if they abide not still in unbelief, shall be grafted in: for God is able to graft them in again. For if thou wert cut out of the olive tree which is wild by nature, and wert grafted contrary to nature into a good olive tree: how much more shall these, which be the natural branches, be grafted into their own olive tree?" Both from King James Version.

27. Joseph E. Williams, "For the Christian Recorder," *Christian Recorder*, Sep. 19, 1863, 149.

28. Thomas H.C. Hinton, "Washington Correspondence," *Christian Recorder*, Aug. 22, 1863, 133. Hebrews 9:22 reads, "And almost all things are by the law purged with blood; and without shedding of blood there is no remission."

29. "The Hand of God," *Christian Recorder*, May 25, 1861, 78.

30. T. Strother, "Why the Great Present Southern Rebellion Has Not Been Long since Crushed," *Christian Recorder*, Jul. 30, 1864, 121.

31. Nicholas Guyatt, *Providence and the Invention of the United States, 1607–1876* (New York: Cambridge University Press, 2007), 6.

32. "Our Country Is Right," *Christian Recorder*, Nov. 23, 1861, 183.

33. "The Glass of Providence. In Which the Nation May See Itself," *Christian Recorder*, Aug. 10, 1861, 121.

34. "Who Stampeded Our Army at Manassas?" *Christian Recorder*, Sep. 28, 1861, 150.

35. "Our Country Is Right," 183.

36. E.W.D., "For the Christian Recorder: Army Correspondence," *Christian Recorder*, Jun. 25, 1864, 101.

37. J.P.C., "The War and Its Design," *Christian Recorder*, Oct. 8, 1864, 162.

38. "Our Government," *Christian Recorder*, Jun. 8, 1861, 85. Weaver began his article by quoting the *German Reformed Messenger*, and it is not clear whether this was his own argument or if he was following the *Messenger's*.

39. "For the Christian Recorder," *Christian Recorder*, May 16, 1863, 77. This argument differs somewhat from Benjamin Fagan's *The Black Newspaper and the Chosen Nation*, which stresses black critiques of the United States. Fagan, *The Black Newspaper and the Chosen Nation* (Athens: University of Georgia Press, 2016), 5–6.

40. On Lincoln's faith, see Gary Scott Smith, *Faith and the Presidency: From George Washington to George W. Bush* (New York: Oxford University Press, 2006), 91–128; and Allen C. Guelzo, *Abraham Lincoln: Redeemer President* (Grand Rapids, MI: Eerdmans, 1999).

41. John C. Brock, "For the Christian Recorder: The Death of the President," *Christian Recorder*, May 6, 1865, 69.

42. Lizzie [Hart], "For the Christian Recorder: Letter from Morrowton, Ohio," *Christian Recorder*, May 27, 1865, 83; W.B. Johnson, "For the Christian Recorder: From the Third U.S.C. Troops," *Christian Recorder*, May 20, 1865, 74. See also "Our National Sacrifice," *Christian Recorder*, Apr. 22, 1865, 62.

43. Junius Albus, "For the Christian Recorder: Colored Troops, No. 8," *Christian Recorder*, Feb. 25, 1865, 30.

44. H.M.T., "For the Christian Recorder: Army Correspondence, By Chaplain H.M. Turner," *Christian Recorder*, Feb. 25, 1865, 29.

45. John C. Brock, "For the Christian Recorder: Soldier's Letter," *Christian Recorder*, Jun. 25, 1864, 101. The reference is to Isaiah 60:2. Brock left out the second half of the verse: "but the LORD shall rise upon thee, and his glory shall be seen upon thee."

46. H.M. Turner, "For the Christian Recorder: From Chaplain Turner," *Christian Recorder*, Jun. 25, 1864, 101.

47. H.M.T., "For the Christian Recorder: Army Correspondence," *Christian Recorder*, May 6, 1865, 69.

48. "Sermon by Bishop Campbell: 'The War and Its Issues,'" *Christian Recorder*, Jun. 3, 1865, 86; see also Junius Albus, "For the Christian Recorder: Colored Troops, No. 7," *Christian Recorder*, Aug. 29, 1863, 137; and Junius Albus, "Colored Troops, No. VI," *Christian Recorder*, Aug. 15, 1863, 130.

49. Mary A. Williams, "For the Christian Recorder: The Union of Church and State," *Christian Recorder*, Sep. 17, 1864, 150.

50. "Rebel Thanksgiving," *Christian Recorder*, Sep. 20, 1862, 150.

51. For a statement of the position (though by a Northerner), see Henry J. Van Dyke, *The Spirituality and Independence of the Church: A Speech Delivered in the Synod of New York, October 18, 1864* (New York: n.p., 1864).

52. "Love of Country Not Love of God," *Christian Recorder*, Aug. 10, 1861, 121.

53. J.K.P., "Christians—The Times," *Christian Recorder*, Nov. 30, 1861, 185.

54. "Our Duty. No. 2," *Christian Recorder*, Feb. 9, 1861, 18.

55. Daniel Alexander Payne, "Welcome to the Ransomed; Or, Duties of the Colored Inhabitants of the District of Columbia," in *Sermons and Addresses, 1853–1891*, ed., Charles Killian (New York: Arno Press, 1972), 12–13.

56. Stephen Ward Angell, *Bishop Henry McNeal Turner and African-American Religion in the South* (Knoxville: University of Tennessee Press, 1992), 1–33.

57. H.M.T., "For the Christian Recorder: The Plagues of This Country," *Christian Recorder*, Jul. 12, 1862, 109.

58. "For the Christian Recorder," *Christian Recorder*, Sep. 20, 1862, 149. See also Frederick Douglass, *Narrative of the Life of Frederick Douglass, An American Slave, Written by Himself*, ed. Houston A. Baker, Jr. (New York: Penguin, 1982), 97–100, 119–20, for a similar critique.

59. F.E.W. Harper, "Mrs. Francis [*sic*] E. Watkins Harper on the War and the President's Colonization Scheme," *Christian Recorder*, Sep. 27, 1862, 153. There are Winthropian echoes here, but they are probably unintentional. See Richard M. Gamble, *In Search of the City on a Hill: The Making and Unmaking of an American Myth* (London: Continuum, 2012). Turner also compared the sufferings of blacks and Indians. See H.M.T., "Washington Correspondence," *Christian Recorder*, Jan. 31, 1863, 18.

60. On this, see Brian Taylor, "A Politics of Service: Black Northerners' Debates over Enlistment in the American Civil War," *Civil War History* 58 (Dec. 2012): 451–80, https://doi.org/10.1353/cwh.2012.0066.

61. M.S.D., "For the Christian Recorder: Colored Soldiers," *Christian Recorder*, Aug. 15, 1863, 129.

62. John H.W.N. Collins, "For the Christian Recorder: A Letter from a Soldier of the 54th Mass. Regt.," *Christian Recorder*, Jul. 23, 1864, 117.

63. "Colored Troops of the United States," *Christian Recorder*, Apr. 2, 1864, 54.

64. G.W. Hatton, "For the Christian Recorder," *Christian Recorder*, Jul. 16, 1864, 114–15. The *Recorder* printed dozens of complaints about unequal wages. For example, "The Pay of Colored Soldiers," *Christian Recorder*, Dec. 26, 1863, 206; "Colored Troops of the United States," 54; "Congress and the Pay of Colored Troops," *Christian Recorder*, Apr. 16, 1864, 62; H.I.W., "For the Christian Recorder: A Letter from a Soldier," *Christian Recorder*, Jul. 23, 1864, 117.

65. Kate Masur suggested that historians have not taken black support for colonization seriously enough. See Masur, "The African American Delegation to Abraham Lincoln: A Reappraisal," *Civil War History* 56 (Jun. 2010): 144, https://doi.org/10.1353/cwh.0.0149. This perspective disagrees with the supposedly unanimous AME opposition to colonization discussed in Walker, *A Rock in a Weary Land*, 37. On black support for colonization in general, see Phillip W. Magness, "The British Honduras Colony: Black Emigrationist Support for Colonization in the Lincoln Presidency," *Slavery & Abolition* 34 (Mar. 2013): 39–60, https://doi.org/10.1080/0144039X.2012.709044.

66. "The Scheme of Colonization—Interview Between the President and a Committee of Colored Men—Remarks of the President," *Christian Recorder*, Aug. 23, 1862, n.p.

67. There was an aborted attempt to colonize about 500 ex-slaves on an island adjacent to Haiti. See Magness, "The British Honduras Colony," 41.

68. H.M. Turner, "For the Christian Recorder," *Christian Recorder*, Dec. 14, 1861, 191. Later Turner seemed more ambivalent about emigration. See H.M.T., "Washington Correspondence," Dec. 6, 1862, 193.

69. West Jersey, "Camden Correspondence," *Christian Recorder*, May 2, 1863, 70.

70. W.C.D., "For the Christian Recorder," *Christian Recorder*, Nov. 8, 1862, 177. See also Observer, "Sketches from Washington," *Christian Recorder*, Apr. 26, 1862, 66.

71. Junius, "For the Christian Recorder: Brooklyn Correspondence," *Christian Recorder*, Nov. 14, 1863, 182. See also Junius, "Brooklyn Correspondence," *Christian Recorder*, Oct. 24, 1863, 170.

72. H.M. Turner, "For the Christian Recorder," *Christian Recorder*, Dec. 14, 1861, 194.

73. J.P.C., "For the Christian Recorder: The President and the Colored People," *Christian Recorder*, Oct. 12, 1861, 158. See also A.F., "The National Fast and the Negro," *Christian Recorder*, Oct. 12, 1861, 158.

74. "The Great Speech: Frederick Douglass on the War," *Christian Recorder*, Jan. 18, 1862, 10. On the *Recorder*'s view of Douglass's speech, see "Speech of Frederick Douglass," *Christian Recorder*, Jan. 18, 1862, 10.

75. James Oakes, *The Radical and the Republican: Frederick Douglass, Abraham Lincoln, and the Triumph of Anti-Slavery Politics* (New York: Norton, 2007), xiii–xxii.

76. Abraham Lincoln, "Message to Congress, March 6, 1862," in *The Collected Works of Abraham Lincoln*, ed. Roy P. Basler (New Brunswick, NJ: Rutgers University Press, 1953): 5: 144–46.

77. H.M.T., "Turner on the President's Message," *Christian Recorder*, Mar. 22, 1862, 46. Ultimately, Turner was right: the District of Columbia was the only entity to adopt the president's plan.

78. H.M.T., "The Plagues of This Country," 109.

79. On this, see James McPherson, *Battle Cry of Freedom: The Civil War Era* (New York: Oxford University Press, 1988), 352–54.

80. H.M.T., "The Plagues of This Country," 109.

81. "For the Christian Recorder," Sep. 20, 1862, 149.

82. William Steward, "For the Christian Recorder: The Negro Soldier," *Christian Recorder*, Mar. 7, 1863, 37.

83. Junius, "For the Christian Recorder: Brooklyn Correspondence," *Christian Recorder*, Feb. 25, 1865, 30.

84. "Catholicity Promotes Union," *New-York Freeman's Journal and Catholic Register*, Nov. 24, 1860, 4; "Sensation Literature Found to be a Nuisance," *Catholic Mirror* (Baltimore), Mar. 9, 1861, 4.

85. William B. Kurtz, *Excommunicated from the Union: How the Civil War Created a Separate Catholic America* (New York: Fordham University Press, 2016), 1–8; Mark A. Noll, "The Catholic Press, the Bible, and Protestant Responsibility for the Civil War," *Journal of the Civil War Era* 7, no. 3 (Sep. 2017): 355–76, https://dio.org/10.1353/cwe.2017.0058. The racism of many white Catholics, of course, represented a stark difference from the AME.

3. "A War of Mercy"

An early version of this chapter was published as "Onward Christian Soldiers: Lyman Abbott's Justification of the Spanish-American War," *Journal of Church & State* 54, no. 3 (Summer 2012): 406–25, https://doi.org/10.1093/jcs/csr110. Used by permission of Oxford University Press.

1. Hannah Fischer, Kim Klarman, and Mari-Jana Oboroceanu, *American War and Military Operations Casualties: Lists and Statistics* (Washington, DC: Congressional Research Service, 2008), 2, http://www.law.umaryland.edu/marshall/crsreports/crsdocuments/RL32492_05142008.pdf.

2. I am largely sympathetic to the argument advanced in Walter LaFeber's *The New Empire* that American intervention in the Spanish-American War was the culmination

of an aggressive foreign policy pursued for the previous half-century. Still, 1898 marked the first time that war resulted in the United States acquiring imperial possessions outside of North America. See Walter LaFeber, *The New Empire: An Interpretation of American Expansion, 1860–1898* (Ithaca, NY: Cornell University Press, 1963).

3. Kristin L. Hoganson, *Fighting for American Manhood: How Gender Politics Provoked the Spanish-American and Philippine-American Wars* (New Haven, CT: Yale University Press, 1998), 1–14. See also Bonnie M. Miller, *From Liberation to Conquest: The Visual and Popular Cultures of the Spanish-American War of 1898* (Amherst: University of Massachusetts Press, 2011), 19–54.

4. Hoganson, *Fighting for American Manhood*, 13.

5. Louis A. Pérez Jr., *The War of 1898: The United States and Cuba in History and Historiography* (Chapel Hill: University of North Carolina Press, 1998); and "Incurring a Debt of Gratitude: 1898 and the Moral Sources of United States Hegemony in Cuba," *American Historical Review* 104, no. 2 (Apr. 1999): 356–98, https://doi.org/10.2307/2650370.

6. Religious interpretations of the Spanish-American War are not entirely absent in the literature, but they are incomplete. For an older study that catalogs a wealth of quotations about the war from religious voices, see William A. Karraker, "The American Churches and the Spanish-American War" (PhD diss., University of Chicago, 1940). For a similar approach, with more awareness of the historical roots of providentialism and humanitarianism, see John Edwin Smylie, "Protestant Churches and America's World Role, 1865–1900: A Study of Christianity, Nationality, and International Relations," (ThD diss., Princeton Theological Seminary, 1959), 389–557. For the use of religion by politicians during the war, see Paul T. McCartney, *Power and Progress: American National Identity, the War of 1898, and the Rise of American Imperialism* (Baton Rouge: Louisiana State University Press, 2006); and McCartney, "Religion, the Spanish-American War, and the Idea of American Mission," *Journal of Church and State* 54 (Spring 2012): 257–78, https://doi.org/10.1093/jcs/csr050. The best account of religion and the war is Matthew McCullough, *The Cross of War: Christian Nationalism and U.S. Expansionism in the Spanish-American War* (Madison: University of Wisconsin Press, 2014). Finally, for studies dealing with religion and imperialism, see Susan K. Harris, *God's Arbiters: Americans and the Philippines, 1898–1902* (New York: Oxford University Press, 2011), 3–37; and Ian R. Tyrrell, *Reforming the World: The Creation of America's Moral Empire* (Princeton, NJ: Princeton University Press, 2010), 1–10.

7. David F. Trask, *The War with Spain in 1898* (New York: Macmillan, 1981), 1.

8. Trask, *War with Spain*, 8–9. The actual figure was closer to 100,000, but this was not known at the time.

9. Trask, *War with Spain*, xii.

10. Quoted in Trask, *War with Spain*, 28.

11. Lewis O. Saum, *The Popular Mood of America, 1860–1890* (Lincoln: University of Nebraska Press, 1990), 13–39.

12. Lyman Abbott, *Reminiscences* (Boston: Houghton Mifflin, 1915), 369–70.

13. Frank Luther Mott, *A History of American Magazines*, vol. 4, *1885–1905* (Cambridge, MA: Harvard University Press, 1957), 290–291, for *Christian Advocate* figure; Mott, *History of American Magazines*, vol. 3, *1865–1885* (Cambridge, MA: Harvard University Press, 1938), 475, for *Century* figure.

14. Finley Peter Dunne, *Mr. Dooley on Lyman Abbott* (n.p., 1899), Plymouth Church of the Pilgrims and Henry Ward Beecher Collection, 1819–1989; ARC.212; box 25, folder 9; Brooklyn Historical Society.

15. Nicholas Guyatt, *Providence and the Invention of the United States, 1607–1876* (New York: Cambridge University Press, 2007), 6.

16. Lyman Abbott, "The Meaning of the War," *Plymouth Morning Pulpit*, May 31, 1898, 1–2.

17. See, for example, Lyman Abbott, ed., *The New Puritanism* (New York: Fords, Howard, and Hulbert, 1898).

18. Abbott, "The Meaning of the War," 1–2.

19. "The New National Policy," *Outlook*, Jun. 18, 1898, 415.

20. Abbott, "The Meaning of the War," 3–5.

21. Thanksgiving for Victories," *Outlook*, Jul. 16, 1898, 666.

22. Lyman Abbott, "The Duty and Destiny of America," *Plymouth Morning Pulpit*, Jun. 15, 1898, 20. The quotation paraphrased Isaiah 60:1, 3.

23. "Thanksgiving for Victories," 667.

24. Lyman Abbott to Edward Abbott, Aug. 3, 1898, box 6, folder 10, Abbott Memorial Collection, George J. Mitchell Department of Special Collections & Archives, Bowdoin College Library (hereafter AMC).

25. "The President's Message," *Outlook*, Apr. 16, 1898, 953.

26. "Sermons on Possible War," *New York Times*, Mar. 14, 1898, 2.

27. "The First Battle," *Outlook*, May 7, 1898, 11–12.

28. On the journal's theology, see "Critical Notes: The Theological Position of the *Bibliotheca Sacra*," *Bibliotheca Sacra* 55:220 (Oct. 1898), 736–39; and William J. Morison, "*Bibliotheca Sacra*," in *The Conservative Press in Twentieth-Century America*, ed. Ronald Lora and William Henry Longton (Westport, CT: Greenwood Press, 1999), 91–101.

29. G. Frederick White, "Sociological Notes: Responsibility of Our National Greatness," *Bibliotheca Sacra* 55:220 (Oct. 1898): 749, 750.

30. "Debate Heated," *Boston Daily Globe*, May 13, 1898, 9; G.W. Duane to Edward Abbott, Apr. 27, 1898, box 6, folder 9, AMC.

31. Josiah Strong, *Expansion under New World-Conditions* (New York: Baker & Taylor, 1900), 271.

32. Strong, *Expansion*, 302.

33. Robert Stuart MacArthur, "The Hand of God in the Nation's Conflict," in American Baptist Publication Society, *The Seventy-fourth Anniversary, Held at Rochester, New York, May 21 and 23, 1898* (Philadelphia: American Baptist Publication Society, [1898?]), 66, quoted in Karraker, "The American Churches and the Spanish-American War," 65.

34. "Thanksgiving for Victory," *New York Times*, Jul. 11, 1898, 10.

35. LeRoy Armstrong, *Pictorial Atlas Illustrating the Spanish-American War: Comprising a History of the Great Conflict of the United States with Spain* (n.p., Souvenir Publishing Co., 1899), 76.

36. "Expansion but Not Imperialism," *Outlook*, Mar. 24, 1900, 662. "The considerate judgment of mankind and the gracious favor of Almighty God" was a line from the Emancipation Proclamation. Ironically, Abbott was thus invoking emancipation to justify the United States' imperial policy in the Philippines.

37. "The Issues Restated," *Outlook*, Jul. 23, 1898, 711.

38. "The Responsibilities of Peace," *Outlook*, Aug. 20, 1898, 958.

39. Lyman Abbott, "Southern Evangelization," *New Englander* 23 (Oct. 1864): 703.

40. Mark Noll, *The Civil War as a Theological Crisis* (Chapel Hill: University of North Carolina Press, 2006), 19.

41. "An Irrepressible Conflict," *Outlook*, May 14, 1898, 113–14.

42. "Santiago," *Outlook*, Jul. 9, 1898, 610.

43. "Santiago," 610. See also similar comments in Abbott, *The Life That Really Is* (New York: Wilbur B. Ketcham, 1899), 197, 268. These sorts of views echoed the conclusions of the major nineteenth-century American survey of Spanish literature, George Ticknor's three-volume *History of Spanish Literature* (1849). On Ticknor's views, see Iván Jaksić, *The Hispanic World and American Intellectual Life, 1820–1880* (New York: Palgrave Macmillan, 2007), 29–51.

44. "An Irrepressible Conflict," 113–14.

45. "An Irrepressible Conflict," 114.

46. "Thanksgiving for Victories," 667.

47. "Liquor in the Army," *Outlook*, Jul. 23, 1898, 715.

48. "Liquor in the Army," 716; "Spanish Prisoners," *Outlook*, Jul. 16, 1898, 654.

49. "The National Holiday," *Outlook*, Jul. 2, 1898, 59.

50. "Christian Work in the Army," *Outlook*, Jul. 30, 1898, 786.

51. "Christian Work in the Army," 786.

52. William B. Millar, "The Army Commission," *Independent*, Jul. 7, 1898, 65–66.

53. White, "Sociological Notes," 748, 750–51.

54. "Sundry War Notes," *Christian Advocate* 73 (May 5, 1898): 718. The Spanish alphabet had more than twenty-six letters.

55. Washington Gladden, *Our Nation and Her Neighbors* (Columbus, OH: Quinius & Ridenour, 1898), 5–6.

56. Gladden, *Our Nation*, 28–29.

57. "Thanksgiving for Victory," 10.

58. The literature on the Social Gospel is extensive. See, for example, Gary Scott Smith, *The Search for Social Salvation: Social Christianity and America, 1880–1925* (Lanham, MD: Lexington Books, 2000); Christopher H. Evans, ed., *Perspectives on the Social Gospel: Papers from the Inaugural Social Gospel Conference at Colgate Rochester Divinity School* (Lewiston, NY: Edwin Mellen Press, 1999); Ralph E. Luker, *The Social Gospel in Black and White: American Racial Reform, 1885–1912* (Chapel Hill: University of North Carolina Press, 1991); Ronald C. White, Jr., *Liberty and Justice for All: Racial Reform and the Social Gospel (1877–1925)* (1990; repr. Louisville, KY: Westminster John Knox Press 2002); Susan Curtis, *A Consuming Faith: The Social Gospel and Modern American Culture* (Baltimore: Johns Hopkins University Press, 1991); Ronald C. White, Jr. and C. Howard Hopkins, *The Social Gospel: Religion and Reform in Changing America* (Philadelphia: Temple University Press, 1976); Robert T. Handy, *The Social Gospel in America, 1870–1920* (New York: Oxford University Press, 1966); Jacob H. Dorn, *Washington Gladden: Prophet of the Social Gospel* (Columbus: Ohio State University Press, 1967); and C. Howard Hopkins, *The Rise of the Social Gospel in American Protestantism, 1865–1915* (New Haven, CT: Yale University Press, 1940). For a new interpretation stressing the working-class origins of the Social Gospel, see Heath W. Carter, *Union Made: Working*

People and the Rise of Social Christianity in Chicago (New York: Oxford University Press, 2015).

Matthew McCullough used the related term "messianic interventionism" to describe the United States' posture toward the rest of the world in this era. I appreciate McCullough's term (as well as Richard Gamble's notion of "a messianic nation") but I stick with the more familiar "social gospel" here. See McCullough, *Cross of War*, 3; and Richard M. Gamble, *The War for Righteousness: Progressive Christianity, the Great War, and the Rise of the Messianic Nation* (Wilmington, DE: ISI Books, 2003).

59. Lyman Abbott, *An Illustrated Commentary on the Gospel According to Matthew* (New York: A.S. Barnes, 1875), 1:87.

60. Josiah Strong, "The Individual and Social Interpretation of Christianity," in *First Year of the Sagamore Sociological Conference, Sagamore Beach, U.S.A., June 18, 19, 20, 1907* (Boston: Arakelyan Press, 1907), 7.

61. For example, Washington Gladden, *Applied Christianity: Moral Aspects of Social Questions* (Boston: Houghton Mifflin, 1886); Walter Rauschenbusch, *Christianity and the Social Crisis* (New York: Macmillan, 1907); *Christianizing the Social Order* (New York: Macmillan, 1912); *A Theology for the Social Gospel* (New York: Macmillan, 1917); Josiah Strong, *Religious Movements for Social Betterment* (New York: Baker & Taylor, 1900); George D. Herron, *The Christian State, A Political Vision of Christ: A Course of Six Lectures Delivered in Churches in Various American Cities* (New York: T.Y. Crowell, 1895).

62. Abbott, "The Meaning of the War," 2; emphasis added.

63. Abbott, "The Meaning of the War," 3.

64. "To the Front," *Outlook*, May 7, 1898, 11.

65. For the biblical context, see Genesis 4:1–16.

66. David R. Spencer, *The Yellow Journalism: The Press and America's Emergence as a World Power* (Evanston, IL: Northwestern University Press, 2007), 144–51.

67. "Untitled," *Outlook*, Feb. 26, 1898, 505–07; "Wait!," 567–68; "Untitled," *Outlook*, Mar. 12, 1898, 651.

68. "The Cuban Question," *Outlook*, Mar. 26, 1898, 759.

69. "The Cuban Question," 760.

70. "Why War?" *Outlook*, Apr. 23, 1898, 1004.

71. "Our Future Policy," *Outlook*, May 21, 1898, 157–58.

72. Abbott, "Duty and Destiny of America," 2.

73. Abbott, *The Life That Really Is*, 109.

74. J.W. Trowbridge, "Cuba," *Independent*, Jul. 7, 1898, 7.

75. "War and Conscience," *Independent*, Jul. 7, 1898, 58–59.

76. Washington Gladden, "The Issues of the War," *Outlook*, Jul. 16, 1898, 673–75.

77. Edgar Gardner Murphy, "The Pulpit and the War," *North American Review* 166 (Jun. 1898): 751–52.

78. Hoganson, *Fighting for American Manhood*; T.J. Jackson Lears, *No Place of Grace: Antimodernism and the Transformation of American Culture* (Chicago: University of Chicago Press, 1994), 47–58, quotation from 48; Gail Bederman, *Manliness & Civilization: A Cultural History of Gender and Race in the United States, 1880–1917* (Chicago: University of Chicago Press, 1995), 84–88, 187–206; Clifford Putney, *Muscular Christianity: Manhood and Sports in Protestant America, 1880–1920* (Cambridge, MA: Harvard University Press, 2001), 39–42, quotation from 42.

79. Harris, *God's Arbiters*, 19.

80. "Peace—and After," *Outlook*, Jul. 16, 1898, 662–65.

81. "Expansion but Not Imperialism," 663.

82. Ira V. Brown, *Lyman Abbott, Christian Evolutionist: A Study in Religious Liberalism* (Cambridge, MA: Harvard University Press, 1953), 163–64; Lyman Abbott to Theodore Roosevelt, Jan. 8, 1907, Reel 71, Theodore Roosevelt Papers, Manuscript Division, Library of Congress, Washington, DC. On the "children" remark, see "Expansion but Not Imperialism," 663. For a call for paying more attention to the interplay of religion and race for whites, see "Forum: American Religion and 'Whiteness,'" *Religion and American Culture: A Journal of Interpretation* 19 (Winter 2009): 1–35. On Anglo-Saxonism and empire, see Paul Kramer, "Empires, Exceptions, and Anglo-Saxons: Race and Rule Between the British and United States Empires, 1880–1910," *Journal of American History* 88 (Mar. 2002): 1315–53, https://doi.org/10.2307/2700600.

83. Paul A. Kramer, *The Blood of Government: Race, Empire, the United States, and the Philippines* (Chapel Hill: University of North Carolina Press, 2006), 1–34.

84. LaFeber, *The New Empire*, 2; Heather Cox Richardson, *West from Appomattox: The Reconstruction of America after the Civil War* (New York: Oxford University Press, 2007), 1–7.

85. Jennifer Graber, *The Gods of Indian Country: Religion and the Struggle for the American West* (New York: Oxford University Press, 2018), 1–18.

86. "The Outlook," *Christian Union*, Jul. 21, 1880, 41; "The Outlook," *Christian Union*, Sep. 4, 1884, 219; "The Outlook," *Christian Union*, Sep. 25, 1884, 291.

87. Brown, *Lyman Abbott*, 90–93.

88. Brown, *Lyman Abbott*, 93–94, quotation from 94. For a dissenting perspective, see Alice C. Fletcher, "The Allotted Indian's Difficulties," *Outlook*, Apr. 11, 1896, 660–61.

89. LaFeber, *The New Empire*.

90. "Peace—and After," 662–65.

91. "The New Monroe Doctrine," *Outlook*, Aug. 7, 1898, 1004.

92. Gary Scott Smith, *Religion in the Oval Office: The Religious Lives of America's Presidents* (New York: Oxford University Press, 2015), 159–83. Against the views of Lewis Gould, Smith sides with Robert Linder, Richard Pierard, and Andrew Preston that McKinley's alleged statement about walking the halls of the White House (which was not published until several years later) is probably accurate. See Smith, *Religion in the Oval Office*, 184.

93. "Our Conditions to Spain," *Independent*, Jul. 21, 1898, 196–97; "Can We 'Let Them Go'?" *Independent*, Jul. 28, 1898, 266.

94. William Jennings Bryan, "Annexation," in *Patriotic Eloquence Relating to the Spanish-American War and its Issues*, ed. Robert I. Fulton and Thomas C. Trueblood (New York: Scribner's, 1900), 39–40, quotations from 40.

95. Charles E. Jefferson, "Temptation from the Mountain Top," in *Patriotic Eloquence*, 174–77.

96. See Gamble, *War for Righteousness*, 1–23.

97. Lyman Abbott, *The Twentieth Century Crusade* (New York: Macmillan, 1918).

98. For a related point, see McCullough, *Cross of War*, 135–41.

99. Finley Peter Dunne, *Mr. Dooley: Now and Forever* (Stanford, CA: Academic Reprints, 1954), 37.

4. "I Look upon This War as an Impudent Crime"

An earlier version of this chapter was published as "A Church Divided: American Catholics Debate the Spanish-American War," *Journal of the Gilded Age and Progressive Era* 14 (Jul. 2015): 348–66, https://www.jstor.org/stable/43903097. Used by permission of Cambridge University Press and the Society for Historians of the Gilded Age and Progressive Era.

1. "Bishop McQuaid's Patriotic Speech," *Boston Pilot*, May 14, 1898, 5.

2. "Bishop McQuaid's Patriotic Speech"; "The Archbishop's Jubilee," *New York Times*, May 5, 1898, 12.

3. Julius Pratt, *Expansionists of 1898: The Acquisition of Hawaii and the Spanish Islands* (Baltimore: Johns Hopkins University Press, 1936), 287–88; William A. Karraker, "The American Churches and the Spanish-American War" (PhD diss., University of Chicago, 1940), 113; Frank T. Reuter, *Catholic Influence on American Colonial Policies, 1898–1904* (Austin: University of Texas Press, 1967); Thomas E. Wangler, "American Catholics and the Spanish-American War," in *Catholics in America: 1776–1976*, ed. Robert Trisco (Washington, DC: United States Catholic Conference, 1976), 251–52; James Hennesey, *American Catholics: A History of the Roman Catholic Community in the United States* (New York: Oxford University Press, 1981), 205; Harvey Rosenfeld, *Diary of a Dirty Little War: The Spanish-American War of 1898* (Westport, CT: Praeger, 2000); Scott Wright, "The *Northwestern Chronicle* and the Spanish-American War: American Catholic Attitudes Regarding the 'Splendid Little War,'" *American Catholic Studies* 116, no. 4 (2005): 55–68; James M. O'Toole, *The Faithful: A History of Catholics in America* (Cambridge: Harvard University Press, 2008), 141–42. Exceptions include Francis Coghlan, "The Impact of the Spanish American War on the Catholic Church in the United States of America" (MA thesis, University of Notre Dame, 1956), 1–31; Darrel Bigham, "American Christian Thinkers and the Function of War, 1861–1920" (PhD diss., University of Kansas, 1970), 154, 169–70; and David Noel Doyle, *Irish Americans, Native Rights and National Empires: The Structure, Divisions and Attitudes of the Catholic Minority in the Decade of Expansion, 1890–1901* (New York: Arno Press, 1976), 165–223.

4. Hennesey, *American Catholics*, 205.

5. Matthew McCullough, *The Cross of War: Christian Nationalism and U.S. Expansion in the Spanish-American War* (Madison: University of Wisconsin Press, 2014), 46–59.

6. Andrew Preston, *Sword of the Spirit, Shield of Faith: Religion in American War and Diplomacy* (New York: Knopf, 2012), 216–18.

7. Preston, *Sword of the Spirit*, 217.

8. Roger Finke and Rodney Stark, *The Churching of America, 1776–2005: Winners and Losers in Our Religious Economy* (New Brunswick, NJ: Rutgers University Press, 2005), 121.

9. See Philip Gleason, "Coming to Terms with American Catholic History," *Societas* 3 (Autumn 1973): 283–312. Wilson D. Miscamble has suggested that Catholics' views on foreign policy be considered a "barometer" of their Americanization in "Catholics and American Foreign Policy from McKinley to McCarthy: A Historiographical Survey," *Diplomatic History* 4 (Summer 1980): 225.

10. Anti-Catholic sentiments were sometimes intertwined with anti-Irish views. See Matthew Frye Jacobson, *Whiteness of a Different Color: European Immigrants and the*

Alchemy of Race (Cambridge, MA: Harvard University Press, 1998), 70. On nineteenth-century anti-Catholicism, see Ray Allen Billington, *The Protestant Crusade, 1800–1860* (New York: Macmillan, 1938); and Jenny Franchot, *Roads to Rome: The Antebellum Protestant Encounter with Catholicism* (Berkeley: University of California Press, 1994).

11. Robert Michaelsen, "Common School, Common Religion? A Case Study in Church-State Relations, Cincinnati, 1869–1870," *Church History* 38 (Jun. 1969): 201–17, https://doi.org/10.2307/3162707; Mark W. Summers, *Rum, Romanism, and Rebellion: The Making of a President, 1884* (Chapel Hill: University of North Carolina Press, 2000); Josiah Strong, *Our Country: Its Possible Future and Its Present Crisis* (1885; repr. New York: Baker & Taylor, 1968); Donald L. Kinzer, *An Episode in Anti-Catholicism: The American Protective Association* (Seattle: University of Washington Press, 1964).

12. On Columbus, see Gerald P. Fogarty, "1892 and 1992: From Celebration of Discovery to Encounter of Cultures," *Catholic Historical Review* 79 (Oct. 1993): 626–42, https://www.jstor.org/stable/25024142. On Gibbons, see Mark A. Noll, "Bishop James Gibbons, the Bible, and Protestant America," *U.S. Catholic Historian* 31 (Summer 2013): 77–104, https://www.jstor.org/stable/24584769. On the Catholic Congress, see *Official Report of the Proceedings of the Catholic Congress, Held at Baltimore, MD., November 11th and 12th, 1889* (Detroit: William H. Hughes, 1889), vi, viii, 8.

13. McCullough, *Cross of War*, 54.

14. James Michael Reardon, *The Catholic Church in the Diocese of St. Paul* (St. Paul: North Central Pub. Co., 1952), 173; "At Point of War," *Northwestern Chronicle* [hereafter *NWC*], Apr. 1, 1898, 8; "Mr. M'Kinley's Latest," *NWC*, Apr. 15, 1898, 4; The Maine Inquiry Report," *NWC*, Apr. 1, 1898, 4; Territorial Expansion of the United States," *NWC*, Jun. 17, 1898, 4; "A Question of Conquest," *NWC*, May 20, 1898, 4; "Editorial Notes," *Catholic World* 67 (Aug. 1898): 725. See also "Editorial Notes," *Catholic World* 67 (Jun. 1898): 426.

15. Gary Gerstle, *American Crucible: Race and Nation in the Twentieth Century* (Princeton, NJ: Princeton University Press, 2001), 9.

16. "All at a Word," *NWC*, Apr. 22, 1898, 4; "Proving Their Patriotism," *Pilot*, Apr. 30, 1898, 8; "Archbishop Ryan of Philadelphia on the War," *Pilot*, May 21, 1898, 1. The papacy remained officially neutral, but the Vatican's Apostolic Delegate to the United States, Sebastian Martinelli, held pro-American feelings. On neutrality, see "The Attitude of the Pope," *New York Times*, May 10, 1898, 2. On Martinelli's views, see "Mgr. Martinelli's Stand," *New York Times*, Apr. 18, 1898, 1; and "Church in Puerto Rico," *New York Times*, Aug. 4, 1898, 1.

17. John Jerome Rooney, "A Catholic Soldier," *Catholic World* 67 (Aug. 1898): 702; "Notes and Remarks," *Ave Maria*, Jul. 9, 1898, 53.

18. "Religion, Patriotism," *Monitor* (San Francisco), Apr. 23, 1898, 71; "Patriotism and Religion," *Boston Pilot*, Jul. 9, 1898, 1; Ibid.; "Bishop Durier's Remarkable Pastoral," *St. Louis Review*, Oct. 6, 1898, 5.

19. John Tracy Ellis, *The Life of James Cardinal Gibbons: Archbishop of Baltimore, 1834–1921* (Milwaukee: Bruce Pub. Co., 1952), 2:86–91.

20. Marvin R. O'Connell, *John Ireland and the American Catholic Church* (St. Paul: Minnesota Historical Society Press, 1988), 5–15, 68–84.

21. R. Scott Appleby, *Church and Age Unite! The Modernist Impulse in American Catholicism* (Notre Dame, IN: University of Notre Dame Press, 1992), 7–8, quotation on

8; Peter R. D'Agostino, *Rome in America: Transnational Catholic Ideology from the Risorgimento to Fascism* (Chapel Hill: University of North Carolina Press, 2004), 57.

22. John Offner, "Washington Mission: Archbishop Ireland on the Eve of the Spanish-American War," *Catholic Historical Review* 73 (Oct. 1987): 562–75, https://www.jstor.org/stable/25022638; Thomas E. Cusack, "Archbishop John Ireland and the Spanish-American War: Peacemaker or Bungler?" (MA thesis, University of Notre Dame, 1974); John T. Farrell, "Archbishop Ireland and Manifest Destiny," *Catholic Historical Review* 33 (Oct. 1947): 269–301, https://www.jstor.org/stable/25014801; and Humphrey Moynihan, "Archbishop Ireland and the Spanish-American War: Some Original Data," *Ireland American Review* 5 (1942–43): 98–118.

23. John Ireland differentiated himself from other prowar advocates by his respect and praise for Spain. See "Defends Spain," *NWC*, July 15, 1898, 8. In private, Ireland substantially qualified his support for the war, although he did not abandon his providential reasoning. In a May 2 letter to Denis J. O'Connell, Ireland acknowledged, "I do not, I confess, like our present war" while also affirming, "Of course now, I am for war—for the Stars and Stripes. I am all right—as an American." On May 11, he told O'Connell that his "sympathies are largely with Spain; but the fact is, she is beaten." Yet, on June 18, he wrote to O'Connell—in the context of discussing his hope that American influence and Americanism would continue to grow around the world— that "Providence overrules wars—and this war is Providence's opportunity to make a new world." Quotations from Farrell, "Archbishop Ireland," 292, 295, 301. This chapter focuses on the public Ireland because his private ruminations were known only to a tiny group.

24. "America and the War," *Boston Pilot*, Jul. 16, 1898, 4; "For Humanity," *NWC*, May 6, 1898, 8.

25. "M'Kinley Points Way of Destiny," *Chicago Tribune*, Oct. 19, 1898, 1–2; John Ireland, *War and Peace: Address of the Most Rev. John Ireland, at the Peace Jubilee, Chicago, October 18th, 1898* (n.p., 1898?), [1].

26. Ireland, *War and Peace*, [4].

27. Ireland, *War and Peace*, [7]–[8], [11].

28. John Ireland, *The Church and Modern Society: Lectures and Addresses* (Chicago: D.H. McBride & Co., 1896), 146–47.

29. "A Bray from a Pulpit," *NWC*, May 13, 1898, 4; "Editorial Notes," *Catholic World* 67 (May 1898): 279; "Editorial Notes," *Catholic World* 67 (Aug. 1898): 715; "Mgr. Gross on Spain," *NWC*, Jun. 3, 1898, 1; "Snubbed by Spain," *NWC*, Jun. 3, 1898, 1; "Spain Violates Catholicism," *New York Times*, May 2, 1898, 12.

30. "At Point of War," 8; "All at a Word," 4.

31. Philip Gleason, "The Crisis of Americanization," in *Contemporary Catholicism in the United States*, ed. Philip Gleason (Notre Dame, IN: University of Notre Dame Press, 1969), 16; Gleason, "American Identity and Americanization," in *Harvard Encyclopedia of American Ethnic Groups*, ed. Stephan Thernstrom (Cambridge, MA: Harvard University Press, 1980), 32. Gleason is referring specifically to the early national period, but his descriptions would seem to hold true for any period of American history.

32. Gleason, "American Identity and Americanization," 35.

On Leo's political aspirations, see Vincent Viaene, "Introduction," in *The Papacy and the New World Order: Vatican Diplomacy, Catholic Opinion and International Politics at the Time of Leo XIII, 1878–1903,* ed. Vincent Viaene (Leuven, Belgium: Leuven University Press, 2005), 10.

33. "The Week," *The Nation,* Mar. 3, 1898, 157–58; Sara Norton and M.A. DeWolfe Howe, eds., *Letters of Charles Eliot Norton* (Boston: Houghton Mifflin, 1913), 2:268–69; Charles Fanning, *Finley Peter Dunne and Mr. Dooley: The Chicago Years* (Lexington: University Press of Kentucky, 1978), 185–99; Finley Peter Dunne, *Mr. Dooley in Peace and War* (Boston: Small, Maynard, & Co., 1914), 42. On Hobson, see Dunne, *Mr. Dooley in the Hearts of His Countrymen* (Boston: Small, Maynard, & Co., 1899), 216–21. Unlike the others, Dunne was not necessarily a consistent opponent of the war.

34. Norton and Howe, *Letters of Charles Eliot Norton,* 2:266; James Turner, *The Liberal Education of Charles Eliot Norton* (Baltimore: Johns Hopkins University Press, 1999), 390–96. Fears of imperialism probably also motivated Norton. See Norton and Howe, eds., *Letters of Charles Eliot Norton,* 2:270, 2:272–73.

35. Michael Wreszin, *Oswald Garrison Villard: Pacifist at War* (Bloomington: Indiana University Press, 1965), 4, 19–21.

36. My research has not led me to conclude that secular opponents of the war cooperated in any meaningful way with Catholic opponents of the war; the two groups seemed to be operating on parallel tracks.

37. Indiscreet Priest Removed," *NWC,* Mar. 4, 1898, 8.

38. "Amerika ist unser Vaterland, sei es durch Geburt oder freier Wahl." My translation, with assistance from Philipp Gollner. "Editorielles," *Katholische Rundschau,* Apr. 28, 1898, 4; "Editorielles," *Katholische Rundschau,* Apr. 14, 1898, 4.

39. Rory T. Conley, *Arthur Preuss: Journalist and Voice of German and Conservative Catholics in America, 1871–1934* (New York: Peter Lang, 1998), 9–18.

40. Conley, *Arthur Preuss,* 28–29; A.K., "A Gloomy View," *St. Louis Review,* May 5, 1898, 7; "Topics of the Day," *St. Louis Review,* Aug. 4, 1898, 2.

41. J. Gabriel Britt, "Hypocrisy versus Truth," *Globe* 32 (Dec. 1898), 423; Judith Wimmer, "Ave Maria," in *Religious Periodicals of the United States: Academic and Scholarly Journals,* ed. Charles H. Lippy (Westport, CT: Greenwood Press, 1986), 43; John W. Cavanaugh, *Daniel E. Hudson, C.S.C.: A Memoir* (Notre Dame, IN: Ave Maria Press, 1960), 3–17; "Untitled," *Ave Maria,* Jun. 25, 1898, 820–21. Britt's reference to Luke 18:11 implied that hypocritical Americans were like a prideful Pharisee in one of Jesus's parables, who thanked God that he was "not as the rest of men."

42. George T. Angell, "Newspaper Lies about the War," *St. Louis Review,* Jul. 28, 1898, 6; "Untitled," *Ave Maria,* Jul. 23, 1898, 719.

43. "Untitled," *Ave Maria,* Aug. 20, 1898, 244–45; "Untitled," *Catholic Record* (Indianapolis), Aug. 11, 1898, 4. The reference was to the notorious agnostic Robert Ingersoll (1833–99).

44. "Untitled," *Ave Maria,* Jul. 2, 1898, 23.

45. "Notes and Remarks," *Ave Maria,* May 7, 1898, 596.

46. C.Ch., "The Protestant Pulpit and the War," *St. Louis Review,* Jun. 30, 1898, 5.

47. Arthur Preuss, "Hyper-Patriotism?" *St. Louis Review,* May 19, 1898, 4; "Topics of the Day," *St. Louis Review,* Apr. 21, 1898, 6; C. CH., "Patriotism Vs. Breeding," *St. Louis Review* Apr. 14, 1898, 5.

48. "Notes and Remarks," *Ave Maria,* Jul. 23, 1898, 116; "Exchange Comment," *St. Louis Review,* Jul. 16, 1898, 5.

49. "Prayers of Two Nations," *St. Louis Review*, May 12, 1898, 3; William Henry Thorne, "Our American-Spanish War," *Globe* 30 (Jun. 1898), 153–54. It should also be noted that in the same article Thorne characterized the Cubans as "half-breed rebels," and that this racism may also have motivated his opposition to American intervention.

50. F.A.M., "Spain and the Catholic Church," *St. Louis Review*, Jul. 21, 1898, 2–3.

51. "Notes and Remarks," *Ave Maria*, Jul. 9, 1898, 53; "Untitled," *Ave Maria*, May 21, 1898, 658–59. This was the same passage that Charles Jefferson referenced in his opposition to imperialism (see chapter 3).

52. Quoted in Frederick J. Zwierlein, *The Life and Letters of Bishop McQuaid* (Rochester, NY: Art Print Shop, 1927), 3:175.

53. George P. Marks III, comp. and ed., *The Black Press Views American Imperialism (1898–1900)* (New York: Ayer, 1971), 51.

54. Marks, *The Black Press*, 51–99.

55. Quoted in *Respect Black: The Writings and Speeches of Henry McNeal Turner*, ed. Edwin S. Redkey (New York: Arno Press, 1971), 172–75.

56. H.T. Johnson, "The Black Man's Burden," *Voice of Missions* 7 (Apr. 1899): 1, quoted in Brad K. Berner and Kalman Goldstein, eds., *The Spanish-American War: A Documentary History with Commentaries* (Madison, NJ: Fairleigh Dickinson University Press, 2014), 90.

57. Edward J. Blum, *Reforging the White Republic: Race, Religion, and American Nationalism, 1865–1898* (Baton Rouge: Louisiana State University Press, 2007), 226–28.

58. Reuben Parsons to D.E. Hudson, Apr. 26, 1898, X-4-b, D.E. Hudson Papers, University of Notre Dame Archives.

5. "A Louder Call for War"

1. "'I Will Run,' Says Roosevelt," *New York Times*, Jan. 10, 1912, 1. This was the second time the Aldine Club held a dinner in Abbott's honor; the first occurred in 1902. "The Dinner to Dr. Abbott," *New York Times*, Mar. 8, 1902, BR8.

2. "I Will Run," 1.

3. Aldine Club, *Some of the Songs Sung at the Dinner to Lyman Abbott and Theodore Roosevelt* (New York: n.p., 1912), held by the New-York Historical Society, Pamphlet Collection.

4. Pearl James, ed., *Picture This: World War I Posters and Visual Culture* (Lincoln: University of Nebraska Press, 2009); Celia Malone Kingsbury, *For Home and Country: World War I Propaganda on the Home Front* (Lincoln: University of Nebraska Press, 2010); Stewart Halsey Ross, *Propaganda for War: How the United States Was Conditioned to Fight the Great War of 1914–1918* (Jefferson, NC: McFarland, 1996), 189–94 only hints at the importance of religion.

5. E. Brooks Holifield, *God's Ambassadors: A History of the Christian Clergy in America* (Grand Rapids, MI: Eerdmans, 2007), 158. Thirty-five percent of clergy served urban congregations by 1925. Holifield, *God's Ambassadors*, 164.

6. Holifield, *God's Ambassadors*, 174–81.

7. Ray H. Abrams, *Preachers Present Arms* (New York: Round Table Press, 1933), xvi.

8. John F. Piper, Jr., *The American Churches in World War I* (Athens: University of Ohio Press, 1985). See also Piper, "The American Churches in World War I," *Journal of*

the American Academy of Religion 38 (June 1970): 147–55, https://www.jstor.org/stable/1461171.

9. William H. Thomas, Jr., *Unsafe for Democracy: World War I and the U.S. Justice Department's Covert Campaign to Suppress Dissent* (Madison: University of Wisconsin Press, 2008), 68–88.

10. Richard M. Gamble, *The War for Righteousness: Progressive Christianity, the Great War, and the Rise of the Messianic Nation* (Wilmington, DE: ISI Books, 2003), 46–47, 251–52. For a similar perspective, see Jonathan H. Ebel, "'The Wreckage and All the Glory': Protestant America and the Legacy of the Great War," *Journal of Presbyterian History* 92 (Spring/Summer 2014): 4–25. For complementary studies of religion and the Great War that do not focus on elite Protestants, see Michael Williams, *American Catholics in the War: National Catholic War Council, 1917–1921* (New York: Macmillan, 1921); and Jonathan H. Ebel, *Faith in the Fight: Religion and the American Soldier in the Great War* (Princeton, NJ: Princeton University Press, 2010).

11. Andrew Preston, *Sword of the Spirit, Shield of Faith: Religion in American War and Diplomacy* (New York: Knopf, 2012), 239–40.

12. The progressive clergy's theological commitments provided some of the motivation for their crusading language, but one could declare the Great War a crusade without espousing progressive theology. For more on Protestant liberalism and the war, see Gamble, *War for Righteousness*, 25–47; on more conservative groups like Pentecostals, see Grant Wacker, *Heaven Below: Early Pentecostals and American Culture* (Cambridge, MA: Harvard University Press, 2001), 240–50; on fundamentalists, see George Marsden, *Fundamentalism and American Culture*, 2nd ed. (New York: Oxford University Press, 2006), 141–53.

13. Ernest L. Tuveson, *Redeemer Nation: The Idea of America's Millennial Role* (Chicago: University of Chicago Press, 1968).

14. Woodrow Wilson, "An Appeal to the American People," Aug. 19, 1914, in *The Papers of Woodrow Wilson*, ed. Arthur S. Link (Princeton, NJ: Princeton University Press, 1979), 30: 394.

15. Theodore Roosevelt [hereafter TR] to Lyman Abbott [hereafter LA], Jan. 3, 1907, reel 344, Theodore Roosevelt Papers, Manuscript Division, Library of Congress, Washington, DC [hereafter Roosevelt Papers, LOC].

16. "The American Crisis: I—Mr. Bryan's Resignation and American Unity," *Outlook*, Jun. 16, 1915, 341; Preston, *Sword of the Spirit, Shield of Faith*, 247.

17. At various times, for example, Arthur Bullard reported from London, Sanford Griffith from Germany, Gino Speranza from Italy, and Joseph H. Odell from France. See Arthur Bullard, "The Neutral Nations of Europe," *Outlook*, Mar. 10, 1915, 583–86; Sanford Griffith, "The Nations at War: I—A Fortnight in Germany," *Outlook*, Dec. 29, 1915, 1039–41; Gino C. Speranza, "The Nations at War: Italia Redenta—The Redeemed Provinces Under the Civil Administration of Their Italian Conquerors," *Outlook*, Feb. 23, 1916, 471–75; and Joseph H. Odell, "Mott, Men, and Millions," *Outlook*, Jul. 31, 1918, 520–21.

18. Steven H. Jaffe, *New York at War: Four Centuries of Combat, Fear, and Intrigue in Gotham* (New York: Basic Books, 2012), 181; "Civilized Warfare and Neutral Nations," *Outlook*, Dec. 30, 1914, 975–76.

19. For Abbott's Anglophilia, see "An Old Friendship Renewed," *Outlook*, May 2, 1917, 10.

20. "Christianity and War," *Outlook*, Jan. 13, 1915, 61–63.

21. "The Lusitania Massacre," *Outlook*, May 19, 1915, 103–4. Although his public utterances did not reflect it, Abbott acknowledged in private that the Germans could make a case that sinking the *Lusitania* did not violate international law. See LA to Ernest Abbott, May 19, 1915, box 9, folder 10, Abbott Memorial Collection, George J. Mitchell Department of Special Collections & Archives, Bowdoin College Library [hereafter AMC].

22. "Interview on WWI, c. 1916," box 29, folder 16, AMC.

23. "How the Message Was Received," *Outlook*, Feb. 14, 1917, 258.

24. Barry Hankins, *Woodrow Wilson: Ruling Elder, Spiritual President* (Oxford: Oxford University Press, 2016), vii; Cara Lea Burnidge, *A Peaceful Conquest: Woodrow Wilson, Religion, and the New World Order* (Chicago: University of Chicago Press, 2016); Malcolm D. Magee, *What the World Should Be: Woodrow Wilson and the Crafting of a Faith-Based Foreign Policy* (Waco, TX: Baylor University Press, 2008).

25. Hankins, *Woodrow Wilson*, 143–45; William G. McLoughlin, *Billy Sunday Was His Real Name* (Chicago: University of Chicago Press, 1955), 255–57; for antiwar advocates in general, see Michael Kazin, *War Against War: The American Fight for Peace, 1914–1918* (New York: Simon & Schuster, 2017).

26. LA to TR, Oct. 28, 1918, Reel 298, Roosevelt Papers, LOC.

27. Abbott, *Twentieth Century Crusade*, 79–80.

28. Abbott, *Twentieth Century Crusade*, 90. The "Predatory Potsdam Gang" phrase was Henry Van Dyke's. See Van Dyke, *Fighting for Peace* (New York: Charles Scribner's Sons, 1917), 8.

29. "Luther's Quadricentennial," *Outlook*, Oct. 3, 1917, 162.

30. "The President's Message," *Outlook*, Apr. 16, 1898, 953.

31. "Bearers of the Message of Christmas," *Outlook*, Dec. 19, 1917, 635.

32. "Bearers of the Message," 635–36.

33. "Bearers of the Message," 636.

34. Lyman Abbott, "The Great Sacrifice," *Outlook*, Aug. 8, 1917, 540.

35. "Easter," *Outlook*, Mar. 27, 1918, 476–77. The phrase is an adaptation of John 11:16.

36. Ebel, *Faith in the Fight*, 95.

37. Abbott, *Twentieth Century Crusade*, 106–107. For the prevalence of this view, see Ebel, *Faith in the Fight*, 95–104.

38. "Salvation by Khaki," *Western Recorder* (Louisville, KY), Mar. 14, 1918.

39. Abbott, *Twentieth Century Crusade*, 104–7.

40. Abbott, *Twentieth Century Crusade*, v–viii.

41. Lyman Abbott, "Knoll Papers: To X.Y.Z.," *Outlook*, Dec. 5, 1917, 554. For another use of the Hebrews 9:22 imagery, see Abbott, *Twentieth Century Crusade*, 60.

42. Abbott, *Twentieth Century Crusade*, ix.

43. Abbott, *Twentieth Century Crusade*, ix.

44. Suggested by Gamble, *The War for Righteousness*, 177.

45. Philip Jenkins, *The Great and Holy War: How World War I Became a Religious Crusade* (New York: HarperOne, 2014), 5–9.

46. Jonathan H. Ebel, "From Covenant to Crusade and Back: American Christianity and the Late Great War," in *From Jeremiad to Jihad: Religion, Violence, and America,*

ed. John D. Carlson and Jonathan H. Ebel (Berkeley: University of California Press, 2012), 62–77. Ebel's statement concerning the American Legion also applies, with some variation, to Abbott: "The Legion subsequently succeeded in cultivating a civil religion that embraced the symbols, texts, and saints of American history, preached the gospel of one-hundred-percent Americanism, and worked to turn the nation away from a sovereign God. In short, the Legion succeeded in making Yahweh a vassal to the sovereign America." Ebel, "From Covenant to Crusade," 75–76.

47. Harold Bell Wright, "The Sword of Jesus," *American Magazine* 85 (Feb. 1918): 56, 57.

48. Albert C. Dieffenbach, "Christ the Combatant," *Christian Register*, Aug. 15, 1918, 775. Because he had such an obviously Germanic surname, perhaps Dieffenbach felt pressure to make his loyalties clear.

49. John Elliott Wishart, "The Christian Attitude toward War," *Bibliotheca Sacra* 75 (April 1918): 194.

50. Wishart, "Christian Attitude," 189.

51. Harry Emerson Fosdick, *The Challenge of the Present Crisis* (New York: Association Press, 1918), 98–99. The phrase "hard bestead" means something like "hard pressed."

52. Harry Emerson Fosdick, "The Trenches and the Church at Home," *Atlantic Monthly* 123 (Jan. 1919): 22.

53. Fosdick, "the Trenches," 26.

54. Ebel, "'The Wreckage and All the Glory,'" 23.

55. "The War Against Popular Rights," *Outlook*, Aug. 15, 1914, 891.

56. The *Outlook* generally focused its fire on Germany rather than Austria-Hungary, the Ottoman Empire, and Bulgaria, although it did advocate declaring war against Austria-Hungary in November 1917 and Turkey in July 1918. See "Declare War on Austria!" *Outlook*, Nov. 14, 1917, 408–9; and "Declare War on Turkey," *Outlook*, Jul. 3, 1918, 378; cf. "Why Not Declare War on Turkey?" *Outlook*, Jul. 10, 1918, 410. The United States declared war against Austria-Hungary in December 1917 but technically remained at peace with the other two Central Powers through the duration of the conflict.

57. On Jastrow, see William Stewart, *A Biographical Dictionary of Psychologists, Psychiatrists and Psychotherapists* (Jefferson, NC: McFarland, 2008), 161.

58. Joseph Jastrow, "Mania Teutonica: A Psychological Study of the War," *Outlook*, Jan. 9, 1918, 58–60; see also Jastrow, "Why the Germans Have Deemed Themselves Superior," *Outlook*, Nov. 20, 1918, 455–58.

59. "A Just Peace," *Outlook*, Sep. 11, 1918, 45.

60. Lyman Abbott, "To Love Is to Hate," *Outlook*, May 15, 1918, 99–100.

61. "Should We Pray for the Kaiser?" *Outlook*, Jul. 17, 1918, 446. Luke 12:10 reads, "And whosoever shall speak a word against the Son of man, it shall be forgiven him: but unto him that blasphemeth against the Holy Ghost it shall not be forgiven." The editorial referenced "blasphemy against the spirit of holiness," almost certainly a garbled translation, which accounts for the application of this text.

62. "Reprisals," *Outlook*, Jun. 12, 1918, 249–50, quotations from 250. See also, "The Moral and Legal Right of Reprisal," *Outlook*, Jul. 31, 1918, 512–13.

63. "No Peace with a Hohenzollernized Germany," *Outlook*, Aug. 15, 1917, 575–76.

64. Pamela Victor Pike, "Should Germany be Abolished?" *Outlook*, Aug. 21, 1918, 639.

65. Forest Crissey, "Newell Dwight Hillis," *Outlook*, Feb. 4, 1899, 270.

66. "Dinner to Rev. Lyman Abbott D.D. and Rev. Newell Dwight Hillis D.D. by the Men of Plymouth Church Germania Club, Nov. 2, 1899," box 29, folder 15, AMC.

67. Gifford N. Gaurel [?] to the Earl of Lytton, Jul. 23, 1918, box 1, folder 7, Newell Dwight Hillis Papers, 1985.004; Brooklyn Historical Society [hereafter Hillis Papers].

68. TR to Newell Dwight Hillis [hereafter NDH], Jun. 29, 1917, box 1, folder 3, Hillis Papers; TR to Whom It May Concern, Jun. 28, 1917, box 1, folder 3, Hillis Papers; TR to NDH, Sep. 13, 1917, box 1, folder 4, Hillis Papers.

69. Gamble, *War for Righteousness*, 161–62; "Dr. Hillis Attacks Britain's Enemies," *New York Times*, Sep. 24, 1917, 13.

70. Oscar A. Price to NDH, Nov. 8, 1917, box 1, folder 4, Hillis Papers. Price was the director of the Publicity Bureau, in charge of promoting the Liberty Loan.

71. NDH to Andrew MacPhail, Apr. 18, 1918, box 1, folder 5, Hillis Papers. Historian Philip Jenkins notes that most of the atrocity accounts were "bogus." Jenkins, *Great and Holy War*, 35.

72. Newell Dwight Hillis, *The Blot on the Kaiser's 'Scutcheon* (New York: Fleming H. Revel, 1918).

73. Hillis, *Blot*, 57.

74. Hillis, *Blot*, 59.

75. Hillis, *Blot*, 59.

76. The Pastor of a City Congregation, "German Propaganda in the Church," *Outlook*, Jan. 30, 1918, 180–81.

77. Abbott, *Twentieth Century Crusade*, 90. The Genesis text states, "And I will put enmity between thee and the woman, and between thy seed and her seed; it shall bruise thy head, and thou shalt bruise his heal."

78. "Justice to Germany," *Outlook*, Oct. 23, 1918, 284. The Jewish high priest Caiaphas played a leading role in capturing and executing Jesus. See, for example, Matthew 26:2–4.

79. "In Hoc Signo Vinces," *Outlook*, Apr. 10, 1918, 574.

80. Volume 1, numbers 65 and 34, in The Congregationalists and the War surveys, 1917–19, RG5026, the Congregational Library & Archives, Boston, MA.

81. Perry Bush, "Mennonites and the Great War," in *American Churches and the First World War*, ed. Gordon L. Heath (Eugene, OR: Pickwick, 2016), 87–106; and Robynne Rogers Healy, "Quakers and World War One: Negotiating Individual Conscience and the Peace Testimony," in *American Churches and the First World War*, 107–28.

82. Charles E. Jefferson, *Christianity and International Peace: Six Lectures at Grinnell College, Grinnell, Iowa, in February 1915, on the George A. Gates Memorial Foundation* (New York: Thomas Y. Crowell, 1915), 37; John Haynes Holmes, *New Wars for Old: Being a Statement of Radical Pacifism in Terms of Force versus Non-Resistance, with Special Reference to the Problems and Facts of the Great War* (New York: Dodd, Mead and Company, 1916), viii.

83. Christopher H. Evans, *The Kingdom Is Always but Coming: A Life of Walter Rauschenbusch* (Grand Rapids, MI: Eerdmans, 2004), 305. As the war progressed he

expressed more condemnation of Germany, but it was not entirely clear whether he actually approved of America's role in the conflict. Evans, *The Kingdom Is Always but Coming*, 308–10.

84. James P. Byrd, *Sacred Scripture, Sacred War: The Bible and the American Revolution* (New York: Oxford University Press, 2013), 76–77, 81–82.

85. "The Curse of Meroz," *Outlook*, Feb. 14, 1917, 264.

86. Lyman Abbott, "The Duty of Christ's Church Today," *Outlook*, May 2, 1917, 14.

87. "The Latest Manifestation of Prussianism," *Outlook*, Jun. 5, 1918, 216.

88. George D. Beattys, "Letters to the Editor: 'When Will the Christ Be Born?'" *Christian Advocate*, Jan. 3, 1918, 19.

89. Shailer Mathews, *Patriotism and Religion* (New York: Macmillan, 1918), 16.

90. Mathews, *Patriotism and Religion*, 16–17. Sennacherib was an Assyrian king who threatened Israel.

91. Quoted in McLoughlin, *Billy Sunday Was His Real Name*, 258, 260; quoted in George Marsden, *Fundamentalism and American Culture*, 2nd ed. (New York: Oxford University Press, 2006), 142.

92. Gamble, *War for Righteousness*, 3; Gamble, "Together for the Gospel of Americanism: Evangelicals and the First World War," in *American Churches and the First World War*, 15–31.

93. Lyman Abbott, "Knoll Papers: Christ's League to Enforce Peace," *Outlook*, Sep. 26, 1917, 122–23.

94. The text reads: "And he came to Nazareth, where he had been brought up: and, as his custom was, he went into the synagogue on the sabbath day, and stood up for to read. And there was delivered unto him the book of the prophet Esaias. And when he had opened the book, he found the place where it is written, 'The Spirit of the Lord is upon me, because he hath anointed me to preach the gospel to the poor; he hath sent me to heal the brokenhearted, to preach deliverance to the captives, and recovering of sight to the blind, to set at liberty them that are bruised, to preach the acceptable year of the Lord.' And he closed the book, and he gave it again to the minister, and sat down. And the eyes of all them that were in the synagogue were fastened on him. And he began to say unto them, 'This day is this scripture fulfilled in your ears.'"

95. Abbott, *Twentieth Century Crusade*, 44–45.

96. "Bondholders of Democracy," *Outlook*, Jun. 6, 1917, 209.

97. "Reflections," 36–37, Sep. 29, 1918, box 25, folder 8, AMC. It is unclear whether he ever preached this sermon; regardless, it shows his thought.

98. Lyman Abbott, "The Call of the Nation," *Outlook*, Aug. 1, 1917, 505.

99. Abbott, *Twentieth Century Crusade*, 86–87.

100. Abbott, *Twentieth Century Crusade*, 87.

101. Mathews, *Patriotism and Religion*, 32–33.

102. Beattys, "Letters to the Editor," 19.

103. Fosdick, "The Trenches and the Church at Home," 27.

104. Quoted in Abrams, *Preachers Present Arms*, 86.

105. LA to Lord Aberdeen, Aug. 13, 1915, AMC.

106. Newspaper clipping located in box 28, folder 16, AMC.

107. LA to Lord Aberdeen, Aug. 13, 1915, AMC.

108. Clifford Putney, *Muscular Christianity: Manhood and Sports in Protestant America, 1880–1920* (Cambridge, MA: Harvard University Press, 2001), 179–181; on Scudder, T.J. Jackson Lears, *No Place of Grace: Antimodernism and the Transformation of American Culture* (1981; Chicago: University of Chicago Press, 1994), 214.

109. Darrel E. Bigham, "American Christian Thinkers and the Function of War, 1861–1920," (PhD diss., University of Kansas, 1970), 3–4, 303; Ann Douglas, *The Feminization of American Culture* (New York: Knopf, 1977), 42–43.

110. Ebel, "'The Wreckage and All the Glory,'" 14–21; cf. Lyman Abbott, "Lenten Lessons—IV," *Outlook*, Mar. 26, 1919, 512–14.

111. Gerald Sittser, *A Cautious Patriotism: The American Churches & the Second World War* (Chapel Hill: University of North Carolina Press, 1997).

112. Ira V. Brown, *Lyman Abbott, Christian Evolutionist: A Study in Religious Liberalism* (Cambridge, MA: Harvard University Press, 1953), 227.

113. Lyman Abbott, "Not Peace but Justice," *Outlook*, Apr. 26, 1922, 683.

6. "There Will Be a Day of Reckoning for Our Country"

1. Eric W. Gritsch, *A History of Lutheranism*, 2nd ed. (Minneapolis: Fortress Press, 2010), 197–98. Some of the Americanizing influences included an emphasis on revivalism, insistence on Sabbath observance, a preference for the English language, and other marks of antebellum evangelicalism. See Gritsch, *A History of Lutheranism*, 193.

2. Frederick C. Luebke, *Bonds of Loyalty: German-Americans and World War I* (DeKalb: Northern Illinois University Press, 1974), 37–38.

3. Th.[eodore] Graebner, comp., *A Testimony and Proof: Bearing on the Relation of the American Church to the German Emperor* (St. Louis: Concordia Publishing House, 1918), 7. Around four and a half million German immigrants had come to the United States between 1845 and 1895. See Alan Graebner, "The Acculturation of an Immigrant Lutheran Church: the Lutheran Church-Missouri Synod, 1917–1929" (PhD diss., Columbia University, 1965), 11.

4. Wayne Wilke, "Changing Understanding of the Church-State Relationship: The Lutheran Church-Missouri Synod, 1914–1969" (PhD diss., University of Michigan, 1990), 88–89; Mark Granquist, "American Lutherans and the First World War," in *American Churches and the First World War*, ed. Gordon L. Heath (Eugene, OR: Pickwick, 2016), 53–54.

5. A. Graebner, "The Acculturation of an Immigrant Lutheran Church," 145.

6. A. Graebner, "The Acculturation of an Immigrant Lutheran Church," 10.

7. s.v. "Fuerbringer, Ludwig Ern(e)st; Graebner, Theodore Conrad; Sommer, Martin Samuel," *Christian Cyclopedia*, the Lutheran Church Missouri Synod, http://cyclopedia.lcms.org/.

8. Carl S. Meyer, *A Brief Historical Sketch of the Lutheran Church-Missouri Synod*, rev. ed. (St. Louis: Concordia, 1970), 19.

9. L. DeAne Lagerquist, *The Lutherans* (Westport, CT: Greenwood Press, 1999), xiii; Tim Grundmeier, "The Problem of American Lutheran Histor(iograph)y," *Religion in American History* (blog), Mar. 20, 2015, http://usreligion.blogspot.com/2015/03/the-problem-of-american-lutheran.html#more. Similarly, Mark Noll observed in 2003 that "there is no truly great monograph" on American Lutheran history. See Noll, "Ameri-

can Lutherans Yesterday and Today," in *Lutherans Today: American Lutheran Identity in the Twenty-First Century*, ed. Richard Cimino (Grand Rapids, MI: Eerdmans, 2003) 19.

10. Wilke, "Changing Understanding of the Church-State Relationship," 39–97.

11. Frederick Nohl, "The Lutheran Church-Missouri Synod Reacts to United States Anti-Germanism During World War I," *Concordia Historical Institute Quarterly* 35 (July 1962): 49–66; A. Graebner, "The Acculturation of an Immigrant Lutheran Church," 6–110; Neil M. Johnson, "The Patriotism and Anti-Prussianism of the Lutheran Church-Missouri Synod, 1914–1918," *Concordia Historical Institute Quarterly* 39 (Oct. 1966): 99–118; E. Clifford Nelson, ed., *The Lutherans in North America*, rev. ed. (Philadelphia: Fortress Press, 1980), 396–405; Lagerquist, *The Lutherans*, 118–19. Much the same picture is given in the most recent treatment of the subject: Mark Granquist, *Lutherans in America: A New History* (Minneapolis: Fortress Press, 2015), 224–27. For a mostly parallel case, see Stephen Gurgel, "The War to End All Germans: Wisconsin Synod Lutherans and the First World War" (MA thesis, University of Wisconsin-Milwaukee, 2012).

12. Ray H. Abrams, *Preachers Present Arms* (New York: Round Table Press, 1933).

13. John F. Piper, Jr.., *The American Churches in World War I* (Athens: University of Ohio Press, 1985), 12, 116. Including Lutheran opinion in this study would actually have buttressed his argument that Abrams overestimated the strength of the extreme prowar clergy.

14. Richard M. Gamble, *The War for Righteousness: Progressive Christianity, the Great War, and the Rise of the Messianic Nation* (Wilmington, DE: ISI Books, 2003).

15. Andrew Preston, *Sword of the Spirit, Shield of Faith: Religion in American War and Diplomacy* (New York: Knopf, 2011), 233–74; Philip Jenkins, *The Great and Holy War: How World War I Became a Religious Crusade* (New York: HarperOne, 2014), 92–96; Martin Greschat, *Der Erste Weltkrieg und die Christenheit: Ein globaler Überblick* (Stuttgart: Verlag W. Kohlhammer, 2014), 92–104.

16. David Kennedy, *Over Here: The First World War and American Society* (New York: Oxford University Press, 1982).

17. David W. Detjen, *The Germans in Missouri, 1900–1918: Prohibition, Neutrality, and Assimilation* (Columbia: University of Missouri Press, 1985), 99, 151; Christopher C. Gibbs, *The Great Silent Majority: Missouri's Resistance to World War I* (Columbia: University of Missouri Press, 1988). Gibbs's work concentrates on consistent opponents of the conflict, but Lutheran nervousness about the possibility of war prior to April 1917 makes their story relevant.

18. Petra DeWitt, *Degrees of Allegiance: Harassment and Loyalty in Missouri's German-American Community during World War I* (Athens: Ohio University Press, 2012), 22–24, 31, 43, 79–80, 163, 165.

19. On these sorts of efforts, see Gaines M. Foster, *Moral Reconstruction: Christian Lobbyists and the Federal Legislation of Morality, 1865–1920* (Chapel Hill: University of North Carolina Press, 2002).

20. Mary Jane Haemig, "The Confessional Basis of Lutheran Thinking on Church-State Issues," in *Church & State: Lutheran Perspectives*, ed. John R. Stumme and Robert W. Tuttle (Minneapolis: Fortress Press, 2003), 8–11. See also C.C. Morhart, "Should Churches Engage in Politics?" *Lutheran Witness*, Jan. 12, 1915, 5–6.

21. Louis Buchheimer, *Christian Warfare: Sermons* (St. Louis: Rudolph Volkening, 1918), 62, 64.

22. L. Feurbringer, "Serious Times," *Der Lutheraner*, Apr. 23, 1918, 142. The paper printed this editorial in English as well as German "for the sake of publicity."

23. "Gottes Wort und Luthers Lehre vergehet nun und nimmermehr." German translations in this chapter are my own, with assistance from Philipp Gollner.

24. G., "President Wilson," *Lutheran Witness*, Nov. 16, 1915, 360–61.

25. "Two-kingdoms" theology and the American separation of church and state are related but not identical concepts. For a helpful explanation of the distinction, see Haemig, "The Confessional Basis," 9.

26. G., "But What of These Words of the Manhattan Club Address," *Lutheran Witness*, Nov. 16, 1915, 361–62.

27. S., "The War," *Lutheran Witness*, Aug. 25, 1914, 138.

28. S., "War's Arithmetic," *Lutheran Witness*, Sep. 8, 1914, 145–46.

29. L.F. "Zur Kirklichen Chronik," May 21, 1918, 178. "Wir haben freilich solche Heimsuchung wohl verdient mit unsern vielen und grossen Sünden; aber sie sind uns alle von Herzen leid und reuen uns sehr. Und weil du gnädig und barmherzig bist, geduldig und von grosser Güte und die Strafe dich bald reuet, so bitten wir dich, du wollest nich handeln mit uns nach unsern Sünden und uns nicht vergelten nach unserer Missetat."

30. G., "Moral Issues and Religious Aspects of the Great War: III. Shall We Go to War 'for Humanity?'" *Lutheran Witness*, May 2, 1916, 126.

31. Romans 13: 1–7, King James Version.

32. G., "Moral Issues and Religious Aspects of the Great War, III," 126.

33. G., "Moral Issues and Religious Aspects of the Great War, III," 128.

34. G., "Moral Issues and Religious Aspects of the Great War, III," 127.

35. Nelson, *The Lutherans in North America*, 399.

36. G., "Press Censorship and Religious Liberty," *Lutheran Witness*, June 12, 1917, 173–74.

37. C.M.Z., "Der 60 Psalm: Ein Lied für Krieg und Sieg," *Der Lutheraner*, Nov. 19, 1918, 386. "Aber wo ist jetzt ein politisches, das heisst, ein in einem Land zussamanwohnendes und unter ein und derselben Obrigkeit stehendes Volk, welches eine Verheissung Gottes hat und zum Panier aufwerfen kann in der Weise wie einst das Volk Israel? Wo ist jetzt ein solches Volk, das in Kriegsnot diesen Psalm beten und des Sieges gewiss sein kann? Nirgends. Denn kein solches Volk ist die Kirche Gottes, wenn auch die Kirche Gottes in seiner Mitte sich findet. Ist denn dieser Psalm jetzt nicht zu gebrauchen, wenn Krieg ist? O ja, aber in rechter und bescheidener Weise."

38. G., "Liberty Loan Sunday," *Lutheran Witness*, June 12, 1917, 182.

39. "The Church and the Government," *Lutheran Witness*, Sept. 18, 1917, 304. See also G., "Liberty Loan—Big Brother—Civic Sunday," *Lutheran Witness*, Nov. 13, 1917, 357–58. The Presbyterian article was originally published in the *Presbyterian of the South*, a publication of the conservative Presbyterian Church in the United States.

40. G., "The War-Time Pulpit," *Lutheran Witness*, Feb. 5, 1918, 42–43.

41. G., "The War-Time Pulpit," 42.

42. S., "Weak Rationalism," *Lutheran Witness*, Nov. 17, 1914, 186.

43. G., "Evolution and Atheism," *Lutheran Witness*, Aug. 8, 1916, 247. For a more favorable statement, see S., "Doctor Lyman Abbott," *Lutheran Witness*, May 4, 1915, 141.

44. S., "Praying for Our Enemies," *Lutheran Witness*, Oct. 15, 1918, 327–28.

45. S., "The Dead Soldier," *Lutheran Witness*, Oct. 15, 1918, 329.

46. "Christian Patriotism," *Lutheran Witness*, June 25, 1918, 198.

47. G., "The Greatest of All Wars: III," *Lutheran Witness*, July 27, 1915, 231. The same editorial acknowledged that Germany's invasion of Belgium violated international law. Although Graebner did not defend Germany on this point, he praised the German leadership for avoiding hypocritical, sanctimonious justifications for its actions.

48. G., "Moral Issues and Religious Aspects of the Great War: II. American Neutrality," *Lutheran Witness*, March 21, 1916, 82.

49. Luebke, *Bonds of Loyalty*, 105.

50. Robert N. Manley, "The Nebraska State Council of Defense: Loyalty Programs and Policies during World War I" (MA thesis, University of Nebraska, 1959), 148.

51. Quoted in A. Graebner, "The Acculturation of an Immigrant Lutheran Church," 74. "Ich hasse dieses Land, ich bin jetst 25 Jahre hier, aber ich hasse dieses Land."

52. Quoted in A. Graebner, "The Acculturation of an Immigrant Lutheran Church," 74.

53. S., "The Christian Soldier," *Lutheran Witness*, Aug. 10, 1915, 254.

54. G., "The Greatest of All Wars: IV," *Lutheran Witness*, Sep. 7, 1915, 278–82; quotation from 281.

55. G., "University Freedom—German and American," *Lutheran Witness*, Nov. 30, 1915, 375–76.

56. G., "Moral Issues and Religious Aspects of the Great War, I: Mr. Warstock's New Prosperity," *Lutheran Witness*, Feb. 22, 1916, 49, 50.

57. G., "American Ammunition Kills American Soldiers," *Lutheran Witness*, May 2, 1916, 136. The authors of *The Lutherans in North America* interpreted such passages as a departure from traditional LCMS "quietism." See Nelson, *Lutherans in North America*, 396.

58. S., "War," *Lutheran Witness*, May 1, 1917, 126.

59. "Our Duty as Our Boys Are Marching to War," *Lutheran Witness*, Nov. 27, 1917, 373.

60. C.M.Z., "Der 60 Psalm," 386. "Soll Gott da nicht zornig werden, nicht strafen, wenn die Masse des Volks sein Gnadenwort verachtet und mit Füssen tritt, wenn die Christen, die so veil Gnade haben, die Früchte nicht bringen, die Gott sucht?"

61. Buchheimer, *Christian Warfare*, 54–61. Quotations from 57, 58.

62. G, "The Greatest of All Wars, III," 231.

63. S., "What Ails America?" *Lutheran Witness*, Oct. 17, 1916, 320, 318.

64. He probably referred to liberal Protestant churches and Roman Catholics.

65. W.M. Czamanske, "Is the United States a Christian Nation?" *Lutheran Witness*, Nov. 16, 1915, 358.

66. R. Jesse, "The Epidemic," *Lutheran Witness*, Oct. 29, 1918, 340.

67. Charles Spencer Smith, *A History of the African Methodist Episcopal Church: Being A Volume Supplemental to* A History of the African Methodist Episcopal Church, *by Daniel Alexander Payne, D.D., LL.D., Late One of Its Bishops, Chronicling the Principal Events in the Advance of the African Methodist Episcopal Church from 1856 to 1922* (New York: Johnson Reprint Corporation, 1968), 310–11.

68. Adriane Lentz-Smith, *Freedom Struggles: African Americans and World War I* (Cambridge, MA: Harvard University Press, 2009), 38–41.

69. Michael Williams, *American Catholics in the War: National Catholic War Council, 1917–1921* (New York: Macmillan, 1921), 4; Patrick Carey, "The First World War and Catholics in the United States," in *American Churches and the First World War*, 32.

70. "War as a Divine Scourge," *Fortnightly Review* (St. Louis), May 15, 1917, 145–46.

71. "'Atrocity Mongering,'" *Fortnightly Review*, Feb. 1, 1917, 33; "Perversity and Patriotism," *Ave Maria*, July 27, 1918, 116–17.

72. "On Hating the Enemy," *Fortnightly Review*, Aug. 15, 1918, 243. See also "The Propagation of Hate," *Ave Maria*, Feb. 2, 1918, 149–50.

73. Theodore Roosevelt, *Fear God and Take Your Own Part* (New York: George H. Doran Company, 1916), 138.

74. Carl Wittke, *German-Americans and the World War (With Special Emphasis on Ohio's German-Language Press)* (Columbus: Ohio State Archaeological and Historical Society, 1936), 195.

75. "Mail Bag," *Lutheran Witness*, Oct. 29, 1918, 349. The pastor of the Ohio church believed that other factors also precipitated its destruction. Nohl, "The Lutheran Church-Missouri Synod Reacts to United States Anti-Germanism," 58n.41. See also Frederick C. Luebke, "Superpatriotism in World War I: The Experience of a Lutheran Pastor," *Concordia Historical Institute Quarterly* 41 (Feb. 1968): 3–11.

76. Nohl, "The Lutheran Church-Missouri Synod Reacts to United States Anti-Germanism," 57.

77. David Treuer, *The Heartbeat of Wounded Knee: Native America from 1890 to the Present* (New York: Penguin, 2019), 187–190.

78. Treuer, *Heartbeat of Wounded Knee*, 56–57. On the changing role of the state as a result of the war, see Christopher Capozzola, *Uncle Sam Wants You: World War I and the Making of the Modern American Citizen* (New York: Oxford University Press, 2008).

79. Luebke, *Bonds of Loyalty*, 312.

80. For an in-depth study, see Manley, "The Nebraska State Council of Defense."

81. G., "Waging War upon the German Language," *Lutheran Witness*, Apr. 30, 1918, 139.

82. G., "Being Clear on These points," *Lutheran Witness*, Apr. 30, 1918, 139.

83. G., "The War, Language, and the Church," *Lutheran Witness*, Sep. 4, 1918, 282–83.

84. E.P., "Zur Kirchlichen Chronik," *Der Lutheraner*, Jul. 30, 1918, 259–60.

85. S., "Exempted from Combat Service," *Lutheran Witness*, Apr. 30, 1918, 138.

86. "Pan-Germanism and Lutheranism," *Lutheran Witness*, Aug. 20, 1918, 261–63; quotation from 263.

87. S., "What Is Wrong with Germany?" *Lutheran Witness*, Oct. 1, 1918, 313.

88. "Light on the Lutheran Church in Germany," *Lutheran Witness*, Aug. 20, 1918, 260–61.

89. G., "The Kaiser's Conception of Christianity," *Lutheran Witness*, Oct. 15, 1918, 328.

90. "A War-Time Program for Our Young People," *Lutheran Witness*, Dec. 25, 1917, 403–5. The article did not explicitly say that the flags and hospitality events were to be present at church buildings, but this seems to be the implication unless the Walther Leagues had their own buildings.

91. G., "'Stop, Look, Listen!'" *Lutheran Witness*, Dec. 25, 1917, 406.

92. "Patriotic Activities of Our Churches," *Lutheran Witness*, Jan. 8, 1918, 3.

93. T. Graebner, *Testimony and Proof*, 8–9. About 165,000 Lutherans served in the war, of whom 30,000 were members of the Missouri Synod. Lutheran laity also raised about $560,000 to care for the spiritual needs of these soldiers. Figures from *Lutheran Witness*, Nov. 26, 1918, 369; Wittke, *German-Americans and the World War*, 142; and Alan Graebner, *Uncertain Saints: The Laity in the Lutheran Church-Missouri Synod, 1900–1970* (Westport, CT: Greenwood Press, 1975), 59.

94. "'Stop, Look, Listen!,'" 106; T. Graebner, *Testimony and Proof*, 32.

95. S., "War," 126.

96. S., "The Day of Prayer," *Lutheran Witness*, May 28, 1918, 168.

97. "Third Liberty Loan," *Lutheran Witness*, Apr. 16, 1918, 119–20; "The Fourth Liberty Loan," *Lutheran Witness*, Oct. 1, 1918, 311.

98. G., "The Reviewer," *Lutheran Witness*, Aug. 6, 1918, 254.

99. G., "Lutheran Loyalty," *Lutheran Witness*, Aug. 7, 1917, 240; Carl Kurth, "Synodical Conference Builds Hall for Soldier Boys at Army City, Kans.," *Lutheran Witness*, May 28, 1918, 120; O. Gruner, "Northern Illinois District Synod," *Lutheran Witness*, Jun. 25, 1918, 201. See also S., "War's Contrasts," *Lutheran Witness*, Oct. 29, 1918, 348.

100. "Following the Flag a Holy Act," *American Lutheran* 1:6 (Jun. 1918): 4.

101. "Untitled," *American Lutheran* 1 (Jun. 1918): 14–15.

102. H.P. Eckhardt, "Service of Remembrance and Prayer," *American Lutheran* 1:11 (Nov. 1918): 5–6.

103. Arthur J. Hall, "Fundamental Factors in World Peace," *Lutheran Quarterly*, 49 (Jan. 1919): 62; G., "The Greatest of All Wars: II," *Lutheran Witness*, Jun. 1, 1915, 167.

104. Only after 1925 were fewer than half of LCMS sermons delivered in German. See Nelson, *Lutherans in North America*, 424.

105. G., "Church, State, and Reconstruction," *Lutheran Witness*, Dec. 24, 1918, 409.

106. Everette Meier and Herbert T. Mayer, "The Process of Americanization," in *Moving Frontiers: Readings in the History of the Lutheran Church-Missouri Synod*, ed. Carl S. Meyer (St. Louis: Concordia Publishing House, 1964), 344.

107. For a related point, see William R. Hutchison, "Preface: From Protestant to Pluralist America," in *Between the Times: The Travail of the Protestant Establishment in America, 1900–1960*, ed. William R. Hutchison (New York: Cambridge University Press, 1989), xii–xiii.

Conclusion

1. Susan Currell, *American Culture in the 1920s* (Edinburgh: Edinburgh University Press, 2009), 1–33.

2. Ezra Pound, "Hugh Selwyn Mauberley," in *Ezra Pound: New Selected Poems and Translations*, ed. Richard Sieburth (New York: New Directions, 2010), 113.

3. William G. McLoughlin, *Billy Sunday Was His Real Name* (Chicago: University of Chicago Press, 1955), 260.

4. Harry Emerson Fosdick, "What the War Did to My Mind," *Christian Century*, Jan. 5, 1928, 11.

5. Elesha Coffman, *The Christian Century and the Rise of the Protestant Mainline* (New York: Oxford University Press, 2013), 82.

6. Reinhold Niebuhr, "What the War Did to My Mind," *Christian Century*, Sep. 27, 1928, 1162.

7. Gary J. Dorrien, *Economy, Difference, Empire: Social Ethics for Social Justice* (New York: Columbia University Press, 2010), 29–30.

8. Coffman, *The* Christian Century, 136–37.

9. Steven Casey, *A Cautious Crusade: Franklin D. Roosevelt, American Public Opinion, and the War Against Nazi Germany* (New York: Oxford University Press, 2001), xxvi; Gerald Sittser, *A Cautious Patriotism: American Churches & the Second World War* (Chapel Hill: University of North Carolina Press, 1997).

10. W. Edward Orser, "World War II and the Pacifist Controversy in the Major Protestant Churches," *American Studies* 14 (Fall 1973): 5–10. For a similar assessment to mine of religion and World War II, see Matthew McCullough, *The Cross of War: Christian Nationalism and U.S. Expansion in the Spanish-American War* (Madison: University of Wisconsin Press, 2014), 140.

11. Council of Bishops, "The Church in Crisis," *Christian Advocate*, Jan. 1, 1942, 6.

12. Sittser, *A Cautious Patriotism*, 3–4, quotation from 3.

13. Council of Bishops, "Church in Crisis," 7.

14. Harry Emerson Fosdick, *Living under Tension: Sermons on Christianity Today* (New York: Harper & Brothers, 1941), vii–viii.

15. Fosdick, *Living under Tension*, vii.

16. Will Herberg, *Protestant, Catholic, Jew: An Essay in American Religious Sociology* (Garden City, NY: Doubleday, 1955). See also Kevin Shultz, *Tri-Faith America: How Catholics and Jews Held Postwar America to Its Protestant Promise* (New York: Oxford University Press, 2011).

17. George M. Marsden, *The Twilight of the American Enlightenment: The 1950s and the Crisis of Liberal Belief* (New York: Basic Books, 2014); David A. Hollinger, *After Cloven Tongues of Fire: Protestant Liberalism in Modern American History* (Princeton, NJ: Princeton University Press, 2013), ix, 18–55; Daniel T. Rodgers, *Age of Fracture* (Cambridge, MA: Harvard University Press, 2011); Hugh McLeod, *The Religious Crisis of the 1960s* (Oxford: Oxford University Press, 2007).

18. E. Brooks Holifield, *God's Ambassadors: A History of the Christian Clergy in America* (Grand Rapids, MI: Eerdmans, 2007), 235–74.

19. Robert Wuthnow, *The Restructuring of American Religion: Society and Faith since World War II* (Princeton, NJ: Princeton University Press, 1988), 71–240; James Davison Hunter, *Culture Wars: The Struggle to Define America* (New York: Basic Books, 1991).

20. Hollinger, *After Cloven Tongues of Fire*, 70–76.

21. On Vietnam, see Holifield, *God's Ambassadors*, 261–62; Mitchell K. Hall, *Because of Their Faith: CALCAV and Religious Opposition to the Vietnam War* (New York: Columbia University Press, 1990); and Charles DeBenedetti with Charles Chatfield, *An American Ordeal: The Antiwar Movement of the Vietnam Era* (Syracuse, NY: Syracuse University Press 1990), 144–45. On Iraq, see Jerry Hames, "Bishops Oppose Iraq War," Episcopal Life, http://arc.episcopalchurch.org/episcopal-life/HOB11'02.html; "United Methodist Council of Bishops Resolution on the Iraq War," United Methodist Church, http://www.umc.org/who-we-are/united-methodist-council-of-bishops-resolution-on-the-iraq-war; and "A Pastoral Letter on the Iraq War From the Collegium of Officers of the United Church of Christ," United Church of Christ, http://www.ucc.org/a-pastoral-letter-on-the-iraq.

22. Warren Goldstein, *William Sloane Coffin, Jr.: A Holy Impatience* (New Haven, CT: Yale University Press, 2004), 145–224.

23. "A Pastoral Letter on the Iraq War," http://www.ucc.org/a-pastoral-letter -on-the-iraq, paragraph 2.

24. David Treuer, *The Heartbeat of Wounded Knee: Native America from 1890 to the Present* (New York: Penguin, 2019), 296 327, 432–37.

25. Jan Nunley, "Closely Tied for Centuries: Museum Shows Mixed Historical Legacy of Church-Native Relations," The Episcopal Church, Nov. 30, 2004, https:// episcopalchurch.org/library/article/closely-tied-centuries; Steven Martin, "NCC and Creation Justice Ministries Applaud Developments at Standing Rock," National Council of Churches of the Churches of Christ in the USA, Dec. 4, 2016, https://national councilofchurches.us/ncc-and-creation-justice-ministries-applaud-developments-at -standing-rock/.

26. John C. Pinheiro, *Missionaries of Republicanism: A Religious History of the Mexican-American War* (New York: Oxford University Press, 2014), 128–48; for other opposition to the conflict, see Amy S. Greenberg, *A Wicked War: Polk, Clay, Lincoln, and the 1846 U.S. Invasion of Mexico* (New York: Knopf, 2012).

27. Pinheiro, *Missionaries of Republicanism*, 132.

28. Pinheiro, *Missionaries of Republicanism*, 130.

29. Pinheiro, *Missionaries of Republicanism*, 145–46.

30. Sydney E. Ahlstrom, *A Religious History of the American People* (New Haven, CT: Yale University Press, 1972), 880.

31. This statement should not be taken as an overall endorsement of Turner's thesis. See John Mack Faragher, ed., *Rereading Frederick Jackson Turner: "The Significance of the Frontier in American History" and Other Essays* (New Haven, CT: Yale University Press, 1998), 1–10.

32. Darren Dochuk, *From Bible Belt to Sunbelt: Plain-Folk Religion, Grassroots Politics, and the Rise of Evangelical Conservatism* (New York: Norton, 2011).

Bibliography

Primary Sources

Manuscript Collections

Brooklyn Historical Society, Brooklyn, NY.
    Plymouth Church of the Pilgrims & Henry Ward Beecher Collection.
    Newell Dwight Hillis Papers.
Congregational Library & Archives, Boston, MA.
    The Congregationalists and the War Surveys, 1917–19.
Library of Congress, Washington, D.C.
    Theodore Roosevelt Papers, Microfilm.
George J. Mitchell Department of Special Collections & Archives, Bowdoin College
    Library, Brunswick, ME.
        Abbott Memorial Collection.
New-York Historical Society, New York, NY.
    Pamphlet Collection.
University of Notre Dame Archives, Notre Dame, IN.
    Daniel Hudson Papers.

News and Editorial Comment from Newspapers and Periodicals

    American Lutheran (New York)
    Ave Maria (Notre Dame, IN)
    Bibliotheca Sacra (Oberlin, OH)
    Boston Daily Globe (Boston)
    Catholic Mirror (Baltimore)
    Catholic Record (Indianapolis)
    Catholic World (New York)
    Chicago Tribune (Chicago)
    Christian Advocate (New York)
    Christian Recorder (Philadelphia)
    Christian Register (Boston)
    La Civiltá Cattolica (Rome)
    The Globe (Philadelphia)
    Independent (New York)
    Katholische Rundschau (San Antonio, TX)
    Lutheran Witness (St. Louis)
    Der Lutheraner (St. Louis)

Monitor (San Francisco)
The Nation (New York)
New-York Freeman's Journal and Catholic Register (New York)
New York Times (New York)
North American Review (Boston)
Northwestern Chronicle (Minneapolis-St. Paul)
Outlook (New York)
Pilot (Boston)
Review / Fortnightly Review (St. Louis)
Weekly Wabash Express (Terre Haute, IN)
Western Recorder (Louisville, KY)

Primary Sources with Listed Authors

A.F. "The National Fast and the Negro." *Christian Recorder*, Oct. 12, 1861, 158.
A.K. "A Gloomy View." *Review*, May 5, 1898, 7.
Abbott, Lyman. "The Call of the Nation." *Outlook*, Aug. 1, 1917, 504–5.
——. "The Crisis—Its Cause and Cure." *Terre Haute Express*, Dec. 19, 1860, 1.
——. "The Duty and Destiny of America." *Plymouth Morning Pulpit*, Jun. 15, 1898, 1–20.
——. "The Duty of Christ's Church Today." *Outlook*, May 2, 1917, 13–15.
——. "The Great Sacrifice." *Outlook*, Aug. 8, 1917, 540.
——. *Henry Ward Beecher*. Boston: Houghton Mifflin, 1903.
——. *An Illustrated Commentary on the Gospel According to Matthew: For Family Use and Reference, and for the Great Body of Christian Workers in All Denominations*. 2 vols. New York: A.S. Barnes, 1875–78.
——. "Knoll Papers: Christ's League to Enforce Peace." *Outlook*, Sep. 26, 1917, 122–23.
——. "Knoll Papers: To X.Y.Z." *Outlook*, Dec. 5, 1917, 554.
——. "Lenten Lessons—IV." *Outlook*, Mar. 26, 1919, 512–14.
——. *The Life That Really Is*. New York: Wilbur B. Ketcham, 1899.
——. "To Love Is to Hate." *Outlook*, May 15, 1918, 99–100.
——. "The Meaning of the War." *Plymouth Morning Pulpit*, May 31, 1898, 1–14.
——. "The Ministry for the South." *The Home Missionary* 38 (Nov. 1865): 157–63.
——. "The New Puritanism." 23–74. In *The New Puritanism*, ed. Lyman Abbott. New York: Fords, Howard, and Hulbert, 1898.
——. "Not Peace but Justice." *Outlook*, Apr. 26, 1922, 683–84.
——. *Reminiscences*. Boston: Houghton Mifflin, 1915.
——. "Southern Evangelization." *New Englander* 24 (Oct. 1864): 699–708.
——. *The Twentieth Century Crusade*. New York: Macmillan, 1918.
The American Annual Cyclopedia and Register of Important Events, of the Year 1866: Embracing Political, Civil, Military, and Social Affairs; Public Documents; Biography, Statistics, Commerce, Finance, Literature, Science, Agriculture, and Mechanical Industry. Vol. 6. New York: D. Appleton, 1869.
Angell, George T. "Newspaper Lies about the War." *Review*, Jul. 28, 1898, 6.
Armstrong, LeRoy. *Pictorial Atlas Illustrating the Spanish-American War: Comprising a History of the Great Conflict of the United States with Spain*. n.p.: Souvenir Publishing Co., 1899.

Bainbridge, Lucy S. "Personal Memories of Lincoln: II—Three Pictures of Abraham Lincoln." *Outlook*, Feb. 13, 1918, 244.

Beattys, George D. "Letters to the Editor: 'When Will the Christ Be Born?'" *Christian Advocate*, Jan. 3, 1918, 19–20.

Beecher, Henry Ward. "Abraham Lincoln." In *Lectures and Orations by Henry Ward Beecher*, ed. Newell Dwight Hillis, 263–83. New York: Fleming H. Revell, 1913.

——. "Address at the Raising of the Union Flag over Fort Sumter." In *Patriotic Addresses in America and England, from 1850–1885, on Slavery, the Civil War, and the Development of Civil Liberty in the United States*, ed. John R. Howard, 676–697. New York: Fords, Howard, and Hulbert, 1887.

——. *Freedom and War: Discourses on Topics Suggested by the Times*. Freeport, NY: Books for Libraries Press, [1863] 1971.

Bonhoeffer, Dietrich. *No Rusty Swords: Letters, Lectures and Notes, 1928–1936 from the Collected Works of Dietrich Bonhoeffer*, ed. Edwin H. Robertson, trans. Edwin H. Roberston and John Bowden. Vol 1. London: Collins, 1965.

Britt, J. Gabriel. "Hypocrisy Versus Truth." *Globe* 32 (Dec. 1898): 423–27.

Brock, John C. "For the Christian Recorder: The Death of the President." *Christian Recorder*, May 6, 1865, 69.

——. "For the Christian Recorder: Soldier's Letter." *Christian Recorder*, Jun. 25, 1864, 101.

Buchheimer, Louis. *Christian Warfare: Sermons*. St. Louis: Rudolph Volkening, 1918.

Bullard, Arthur. "The Neutral Nations of Europe." *Outlook*, Mar. 10, 1915, 583–86.

Bushnell, Horace. "Our Obligations to the Dead." In *God's New Israel: Religious Interpretations of American Destiny*, ed. Conrad Cherry, 203–14. Rev. ed. Chapel Hill: University of North Carolina Press, 1998.

——. *Reverses Needed: A Discourse Delivered on the Sunday after the Disaster at Bull Run, in the North Church, Hartford*. Hartford, CT: L.E. Hunt, 1861.

——. *The Vicarious Sacrifice, Grounded in Principles of Universal Obligation*. New York: Charles Scribner & Co., 1866.

——. *Work and Play: Or, Literary Varieties*. New York: Charles Scribner, 1864.

C.Ch. "Patriotism Vs. Breeding." *Review*, Apr. 14, 1898, 5.

——. "The Protestant Pulpit and the War." *Review*, Jun. 30, 1898, 5.

C.M.Z. "Der 60 Psalm: Ein Lied für Krieg und Sieg." *Der Lutheraner*, Nov. 19, 1918, 385–86.

Collins, John H.W.N. "For the Christian Recorder: A Letter from a Soldier of the 54th Mass. Rgt." *Christian Recorder*, Jul. 23, 1864, 117.

Council of Bishops. "The Church in Crisis." *Christian Advocate*, Jan. 1, 1942, 6–9.

Crissey, Forrest. "Newell Dwight Hillis." *Outlook*, Feb. 4, 1899, 270.

Czamanske, W.M. "Is the United States a Christian Nation?" *Lutheran Witness*, Nov. 16, 1915, 358.

Dieffenbach, Albert C. "Christ the Combatant." *Christian Register*, Aug. 15, 1918, 775.

Douglass, Frederick. *Narrative of the Life of Frederick Douglass, An American Slave, Written by Himself*, ed. Houston A. Baker, Jr. New York: Penguin, 1982.

Dunne, Finley Peter. *Mr. Dooley in the Hearts of His Countrymen*. Boston: Small, Maynard, 1899.

——. *Mr. Dooley Now and Forever*. Stanford, CA: Academic Reprints, 1957.

——. *Mr. Dooley in Peace and War.* Boston: Small, Maynard, & Co., 1914.

E.P. "Zur Kirchlichen Chronik." *Der Lutheraner,* Jul. 30, 1918, 259–60.

E.W.D. "For the Christian Recorder: Army Correspondence." *Christian Recorder,* Jun. 25, 1864, 101.

Eckhardt, H.P. "Service of Remembrance and Prayer." *American Lutheran* 1, no. 11 (Nov. 1918): 5–6.

F.A.M. "Spain and the Catholic Church." *Review,* Jul. 21, 1898, 2–3.

Fosdick, Harry Emerson. *The Challenge of the Present Crisis.* New York: Association Press, 1918.

——. *Living under Tension: Sermons on Christianity Today.* New York: Harper & Brothers, 1941.

——. "The Trenches and the Church at Home." *Atlantic Monthly* 123 (Jan. 1919): 22–33.

——. "What the War Did to My Mind." *Christian Century,* Jan. 5, 1928, 10–11.

Gladden, Washington. *Applied Christianity.* Boston: Houghton Mifflin, 1886.

——. "The Issues of the War." *Outlook,* Jul. 16, 1898, 673–75.

——. *Our Nation and Her Neighbors.* Columbus, OH: Quinius & Ridenour, 1898.

Graebner, Theodore, comp. *A Testimony and Proof: Bearing on the Relation of the American Church to the German Emperor.* St. Louis: Concordia Publishing House, 1918.

Griffith, Sanford A. "The Nations at War: I—A Fortnight in Germany." *Outlook,* Dec. 29, 1915, 1039–41.

Gruner, O. "Northern Illinois District Synod." *Lutheran Witness,* Jun. 25, 1918, 201.

H.I.W. "For the Christian Recorder: A Letter from a Soldier." *Christian Recorder,* Jul. 23, 1864, 117.

Hall, Arthur J. "Fundamental Factors in World Peace." *Lutheran Quarterly* 49 (Jan. 1919): 61–72.

Harper, F.E.W. "Mrs. Francis [*sic*] E. Watkins Harper on the War and the President's Colonization Scheme." *Christian Recorder,* Sep. 27, 1862, 153.

Hart, Lizzie. "For the Christian Recorder." *Christian Recorder,* Apr. 8, 1865, 2.

——. "For the Christian Recorder: Letter from Morrowtown, Ohio." *Christian Recorder,* May 27, 1865, 83.

Hatton, G.W. "For the Christian Recorder." *Christian Recorder,* Jul. 16, 1864, 114–15.

Herberg, Will. *Protestant, Catholic, Jew: An Essay in American Religious Sociology.* Garden City, NY: Doubleday, 1955.

Herron, George D. *The Christian State, a Political Vision of Christ: A Course of Six Lectures Delivered in Churches in Various American Cities.* New York: T.Y. Crowell, 1895.

Hillis, Newell Dwight. *The Blot on the Kaiser's 'Scutcheon.* New York: Fleming H. Revell, 1918.

——. *German Atrocities: Their Nature and Philosophy.* New York: Fleming H. Revell, 1918.

Hinton, Thomas H.C. "Washington Correspondence." *Christian Recorder,* Aug. 22, 1863, 133.

Holmes, John Haynes. *New Wars for Old: Being a Statement of Radical Pacifism in Terms of Force versus Non-Resistance, With Special Reference to the Problems and Facts of the Great War.* New York: Dodd, Mead and Company, 1916.

Ireland, John. *The Church and Modern Society: Lectures and Addresses.* Chicago: D.H. McBride & Co., 1896.

——. *War and Peace: Address of the Most Rev. John Ireland, at the Peace Jubilee, Chicago, October 18th, 1898.* n.p., 1898?

J.K.P. "Christians—The Times." *Christian Recorder*, Nov. 30, 1861, 185.

J.P.C. "For the Christian Recorder: The President and the Colored People." *Christian Recorder*, Oct. 12, 1861, 158.

——. "The War and Its Design." *Christian Recorder*, Oct. 8, 1864, 162.

Jastrow, Joseph. "Mania Teutonica: A Psychological Study of the War." *Outlook*, Jan. 9, 1918, 58–60.

——. "Why the Germans Have Deemed Themselves Superior." *Outlook*, Nov. 20, 1918, 455–58.

Jefferson, Charles E. *Christianity and International Peace: Six Lectures at Grinnell College, Grinnell, Iowa, in February 1915, on the George A. Gates Memorial Foundation.* New York: Thomas Y. Crowell, 1915.

Jesse, R. "The Epidemic." *Lutheran Witness*, Oct. 29, 1918, 339–40.

Johnson, W.B. "For the Christian Recorder: From the Third U.S.C. Troops." *Christian Recorder*, May 20, 1865, 74.

Junius. "Brooklyn Correspondence." *Christian Recorder*, Oct. 24, 1863, 170.

——. "For the Christian Recorder: Brooklyn Correspondence." *Christian Recorder*, Nov. 14, 1863, 182.

Junius Albus. "For the Christian Recorder: Colored Troops, No. VI." *Christian Recorder*, Aug. 15, 1863, 130.

——. "For the Christian Recorder: Colored Troops, No. 7." *Christian Recorder*, Aug. 29, 1863, 137.

——. "For the Christian Recorder: Colored Troops, No. 8." *Christian Recorder*, Feb. 25, 1865, 30.

Kurth, Carl. "Synodical Conference Builds Hall for Soldier Boys at Army City, Kans." *Lutheran Witness*, May 28, 1918, 120.

Lincoln, Abraham. "Message to Congress, Mar. 6, 1862." In *The Collected Works of Abraham Lincoln*, ed. Roy P. Basler, vol. 5, 144–46. New Brunswick, NJ: Rutgers University Press, 1953.

M.S.D. "For the Christian Recorder: Colored Soldiers." *Christian Recorder*, Aug. 15, 1863, 129.

Mathews, Shailer. *Patriotism and Religion.* New York: Macmillan, 1918.

Millar, William B. "The Army Commission," *Independent*, Jul. 7, 1898, 65–66.

Morhart, C.C. "Should Churches Engage in Politics?" *Lutheran Witness*, Jan. 12, 1915, 5–6.

Murphy, Edgar Gardner. "The Pulpit and the War." *North American Review* 166, no. 499 (Jun. 1898): 751–52.

Niebuhr, Reinhold. "What the War Did to My Mind." *Christian Century*, Sep. 27, 1928, 1161–63.

Norton, Sara, and M.A. DeWolfe Howe, eds. *Letters of Charles Eliot Norton.* 2 vols. Boston: Houghton Mifflin, 1913.

Observer. "Sketches from Washington." *Christian Recorder*, Apr. 26, 1862, 66.

Odell, Joseph H. "Mott, Men, and Millions." *Outlook*, Jul. 31, 1918, 520–21.

Official Report of the Proceedings of the Catholic Conference, Held at Baltimore, MD., November 11th and 12th, 1889. Detroit: William H. Hughes, 1889.

Palfrey, John Gorham. *History of New England*. 5 Vols. Boston: Houghton Mifflin, 1858–89.

The Pastor of a City Congregation. "German Propaganda in the Church." *Outlook*, Jan. 30, 1918, 180–81.

Payne, Daniel Alexander. *History of the African Methodist Episcopal Church*. New York: Johnson Reprint Corporation, 1968.

——. "Welcome to the Ransomed; Or, Duties of the Colored Inhabitants of the District of Columbia." 1–16. In *Sermons and Addresses, 1853–1891*, ed. Charles Killian. New York: Arno Press, 1972.

Pike, Pamela Victor. "Should Germany Be Abolished?" *Outlook*, Aug. 28, 1918, 639.

Pound, Ezra. "Hugh Selwyn Mauberley." In *Ezra Pound: New Selected Poems and Translations*, ed. Richard Sieburth, 109–23. New York: New Directions, 2010.

Rauschenbusch, Walter. *Christianity and the Social Crisis*. New York: Macmillan, 1907.

Remensnyder, Junius B. "Personal Memories of Lincoln: I—President Lincoln's Address at Gettysburg," *Outlook*, Feb. 13, 1918, 243–44.

Rooney, John Jerome. "A Catholic Soldier." *Catholic World* 67 (Aug. 1898): 698–702.

Roosevelt, Theodore. *Fear God and Take Your Own Part*. New York: George H. Doran Co., 1916.

Smith, Charles Spencer. *A History of the African Methodist Episcopal Church: Being a Volume Supplemental to* A History of the African Methodist Episcopal Church, *By Daniel Alexander Payne, D.D., LL.D., Late One of Its Bishops, Chronicling the Principles Events in the Advance of the African Methodist Episcopal Church from 1856–1922*. New York: Johnson Reprint Corporation, 1968.

Speranza, Gino C. "The Nations at War: Italia Redenta—The Redeemed Provinces Under the Civil Administration of Their Italian Conquerors." *Outlook*, Feb. 23, 1916, 471–75.

Steward, William. "For the Christian Recorder: the Negro Soldier." *Christian Recorder*, Mar. 7, 1863, 37.

Strong, Josiah. *Expansion Under New World Conditions*. New York: Baker & Taylor, 1900.

——. "The Individual and Social Interpretation of Christianity." 7–10. In *First Year of the Sagamore Sociological Conference, Sagamore Beach, U.S.A., June 18, 19, 20, 1907*. Boston: Arakelyan Press, 1907.

——. *Our Country: Its Possible Future and Its Present Crisis*. 1885. Reprint, Cambridge, MA: Harvard University Press, 1963.

——. *Religious Movements for Social Betterment*. New York: Baker & Taylor, 1900.

Strother, T. "Why the Great Present Southern Rebellion Has Not Been Long since Crushed." *Christian Recorder*, Jul. 30, 1864, 121.

Trowbridge, J.W. "Cuba." *Independent*, Jul. 7, 1898, 7.

Turner, Henry McNeal. "For the Christian Recorder." *Christian Recorder*, Dec. 14, 1861, 191.

——. "For the Christian Recorder: Army Correspondence." *Christian Recorder*, May 6, 1865, 69.

——. "For the Christian Recorder: Army Correspondence, by Chaplain H.M. Turner." *Christian Recorder*, Feb. 25, 1865, 29.

——. "For the Christian Recorder: From Chaplain Turner." *Christian Recorder*, Jun. 25, 1864, 101.

———. "For the Christian Recorder: The Plagues of This Country." *Christian Recorder*, Jul. 12, 1862, 109.

———. "The Negro and the Army." In *Respect Black: The Writings and Speeches of Henry McNeal Turner*, ed. Edwin S. Redkey, 184–85. New York: Arno Press, 1871.

———. "Turner on the President's Message." *Christian Recorder*, Mar. 22, 1862, 46.

———. "Washington Correspondence." *Christian Recorder*, Dec. 6, 1862, 193.

———. "Washington Correspondence." *Christian Recorder*, Jan. 31, 1863, 18.

Van Dyke, Henry [Jr.]. *Fighting for Peace*. New York: Charles Scribner's Sons, 1917.

Van Dyke, Henry [Sr.]. *The Spirituality and Independence of the Church: A Speech Delivered in the Synod of New York, October 18, 1864*. New York: n.p., 1864.

W.C.D. "For the Christian Recorder." *Christian Recorder*, Nov. 8, 1862, 177.

Watts, Samuel. "Ohio Correspondence." *Christian Recorder*, Aug. 6, 1864, 125.

West Jersey. "Camden Correspondence." *Christian Recorder*, May 2, 1863, 70.

White, G. Frederick. "Sociological Notes: Responsibility for National Greatness." *Bibliotheca Sacra* 55, no. 220 (Oct. 1898): 748–52.

Williams, Joseph E. "For the Christian Recorder." *Christian Recorder*, Sep. 19, 1863, 149.

Williams, Mary A. "For the Christian Recorder: The Union of Church and State." *Christian Recorder*, Sep. 17, 1864, 150.

Wilson, Woodrow. "An Appeal to the American People." In *The Papers of Woodrow Wilson*, vol. 30, ed. Arthur S. Link, 393–94. Princeton, NJ: Princeton University Press, 1979.

Wishart, John Elliott. "The Christian Attitude toward War." *Bibliotheca Sacra* 75 (Apr. 1918): 171–94.

Wright, Harold Bell. "Sword of Jesus." *American Magazine* 85 (Feb. 1918): 7–9.

Secondary Sources

Aamodt, Terrie Dopp. *Righteous Armies, Holy Cause: Apocalyptic Imagery and the Civil War*. Macon, GA: Mercer University Press, 2002.

Abrams, Ray H. *Preachers Present Arms*. New York: Round Table Press, 1933.

Ahlstrom, Sydney. *A Religious History of the American People*. New Haven, CT: Yale University Press, 1972.

Angell, Stephen W. *Bishop Henry McNeal Turner and African-American Religion in the South*. Knoxville: University of Tennessee Press, 1992.

Angell, Stephen W., and Anthony B. Pinn, eds. *Social Protest Thought in the African Methodist Episcopal Church, 1862–1939*. Knoxville: University of Tennessee Press, 2000.

Appleby, R. Scott. *Church and Age Unite! The Modernist Impulse in American Catholicism*. Notre Dame, IN: University of Notre Dame Press, 1992.

Applegate, Debby. *The Most Famous Man in America: The Biography of Henry Ward Beecher*. New York: Doubleday, 2006.

Ayers, Edward L. *What Caused the Civil War? Reflections on the South and Southern History*. New York: Norton, 2005.

Bailey, Julius. *Race Patriotism: Protest and Print Culture in the AME Church*. Knoxville: University of Tennessee Press, 2012.

Bederman, Gail. *Manliness & Civilization: A Cultural History of Gender and Race in the United States, 1880–1917.* Chicago: University of Chicago Press, 1995.

Berner, Brad K., and Kalman Goldstein, eds. *The Spanish-American War: A Documentary History with Commentaries.* Madison, NJ: Fairleigh Dickinson University Press, 2014.

Bigham, Darrel E. "American Christian Thinkers and the Function of War, 1861–1920." PhD diss., University of Kansas, 1970.

Billington, Ray Allen. *The Protestant Crusade, 1800–1860.* New York: Macmillan, 1938.

Blight, David. *Race and Reunion: The Civil War in American Memory.* Cambridge, MA: Harvard University Press, 2001.

Blum, Edward J. *Reforging the White Republic: Race, Religion, and American Nationalism, 1865–1898.* Baton Rouge: Louisiana State University Press, 2007.

Bogaski, George. *American Protestants and the Debate over the Vietnam War: Evil Was Loose in the World.* Lanham, MD: Lexington Books, 2014.

Bowden, Henry Warner. *American Indians and Christian Missions: Studies in Cultural Conflict.* Chicago: University of Chicago Press, 1981.

Brown, Ira V. *Lyman Abbott, Christian Evolutionist: A Study in Religious Liberalism.* Cambridge, MA: Harvard University Press, 1953.

Burnidge, Cara Lea. *A Peaceful Conquest: Woodrow Wilson, Religion, and the New World Order.* Chicago: University of Chicago Press, 2016.

Butler, Jon. *God in Gotham: The Miracle of Religion in Modern Manhattan.* Cambridge, MA: Harvard University Press, 2020.

Byrd, James P. *Sacred Scripture, Sacred War: The Bible and the American Revolution.* New York: Oxford University Press, 2013.

Capozzola, Christopher. *Uncle Sam Wants You: World War I and the Making of the Modern American Citizen.* New York: Oxford University Press, 2008.

Carter, Heath W. *Union Made: Working People and the Rise of Social Christianity in Chicago.* New York: Oxford University Press, 2015.

Casey, Steven. *A Cautious Crusade: Franklin D. Roosevelt, American Public Opinion, and the War Against Nazi Germany.* New York: Oxford University Press, 2001.

Cavanaugh, John W. *Daniel E. Hudson, C.S.C.: A Memoir.* 2nd ed. Notre Dame, IN: Ave Maria Press, 1960.

Chapell, Colin B. "The Third Strand: Race, Gender, and Self-Government in the Mind of Lyman Abbott." *Fides et Historia* 42 (Summer/Fall 2010): 27–54.

Cherry, Conrad, ed. *God's New Israel: Religious Interpretations of American Destiny.* Rev. ed. Chapel Hill: University of North Carolina Press, 1998.

——. "The Structure of Organic Thinking: Horace Bushnell's Approach to Language, Nature, and Nation." *Journal of the American Academy of Religion* 40 (Mar. 1972): 3–20.

Clark, Clifford E., Jr. *Henry Ward Beecher: Spokesman for a Middle-Class America.* Urbana: University of Illinois Press, 1978.

Clebsch, William Anthony. "Baptism of Blood: A Study of Christian Contributions to the Interpretation of the Civil War in American History." ThD diss., Union Theological Seminary, 1957.

Coffman, Elesha J. *The Christian Century and the Rise of the Protestant Mainline.* New York: Oxford University Press, 2013.

Coghlan, Francis. "The Impact of the Spanish-American War on the Catholic Church in the United States of America." MA thesis, University of Notre Dame, 1956.

Cole, Jean Lee, and Aaron Sheehan-Dean, eds. *Freedom's Witness: The Civil War Writings of Henry McNeal Turner*. Morgantown: University of West Virginia Press, 2013.

Conley, Rory T. *Arthur Preuss: Journalist and Voice of German and Conservative Catholics in America, 1871–1934*. New York: Peter Lang, 1998.

Cross, Barbara M. *Horace Bushnell: Minister to a Changing America*. Chicago: University of Chicago Press, 1958.

Currell, Susan. *American Culture in the 1920s*. Edinburgh: Edinburgh University Press, 2009.

Curtis, Susan. *A Consuming Faith: The Social Gospel and Modern American Culture*. Baltimore: Johns Hopkins University Press, 1991.

Cusack, Thomas E. "Archbishop John Ireland and the Spanish-American War: Peacemaker or Bungler?" MA thesis, University of Notre Dame, 1974.

D'Agostino, Peter R. *Rome in America: Transnational Catholic Ideology from the Risorgimento to Fascism*. Chapel Hill: University of North Carolina Press, 2004.

DeBenedetti, Charles, with Charles Chatfield. *An American Ordeal: The Antiwar Movement of the Vietnam Era*. Syracuse, NY: Syracuse University Press, 1990.

Detjen, David W. *The Germans in Missouri, 1900–1918: Prohibition, Neutrality, and Assimilation*. Columbia: University of Missouri Press, 1985.

DeWitt, Petra. *Degrees of Allegiance: Harassment and Loyalty in Missouri's German-American Community during World War I*. Athens: Ohio University Press, 2012.

Dicken-Garcia, Hazel, and Linus Abraham. "African Americans and the Civil War as Reflected in the *Christian Recorder*, 1861–1862." In *Words at War: The Civil War and American Journalism*, ed. David B. Sachsman, S. Kittrell Rushing, and Roy Morris Jr., 249–60. West Lafayette, IN: Purdue University Press, 2008.

Dolan, Jay P. *In Search of an American Catholicism: A History of Religion and Culture in Tension*. New York: Oxford University Press, 2002.

Dorn, Jacob H. *Washington Gladden: Prophet of the Social Gospel*. Columbus: Ohio State University Press, 1967.

Dorrien, Gary. *Economy, Difference, Empire: Social Ethics for Social Justice*. New York: Columbia University Press, 2010.

Douglas, Ann. *The Feminization of American Culture*. New York: Knopf, 1977.

Doyle, David Noel. *Irish Americans, Native Rights and National Empires: The Structure, Divisions and Attitudes of the Catholic Minority in the Decade of Expansion, 1890–1901*. New York: Arno Press, 1976.

Dunham, Chester Forrester. *The Attitude of the Northern Clergy Toward the South, 1860–1865*. Philadelphia: Porcupine Press, 1974.

Ebel, Jonathan H. *Faith in the Fight: Religion and the American Scholar in the Great War*. Princeton, NJ: Princeton University Press, 2010.

———. "From Covenant to Crusade and Back: American Christianity and the Late Great War." In *From Jeremiad to Jihad: Religion, Violence, and America*, ed. John D. Carlson and Jonathan H. Ebel, 62–77. Berkeley: University of California Press, 2012.

——. "'The Wreckage and All the Glory': Protestant America and the Legacy of the Great War." *Journal of Presbyterian History* 92 (Spring/Summer 2014): 4–25.

Edwards, Rebecca. *New Spirits: Americans in the "Gilded Age," 1865–1905.* 2nd ed. New York: Oxford University Press, 2011.

Ellis, John Tracy. *American Catholicism.* Chicago: University of Chicago Press, 1956.

——. *The Life of James Cardinal Gibbons: Archbishop of Baltimore, 1834–1921.* 2 Vols. Milwaukee: Bruce Pub. Co., 1952.

Evans, Christopher H. *The Kingdom Is Always but Coming: A Life of Walter Rauschenbusch.* Grand Rapids, MI: Eerdmans, 2004.

——, ed. *Perspectives on the Social Gospel: Papers from the Inaugural Social Gospel Conference at Colgate Rochester Divinity School.* Lewiston, NY: Edwin Mellen Press, 1999.

Fagan, Benjamin. *The Black Newspapers and the Chosen Nation.* Athens: University of Georgia Press, 2016.

Fanning, Charles. *Finley Peter Dunne and Mr. Dooley: The Chicago Years.* Lexington: University Press of Kentucky, 1978.

Faragher, John Mack, ed. *Rereading Frederick Jackson Turner: "The Significance of the Frontier in American History" and Other Essays.* New Haven, CT: Yale University Press, 1998.

Farrell, John T. "Archbishop Ireland and Manifest Destiny." *Catholic Historical Review* 33 (Oct. 1947): 269–301.

Finke, Roger, and Rodney Stark. *The Churching of America, 1776–2005: Winners and Losers in our Religious Economy.* New Brunswick, NJ: Rutgers University Press, 2005.

Fischer, Hannah, Kim Klarman, and Mari-Jana Oboroceanu. *American War and Military Operations Casualties: Lists and Statistics.* Washington, DC: Congressional Research Service, 2008. http://www.law.umaryland.edu/marshall/crsreports/crsdocuments/RL32492_05142008.pdf.

Fogarty, Gerald P. "1892 and 1992: From Celebration of Discovery to Encounter of Cultures." *Catholic Historical Review* 79 (Oct. 1993): 621–47.

Foner, Eric. *Free Soil, Free Labor, Free Men: The Ideology of the Republican Party Before the Civil War.* 2nd ed. New York: Oxford University Press, 1995.

Foster, Gaines M. *Moral Reconstruction: Christian Lobbyists and the Federal Legislation of Morality, 1865–1920.* Chapel Hill: University of North Carolina Press, 2002.

Franchot, Jenny. *Roads to Rome: The Antebellum Protestant Encounter with Catholicism.* Berkeley: University of California Press, 1994.

Franklin, John Hope [and Evelyn Higginbotham]. *From Slavery to Freedom: A History of African Americans.* 9th ed. New York: McGraw-Hill, 2011.

Frederickson, George M. "The Coming of the Lord: The Northern Protestant Clergy and the Civil War Crisis." In *Religion and the American Civil War,* ed. Randall M. Miller, Harry S. Stout, and Charles Reagan Wilson, 110–30. New York: Oxford University Press, 2008.

Fulton, Robert I., and Thomas C. Trueblood, eds. *Patriotic Eloquence Relating to the Spanish-American War and its Issues.* New York: Scribner's, 1900.

Gamble, Richard M. *A Fiery Gospel: The Battle Hymn of the Republic and the Road to Righteous War.* Ithaca, NY: Cornell University Press, 2019.

——. *In Search of the City on a Hill: The Making and Unmaking of an American Myth.* London: Continuum, 2012.

——. *The War for Righteousness: Progressive Christianity, the Great War, and the Rise of the Messianic Nation.* Wilmington, DE: ISI, 2003.

Gardner, Eric. *Black Print Unbound: The* Christian Recorder, *African American Literature, and Periodical Culture.* New York: Oxford University Press, 2015.

——. "Remembered (Black) Readers: Subscribers to the *Christian Recorder,* 1864–1865." *American Literary History* 23 (Summer 2011): 229–59.

——. *Unexpected Places: Relocating Nineteenth-Century African American Literature.* Jackson: University Press of Mississippi, 2009.

——. "'Yours, for the Cause': The *Christian Recorder* Writings of Lizzie Hart." *Legacy: A Journal of American Women Writers,* 27, no. 2 (2010): 367–75.

Gerstle, Gary. *American Crucible: Race and Nation in the Twentieth Century.* Princeton, NJ: Princeton University Press, 2001.

Gibbs, Christopher C. *The Great Silent Majority: Missouri's Resistance to World War I.* Columbia: University of Missouri Press, 1988.

Gleason, Philip. "American Identity and Americanization." In *Harvard Encyclopedia of American Ethnic Groups,* ed. Stephan Thernstrom, 31–58. Cambridge, MA: Harvard University Press, 1980.

——. "Coming to Terms with American Catholic History." *Societas* 3 (Autumn 1973): 283–312.

——. "The Crisis of Americanization." In *Contemporary Catholicism in the United States,* ed. Philip Gleason, 3–31. Notre Dame, IN: University of Notre Dame Press, 1969.

Goldstein, Warren. *William Sloane Coffin, Jr.: A Holy Impatience.* New Haven, CT: Yale University Press, 2004.

Graber, Jennifer. *The Gods of Indian Country: Religion and the Struggle for the American West.* New York: Oxford University Press, 2018.

Graebner, Alan. "The Acculturation of an Immigrant Lutheran Church: The Lutheran Church-Missouri Synod, 1917–1929." PhD diss., Columbia University, 1965.

——. *Uncertain Saints: The Laity in the Lutheran Church-Missouri Synod, 1900–1970.* Westport, CT: Greenwood Press, 1975.

Granquist, Mark. *Lutherans in America: A New History.* Minneapolis: Fortress Press, 2015.

Greenberg, Amy S. *A Wicked War: Polk, Clay, Lincoln, and the 1846 U. S. Invasion of Mexico.* New York: Knopf, 2012.

Greschat, Martin. *Der Erste Weltkrieg und die Christenheit: Ein globaler Überblick.* Stuttgart: Verlag W. Kohlhammer, 2014.

Gribbin, William. *The Churches Militant: The War of 1812 and American Religion.* New Haven, CT: Yale University Press, 1973.

Gritsch, Eric W. *A History of Lutheranism.* 2nd ed. Minneapolis: Fortress Press, 2010.

Grosjean, Paul Eugene. "The Concept of American Nationhood: Theological Interpretation as Reflected by the Northern Mainline Protestant Preachers in the Late Civil War Period." PhD diss., Drew University, 1977.

Guelzo, Allen C. *Abraham Lincoln: Redeemer President.* Grand Rapids, MI: Eerdmans, 1999.

——. "Did Religion Make the American Civil War Worse?" *The Atlantic,* Aug. 23, 2015. http://www.theatlantic.com/politics/archive/2015/08/did-religion-make-the-american-civil-war-worse/401633/

Gurgel, Stephen. "The War to End All Germans: Wisconsin Synod Lutherans and the First World War." MA thesis, University of Wisconsin-Milwaukee, 2012.

Guyatt, Nicholas. *Providence and the Invention of the United States, 1607–1876.* Cambridge, MA: Cambridge University Press, 2007.

Haberski, Raymond J. *God and War: American Civil Religion Since 1945.* New Brunswick, NJ: Rutgers University Press, 2012.

Haemig, Mary Jane. "The Confessional Basis of Lutheran Thinking on Church-State Issues." In *Church & State: Lutheran Perspectives,* ed. John R. Stumme and Robert W. Tuttle, 3–19. Minneapolis: Fortress Press, 2003.

Hall, Mitchell K. *Because of Their Faith: CALCAV and Religious Opposition to the Vietnam War.* New York: Columbia University Press, 1990.

Handy, Robert T. *The Social Gospel in America, 1870–1920.* New York: Oxford University Press, 1966.

Hankins, Barry. *Woodrow Wilson: Ruling Elder, Spiritual President.* Oxford: Oxford University Press, 2016.

Hanley, Mark Y. *Beyond a Christian Commonwealth: The Protestant Quarrel with the American Republic, 1830–1860.* Chapel Hill: University of North Carolina Press, 1994.

Harris, Susan K. *God's Arbiters: Americans and the Philippines, 1898–1902.* New York: Oxford University Press, 2011.

Haselby, Sam. *The Origins of American Religious Nationalism.* New York: Oxford University Press, 2015.

Heath, Gordon L., ed. *American Churches and the First World War.* Eugene, OR: Pickwick, 2016.

Hennesey, James. *American Catholics: A History of the Roman Catholic Community in the United States.* New York: Oxford University Press, 1981.

Hofstadter, Richard. *The Age of Reform: From Bryan to F.D.R.* New York: Knopf, 1955.

Hoganson, Kristin L. *Fighting for American Manhood: How Gender Politics Provoked the Spanish-American and Philippine-American Wars.* New Haven, CT: Yale University Press, 1998.

Holifield, E. Brooks. *God's Ambassadors: A History of the Christian Clergy in America.* Grand Rapids, MI: Eerdmans, 2007.

Hollinger, David A. *After Cloven Tongues of Fire: Protestant Liberalism in Modern American History.* Princeton, NJ: Princeton University Press, 2013.

Hopkins, C. Howard. *The Rise of the Social Gospel in American Protestantism, 1865–1915.* New Haven, CT: Yale University Press, 1940.

Horsman, Reginald. *Race and Manifest Destiny: The Origins of American Racial Anglo-Saxonism.* Cambridge, MA: Harvard University Press, 1981.

Hunter, James Davison. *Culture Wars: The Struggle to Define America.* New York: Basic Books, 1991.

Hutchison, William R. "Cultural Strain and Protestant Liberalism." *American Historical Review* 76 (Apr. 1971): 386–411.

——. "Preface: From Protestant to Pluralist America." In *Between the Times: The Travail of the Protestant Establishment in America, 1900–1960,* ed. William R. Hutchison, vii–xv. New York: Cambridge University Press, 1989.

Hutchison, William R. and Hartmut Lehmann, eds. *Many Are Chosen: Divine Election and Western Nationalism.* Minneapolis: Fortress Press, 1994.

Jacobson, Matthew Frye. *Whiteness of a Different Color: European Immigrants and the Alchemy of Race*. Cambridge, MA: Harvard University Press, 1998.

Jaffe, Steven H. *New York at War: Four Centuries of Combat, Fear, and Intrigue in Gotham*. New York: Basic Books, 2012.

Jaksić, Iván. *The Hispanic World and American Intellectual Life, 1820–1880*. New York: Palgrave Macmillan, 2007.

James, Pearl, ed. *Picture This: World War I Posters and Visual Culture*. Lincoln: University of Nebraska Press, 2009.

Jenkins, Philip. *The Great and Holy War: How World War I Became a Religious Crusade*. New York: HarperOne, 2014.

Johnson, Neil M. "The Patriotism and Anti-Prussianism of the Lutheran Church-Missouri Synod, 1914–1918." *Concordia Historical Institute Quarterly* 39 (Oct. 1966): 99–118.

Karraker, William Archibald. "The American Churches and the Spanish-American War." PhD diss., University of Chicago, 1940.

Kazin, Michael. *War Against War: The American Fight for Peace, 1914–1918*. New York: Simon & Schuster, 2017.

Kennedy, David. *Over Here: The First World War and American Society*. New York: Oxford University Press, 1982.

Kidd, Thomas S. *God of Liberty: A Religious History of the American Revolution*. New York: Basic Books, 2010.

Kingsbury, Celia Malone. *For Home and Country: World War I Propaganda on the Home Front*. Lincoln: University of Nebraska Press, 2010.

Kinzer, Donald L. *An Episode in Anti-Catholicism: The American Protective Association*. Seattle: University of Washington Press, 1964.

Kramer, Paul A. *The Blood of Government: Race, Empire, the United States, and the Philippines*. Chapel Hill: University of North Carolina Press, 2006.

Kurtz, William B. *Excommunicated from the Union: How the Civil War Created a Separate Catholic America*. New York: Fordham University Press, 2016.

LaFantasie, Glenn W. "Good Fortune and Great Sorrow: The Civil War Generation's Place in History." *Wilson Quarterly* (Spring 2016). http://wilsonquarterly.com /quarterly/looking-back-moving-forward/good-fortune-and-great-sorrow-the -civil-war-generations-place-in-history/.

LaFeber, Walter. *The New Empire: An Interpretation of American Expansion, 1860–1898*. Ithaca, NY: Cornell University Press, 1963.

Lagerquist, L. DeAne. *The Lutherans*. Westport, CT: Greenwood Press, 1999.

Lears, T.J. Jackson. *No Place of Grace: Antimodernism and the Transformation of American Culture, 1880–1920*. New York: Pantheon, 1981.

Lentz-Smith, Adriane. *Freedom Struggles: African Americans and World War I*. Cambridge, MA: Harvard University Press, 2009.

Luebke, Frederick C. *Bonds of Loyalty: German Americans and World War I*. DeKalb: Northern Illinois University Press, 1974.

——. "Superpatriotism in World War I: The Experiences of a Lutheran Pastor." *Concordia Historical Institute Quarterly* 41 (Feb. 1968): 3–11.

Luker, Ralph E. *The Social Gospel in Black and White: American Racial Reform, 1885–1912*. Chapel Hill: University of North Carolina Press, 1991.

Magee, Malcolm. *What the World Should Be: Woodrow Wilson and the Crafting of a Faith-Based Foreign Policy.* Waco, TX: Baylor University Press, 2008.

Magness, Phillip W. "The British Honduras Colony: Black Emigrationist Support for Colonization in the Lincoln Presidency." *Slavery & Abolition* 34 (Mar. 2013): 39–60.

Manley, Robert N. "The Nebraska State Council of Defense: Loyalty Programs and Policies during World War I." MA thesis, University of Nebraska, 1959.

Manning, Chandra. *What This Cruel War Was Over: Soldiers, Slavery, and the Civil War.* New York: Vintage, 2007.

Marks, George P. III, comp. and ed. *The Black Press Views American Imperialism (1898–1900).* New York: Ayer, 1971.

Marsden, George M. *Fundamentalism and American Culture.* 2nd ed. New York: Oxford University Press, 2006.

——. *The Twilight of the American Enlightenment: The 1950s and the Crisis of Liberal Belief.* New York: Basic Books, 2014.

Martin, Sandy Dwayne. "Black Churches and the Civil War: Theological and Ecclesiastical Significance of Black Methodist Involvement, 1861–1865." *Methodist History* 32 (Apr. 1994): 174–86.

Masur, Kate. "The African American Delegation to Abraham Lincoln: A Reappraisal." *Civil War History* 56 (Jun. 2010): 117–44.

McCartney, Paul T. *Power and Progress: American National Identity, the War of 1898, and the Rise of American Imperialism.* Baton Rouge: Louisiana State University Press, 2006.

——. "Religion, the Spanish-American War, and the Idea of American Mission." *Journal of Church and State* 54 (Spring 2012): 257–78.

McCullough, Matthew. *The Cross of War: Christian Nationalism and U.S. Expansion during the Spanish-American War.* Madison: University of Wisconsin Press, 2014.

McHenry, Elizabeth. *Forgotten Readers: Recovering the Lost History of African American Literary Societies.* Durham, NC: Duke University Press, 2002.

McLeod, Hugh. *The Religious Crisis of the 1960s.* Oxford: Oxford University Press, 2007.

McLoughlin, William G. *Billy Sunday Was His Real Name.* Chicago: University of Chicago Press, 1955.

——. *The Meaning of Henry Ward Beecher: An Essay on the Shifting Values of Mid-Victorian America, 1840–1870.* New York: Knopf, 1970.

Mead, Sidney E. *The Lively Experiment: The Shaping of Christianity in America.* New York: Harper & Row, 1963.

Meier, Everette, and Herbert T. Mayer. "The Process of Americanization." In *Moving Frontiers: Readings in the History of the Lutheran Church-Missouri Synod*, ed. Carl S. Meyer, 344–85. St. Louis: Concordia Publishing House, 1964.

Menand, Louis. *The Metaphysical Club.* New York: Farrar, Straus and Giroux, 2001.

Meyer, Carl S. *A Brief Historical Sketch of the Lutheran Church-Missouri Synod.* Rev. ed. St. Louis: Concordia Publishing House, 1970.

Michaelsen, Robert. "Common School, Common Religion? A Case Study in Church-State Relations, Cincinnati, 1869–1870." *Church History* 38 (Jun. 1969): 201–17.

Miller, Bonnie M. *From Liberation to Conquest: The Visual and Popular Cultures of the Spanish-American War of 1898.* Amherst: University of Massachusetts Press, 2011.

Miscamble, Wilson D. "Catholics and American Foreign Policy from McKinley to McCarthy: A Historiographical Survey." *Diplomatic History* 4 (Summer 1980): 223–40.

Moore, Christopher M. "'Blood, Blood, Rivers of Blood': Horace Bushnell and the Atonement of America," *Fides et Historia* 50, no. 1 (Winter/Spring 2018): 1–14.

Moorhead, James H. *American Apocalypse: Yankee Protestants and the Civil War, 1860–1869.* New Haven, CT: Yale University Press, 1978.

———. "Between Progress and Apocalypse: A Reassessment of Millennialism in American Religious Thought, 1800–1860." *Journal of American History* 71:3 (Dec. 1984): 524–42.

Moran, Katherine D. "Catholicism and the Making of the U.S. Pacific." *Journal of the Gilded Age and Progressive Era* 12 (Oct. 2013): 434–74.

Morgan, Edmund S. *American Slavery, American Freedom: The Ordeal of Colonial Virginia.* New York: Norton, 1975.

Morison, William J. "*Bibliotheca Sacra.*" In *The Conservative Press in Twentieth-Century America,* ed. Ronald Lora and William Henry Longton, 91–101. Westport, CT: Greenwood Press, 1999.

Mott, Frank Luther. *A History of American Magazines.* 5 vols. Cambridge, MA: Harvard University Press, 1938–68.

Moynihan, Humphrey. "Archbishop Ireland the Spanish-American War: Some Original Data." *Ireland American Review* 5 (1942–43): 98–118.

Nagel, Paul C. *This Sacred Trust: American Nationality, 1798–1898.* New York: Oxford University Press, 1971.

Nelson, E. Clifford, ed. *The Lutherans in North America.* Rev. ed. Philadelphia: Fortress Press, 1980.

Nohl, Frederick. "The Lutheran Church-Missouri Synod Reacts to United States Anti-Germanism during World War I." *Concordia Historical Institute Quarterly* 35 (Jul. 1962): 49–66.

Noll, Mark A. "American Lutherans Yesterday and Today." In *Lutherans Today: American Lutherans in the Twenty-First Century,* ed. Richard Cimino, 3–25. Grand Rapids, MI: Eerdmans, 2003.

———. *America's God: From Jonathan Edwards to Abraham Lincoln.* New York: Oxford University Press, 2002.

———. "Bishop James Gibbons, the Bible, and Protestant America." *U.S. Catholic Historian* 31 (Summer 2013): 77–104.

———. "The Catholic Press, the Bible, and Protestant Responsibility for the Civil War." *Journal of the Civil War Era* 7, no. 3 (Spring 2017): 355–76.

———. *The Civil War as a Theological Crisis.* Chapel Hill: University of North Carolina Press, 2006.

Oakes, James. *Freedom National: The Destruction of Slavery in the United States, 1861–1865.* New York: Norton, 2013.

———. *The Radical and the Republican: Frederick Douglass, Abraham Lincoln, and the Triumph of Anti-Slavery Politics.* New York: Norton, 2007.

O'Connell, Marvin R. *John Ireland and the American Catholic Church.* St. Paul: Minnesota Historical Society Press, 1988.

Offner, John. "Washington Mission: Archbishop Ireland on the Eve of the Spanish-American War." *Catholic Historical Review* 73 (Oct. 1987): 562–75.

Orser, W. Edward. "World War II and the Pacifist Controversy in the Major Protestant Churches." *American Studies* 14 (Fall 1973): 5–24.

O'Toole, James M. *The Faithful: A History of Catholics in America.* Cambridge, MA: Harvard University Press, 2008.

Owens, A. Nevell. *Formation of the African Methodist Episcopal Church in the Nineteenth Century: Rhetoric of Identification.* New York: Palgrave Macmillan, 2014.

Parish, Peter J. "The Just War." In *The North and the Nation in the Era of the Civil War,* ed. Adam I.P. Smith and Susan-Mary Grant, 171–99. New York: Fordham University Press, 2003.

Pérez, Louis A. "Incurring a Debt of Gratitude: 1898 and the Moral Sources of United States Hegemony in Cuba." *American Historical Review* 104, no. 2 (Apr. 1999): 356–98.

——. *The War of 1898: The United States and Cuba in History and Historiography.* Chapel Hill: University of North Carolina Press, 1998.

Pinheiro, John C. *Missionaries of Republicanism: A Religious History of the Mexican-American War.* New York: Oxford University Press, 2014.

Piper, John F., Jr. "The American Churches in World War I." *Journal of American Religion* 38 (Jun. 1970): 147–55.

——. *The American Churches in World War I.* Athens: University of Ohio Press, 1985.

Pratt, Julius. *Expansionists of 1898: The Acquisition of Hawaii and the Spanish Islands.* Baltimore: Johns Hopkins University Press, 1938.

Preston, Andrew. *Sword of the Spirit, Shield of Faith: Religion in American War and Diplomacy.* New York: Knopf, 2012.

Putney, Clifford. *Muscular Christianity: Manhood and Sports in Protestant America, 1880–1920* Cambridge, MA: Harvard University Press, 2001.

Rable, George C. *God's Almost Chosen Peoples: A Religious History of the American Civil War.* Chapel Hill: University of North Carolina, 2010.

Redkey, Edwin S., ed. *A Grand Army of Black Men: Letters from African-American Soldiers in the Union Army, 1861–1865.* New York: Cambridge University Press, 1992.

Reuter, Frank T. *Catholic Influence on American Colonial Policies, 1898–1904.* Austin: University of Texas Press, 1967.

Richardson, Heath Cox. *West from Appomattox: The Reconstruction of American after the Civil War.* New York: Oxford University Press, 2007.

Rodgers, Daniel T. *Age of Fracture.* Cambridge, MA: Harvard University Press, 2011.

Rosenfeld, Harvey. *Diary of a Dirty Little War: The Spanish-American War of 1898.* Westport, CT: Praeger, 2000.

Ross, Stewart Halsey. *Propaganda for War: How the United States Was Conditioned to Fight the War of 1914–1918.* Jefferson, NC: McFarland, 1996.

Saum, Lewis O. *The Popular Mood of America, 1860–1890.* Lincoln: University of Nebraska Press, 1990.

——. *The Popular Mood of Pre-Civil War America.* Westport, CT: Greenwood Press, 1980.

Shalev, Eran. *American Zion: The Old Testament as a Political Text from the American Revolution to the Civil War.* New Haven, CT: Yale University Press, 2013.

Shultz, Kevin. *Tri-Faith America: How Catholics and Jews Held Postwar America to its Protestant Promise.* New York: Oxford University Press, 2011.

Sittser, Gerald. *A Cautious Patriotism: The American Churches & The Second World War.* Chapel Hill: University of North Carolina Press, 1997.

Smith, Gary Scott. *Faith and the Presidency: From George Washington to George W. Bush.* New York: Oxford University Press, 2006.

——. *Religion in the Oval Office: The Religious Lives of America's Presidents.* New York: Oxford University Press, 2015.

——. *The Search for Social Salvation: Social Christianity and America, 1880–1925.* Lanham, MD: Lexington Books, 2000.

Smylie, John Edwin. "Protestant Churches and America's World Role, 1865–1900: A Study of Christianity, Nationality, and International Relations." ThD diss., Princeton Theological Seminary, 1959.

Spencer, David R. *The Yellow Journalism: The Press and America's Emergence as a World Power.* Evanston, IL: Northwestern University Press, 2007.

Stewart, William. *A Biographical Dictionary of Psychologists, Psychiatrists and Psychotherapists.* Jefferson, NC: McFarland, 2008.

Stout, Harry S. "Review Essay: Religion, War, and the Meaning of America." *Religion and American Culture: A Journal of Interpretation* 19 (Summer 2009): 275–89.

——. *Upon the Altar of the Nation: A Moral History of the Civil War.* New York: Penguin, 2006.

Stowell, Daniel W. *Rebuilding Zion: The Religious Reconstruction of the South, 1863–1877.* New York: Oxford University Press, 1998.

Strobert, Nelson T. *Daniel Alexander Payne: The Venerable Preceptor of the African Methodist Episcopal Church.* Lanham, MD: University Press of America, 2012.

Summers, Mark W. *Rum, Romanism, and Rebellion: The Making of a President, 1884.* Chapel Hill: University of North Carolina Press, 2000.

Sweet, William Warren. *The Story of Religion in America.* Rev. ed. New York: Harper & Brothers, 1950.

Taylor, Brian. "A Politics of Service: Black Northerners' Debates over Enlistment in the American Civil War." *Civil War History* 58 (Dec. 2012): 451–80.

Thomas, William H., Jr. *Unsafe for Democracy: World War I and the U.S. Justice Department's Covert Campaign to Suppress Dissent.* Madison: University of Wisconsin Press, 2008.

Trask, David F. *The War with Spain in 1898.* New York: Macmillan, 1981.

Treuer, David. *The Heartbeat of Wounded Knee: Native America from 1890 to the Present.* New York: Penguin, 2019.

Turner, James. *The Liberal Education of Charles Eliot Norton.* Baltimore: Johns Hopkins University Press, 1999.

Tuveson, Ernest. *Redeemer Nation: The Idea of America's Millennial Role.* Chicago: University of Chicago Press, 1968.

Tweed, Thomas A. *The American Encounter with Buddhism, 1844–1912: Victorian Culture and the Limits of Dissent.* 2nd ed. Bloomington: Indiana University Press, 1992.

Tyrrell, Ian R. *Reforming the World: The Creation of America's Moral Empire.* Princeton, NJ: Princeton University Press, 2010.

Viaene, Vincent. "Introduction." In *The Papacy and the New World Order: Vatican Diplomacy, Catholic Opinion and International Politics at the Time of Leo XIII, 1878–1903,* ed. Vincent Viaene, 9–29. Leuven, Belgium: Leuven University Press, 2005.

Wacker Grant. *Heaven Below: Early Pentecostals and American Culture.* Cambridge, MA: Harvard University Press, 2001.

Walker, Clarence E. *A Rock in a Weary Land: The African Methodist Episcopal Church during the Civil War and Reconstruction.* Baton Rouge: Louisiana University Press, 1982.

Wangler, Thomas E. "American Catholics and the Spanish-American War." In *Catholics in America, 1776–1876,* ed. Robert Trisco, 249–53. Washington, DC: United States Catholic Conference, 1976.

Wesley, Timothy L. *The Politics of Faith During the Civil War.* Baton Rouge: Louisiana State University Press, 2013.

West, Elliott. "Reconstructing Race." *Western Historical Quarterly* 31, no. 1 (2003): 6–26.

Wetzel, Benjamin J. "A Church Divided: American Catholics Debate the Spanish-American War." *Journal of the Gilded Age and Progressive Era* 14, no. 3 (Jul. 2015): 348–66.

——. "Onward Christian Soldiers: Lyman Abbott's Justification of the Spanish-American War." *Journal of Church & State* 54, no. 3 (Summer 2012): 406–25.

Wheeler, Rachel. "Hendrick Aupaumut: Christian-Mahican Prophet." In *Native Americans, Christianity, and the Reshaping of the American Religious Landscape,* eds. Joel W. Martin and Mark A. Nichols, 225–49. Chapel Hill: University of North Carolina Press, 2010.

White, Richard. *The Republic for Which It Stands: The United States during Reconstruction and the Gilded Age, 1865–1896.* New York: Oxford University Press, 2017.

White, Ronald C., Jr. *Liberty and Justice for All: Racial Reform and the Social Gospel (1877–1925).* 1990. Reprint, Louisville, KY: Westminster John Knox Press, 2002.

White, Ronald C., Jr., and C. Howard Hopkins, with an Essay by John C. Bennett. *The Social Gospel: Religion and Reform in Changing America.* Philadelphia: Temple University Press, 1976.

Wilke, Wayne. "Changing Understanding of the Church-State Relationship: The Lutheran Church-Missouri Synod, 1914–1969." PhD diss., University of Michigan, 1990.

Williams, Gilbert Anthony. *The* Christian Recorder, *A.M.E. Church, 1854–1902.* Jefferson, NC: McFarland, 1996.

Williams, Michael. *American Catholics in the War: National Catholic War Council, 1917–1921.* New York: Macmillan, 1921.

Wilson, John F. *Public Religion in American Culture.* Philadelphia: Temple University Press, 1979.

Wimmer, Judith. "*Ave Maria.*" In *Religious Periodicals of the United States: Academic and Scholarly Journals,* ed. Charles H. Lippy, 43. Westport, CT: Greenwood Press, 1986.

Wittke, Carl. *German-Americans and the World War (With Special Emphasis on Ohio's German-Language Press).* Columbus: Ohio State Archaeological and Historical Society, 1936.

Wreszin, Michael. *Oswald Garrison Villard: Pacifist at War.* Bloomington: Indiana University Press, 1965.

Wright, Scott. "The *Northwestern Chronicle* and the Spanish-American War: American Catholic Attitudes Regarding the 'Splendid Little War.'" *American Catholic Studies* 116 (Winter 2005): 55–68.

Wuthnow, Robert. *The Restructuring of American Religion: Society and Faith Since World War II.* Princeton, NJ: Princeton University Press, 1988.

Zwierlein, Frederick J. *The Life and Letters of Bishop McQuaid.* Rochester, NY: Art Print Shop, 1927.

Index

CPSIA information can be obtained
at www.ICGtesting.com
Printed in the USA
LVHW111726160822
26093LV00020B/439/J

9 781501 763946